FATE AND FAITH

The Contemporary Jewish Scene

FATE AND FAITH

The Contemporary Jewish Scene

By

JUDAH PILCH

Published for
THE AMERICAN ASSOCIATION FOR JEWISH EDUCATION
by
BLOCH PUBLISHING COMPANY
NEW YORK

To the sacred memory of
MY MOTHER, BAT-SHEVA
MY SISTER, RATZIAH
In grateful appreciation
of their love and devotion

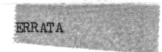

ERRATA

Page 17

In the statistical table the percentage
of the Jewish population of Israel is
88.76, instead of 96.28.

Page 140 ("Scope of Religious Life Today")

Line 1 - should read 9,600 synagogues in
        the world, instead of 29,000
Line 3 - 4,079 synagogues instead of
        23,000
Line 5 - a total of about 8,000 instead
        of 27,000.

Acknowledgements

Our grateful appreciation is expressed to the following publishers for the generous permission granted to quote from their respective publications: Abingdon Press (*Religious Education,* edited by Marvin J. Taylor, 1960, quotations from essay by Judah Pilch on *Jewish Religious Education*); Behrman's Jewish Book House (for reproduction of scattered parts of paragraphs from *Jewish Life in Our Times,* by Judah Pilch, 1943); and to the National Curriculum Research Institute, sponsored by the American Association for Jewish Education, under whose auspices the material for this volume was used in an experimental edition and subsequently revised and edited.

Contents

9

PART II — FAITH

Preface

More than twenty years ago, when the ravages of the war laid waste cities and villages in most areas of our globe, and the European Jewish communities were brought face to face with the Nazi hordes, the teachers engaged in secondary and higher Jewish education had to deal with groups of frustrated, confused and depressed students. Reverberations of Jewish woe echoed throughout our atmosphere and agitated our spirits. It was then that I, a teacher of history, decided to discuss with my students the nature of the Jewish problem in the light of the past and in relation to the actualities of Jewish life between the two world wars. By so doing, I hoped to bolster our common morale, teacher and pupil alike. My lecture notes were subsequently revised and edited and, in 1943, my book *Jewish Life in Our Times* was published.

In that volume I surveyed the religio-cultural and organizational life of the Jews, endeavoring to strike a note of optimism by pointing up those values of our heritage which stood the test of time and which motivated our people not to despair but to keep on struggling for survival. In the preface to that book I expressed the hope that "justice and righteousness will emerge victorious and that Jewish life will be more secure in the world of tomorrow."

Twenty years have elapsed. Radical changes have taken place in the Jewish world. While justice emerged victorious and the Allied Forces defeated the Nazis and set out to heal the wounds inflicted by the war, the Jews had meanwhile paid the price with their very lives. The great European Jewish community was destroyed. Six million Jews met a horrible death at the hands of the Nazi savages and their collaborators. But after this unprecedented annihilation of more than one-third of the world Jewish population, and out of the depths of our people's sorrow, there came into being the State of Israel. These two historic events, the liquidation of the

11

European Jewish community and the rise of the State of Israel, brought to the fore problems of readjustment to these major developments. These new problems called for reorientation with regard to the future of Jewish life the world over and to the nature of Diaspora Jewry's relationship to the new State.

The American Jewish community, the largest Jewish population center in the world, is destined to play an important role in molding a new Jewish personality in Diaspora and in shaping the destiny of Jews everywhere, including Israel. This significant task presupposes a keen understanding of the modern Jewish scene. Jewish men and women, young and old, must become better informed through a careful examination and analysis of the facts of Jewish life today against the background of yesterday and thus meet the challenge of our generation more intelligently and more effectively.

The present volume is designed for teen agers and young adults. Its contents is intended to help them orient themselves to the problems of the larger Jewish group of which they are an integral part. The book presents an evaluation of major aspects of Jewish life— demographic, political, economic and religio-cultural. Most of the issues discussed in these pages were not dealt with in my original presentation in 1943. Some of the material which was incorporated in that volume has been completely revised and brought up to date. Part II, which the author is now preparing for early publication, will dwell on the American Jewish community which has become of age, and the new Israel.

Grateful acknowledgement is made to Drs. Isidor Chein and Louis L. Kaplan for their encouragement in preparing instruction units on this subject and in experimenting with these materials in a number of senior high schools and junior colleges; (the contents and organization of the present volume are a by-product of this action-research program, incorporating the reactions of the students and teachers who studied the text in a mimeographed form for two consecutive years) to Dr. Meir Ben-Horin, Mr. Isaac Toubin and Mr. Sam Steinberg who read the manuscript, and whose assistance and suggestions were invaluable in preparing this volume for publication; and to my devoted wife, Bernice, for her patience and love.

J. P.

New York, May, 1963

PART I
Fate

Jews in Numbers

Jews in the World Population

The Jews are a unique and a richly endowed people. They have survived centuries of persecution, humiliation and oppression, yet have met their attackers with restraint and hope. They seem to have developed an immunity against the merciless forces of oppression directed against them and to have acquired an inner strength which has made them indestructible as a people. Despite millenia of persecution and the accompanying threat to their spiritual integrity, they retained their identity in the face of all odds. They have manifested rare qualities of spiritual power in the course of their history, notwithstanding the calamities that were their lot. The new State of Israel is a concrete manifestation of the Jewish will to survive as a people.

Despite the great losses sustained through continued persecutions, the Jewish people remains, even today, numerically strong. In the pre-Nazi period they numbered more than sixteen and a half million. While the Nazi holocaust reduced their numbers by more than six million, due to natural increase since the Second World War, they form today a distinctive group of more than twelve and a half million.

There are Jews in many parts of the world. The number of Jewish people, dispersed though they are, equals the combined populace of several nations. The Scandinavian peoples together have a smaller population than world Jewry. The Jewish people is larger in number than the Greeks or the Belgians, the Bulgarians, the Tunisians, the Finns or the Dutch, the Peruvians, the Cubans, or the Yemenis.

The Jews are now the only people over whose communities the sun never sets. In the 1930's, prior to the great calamity that befell the Jews at the hands of the Nazis, Jews could be found in every

15

country of importance. The liquidation of large centers of Jewish population in central and eastern Europe and the rise of anti-Jewish discrimination in both Arab and Iron Curtain lands has reduced the number of Jewish communities in the world. But even today, small groups of Jews may be found practically everywhere on earth. There are Jews in Ethiopia, India and China. There are Jews in Australia and the Philippine Islands. There are Jews in Iran, in Iceland, in the Congo, in Japan, in Pakistan, in Kenya, let alone among the great nations of western Europe and the Americas. There is, of course, the new Jewish center in the new Jewish State—Israel.

The following figures show an estimated dispersion of the Jewish people in the different continents of the world: [1]

Continents	Jewish Inhabitants	General Population	Percentage of Jewish Population
Europe (excluding USSR)	1,400,000	421,000,000	0.33
Africa	400,000	236,000,000	0.17
North, Central and South America	6,400,000	398,000,000	1.61
Asia (principally in Israel)	2,300,000	1,624,000,000	0.14
Oceania (principally in Australia & New Zealand)	71,000	16,000,000	0.44
USSR (including Asian regions)	2,345,000	210,000,000	1.17
Total	12,915,000	2,905,000,000	0.44

Scattered in virtually all parts of the world, living in 85 lands, and in the midst of hundreds of ethnic groups, the Jews exist, nonetheless, as one people. The individual members of the Jewish people are well integrated into the cultures, economies and political lives of the countries they live in, yet retain a group consciousness of their own. For, no matter how diverse their conditions, their educational and cultural backgrounds, they have a common history, a common religio-cultural tradition, and common hopes. Together they still have to face much hostility, but they also have a stake in the Jewish State of Israel, its security, its welfare, its trials and triumphs.

The largest centers of Jewish habitation in the not too distant past were in Europe and America. Today they are in America and Israel. Over two-thirds of world Jewry are to be found in these two centers. There are more than two million Jews in Soviet Russia, but due to the Soviet policy of keeping all its people behind an Iron Curtain, there is little contact, if any, between the Jews of Russia and the main body of Jewry in other lands.

The Jews form an ethnic and religious minority everywhere, except in the State of Israel. There is no place in the world where the Jews constitute a sizable majority group in the general population, except in Israel where, according to the census of May, 1962, out of a general population of 2,332,000 there were 2,070,000 Jews. The greatest part of world Jewry lives in the United States, numbering more than five and one-half million.

Countries with a Jewish Population Over 70,000

The following countries have a Jewish population of 70,000 or more:

Countries	Jewish Population	General Population	Percentage of Jewish Population
United States of America	5,500,000	180,000,000	3.1
Soviet Russia (including Asian region)	2,345,000	210,000,000	1.1
Israel	2,070,000	2,332,000	96.28
France	500,000	45,500,000	1.1
England	450,000	52,400,000	0.86
Argentina	450,000	21,000,000	2.14
Canada	275,000	18,000,000	1.53
Rumania	150,000	18,400,000	0.82
Brazil	140,000	65,000,000	0.22
Morocco (including Tangiers)	125,000	11,000,000	1.1
Union of South Africa	110,000	15,000,000	0.73
Iran	80,000	20,000,000	0.40
Hungary	75,000	10,000,000	0.75
Australia and New Zealand	70,000	13,500,000	0.49

In these fourteen lands we find the bulk of world Jewry, over 90 per cent of all Jews. The rest of the Jews in the world form very small communities.

Growth of the Jewish Population

In the days of the Second Commonwealth, over 4,500,000 Jews lived in Palestine, the Near East and other Roman provinces. After the fall of the Jewish State (70 C.E.) and until the beginning of their emancipation, for a period of 1,700 years, continuous persecution and oppression prevented an increase in numbers. In 1800, a mere century and a half ago, the total number of Jews in the world was not larger than 2,500,000. Since then, however, the number of Jews has grown rapidly. Emancipation, the formation of new Jewish centers, (especially in the Americas) and the improved sanitary and living conditions which prolonged the life span of all people, have brought about a continual growth of Jewish population. The figure for 1840 was four and one-half million; in 1900 it was 10,500,000; in 1939, at the outbreak of the Second World War, it had risen to more than 16,500,000. It is worth noting in this connection that had the Jews, who numbered about 4,500,000 in the hey-day of the Roman Empire, increased relatively as fast as the other populations of the world, "there would have been 75,000,000 Jews today only in the countries which once were included in the orbit of the Roman Empire. That orbit, it is well to note, did not include Russia and the United States, in which today more than 60% of all the Jews in the world live." [2] By the same token, one might reason that had the Jews of *all lands* lived a normal life, free from discrimination and overt acts of violence, their number today would have reached the 225 million mark. But, as we shall see in a subsequent chapter, the Church, for many years, in her conversionist zeal, was determined to destroy the Jewish religion and thus obstructed the numerical growth of the Jewish People. The policy of the Church was followed by many a secular state. Increase in Jewish population was therefore arrested.

The following table shows the status of the Jewish population since the destruction of the Second Commonwealth.[3 & 4]

Year	Number of Jews	Year	Number of Jews
70	4,500,000	1840	4,500,000
1170	1,500,000	1860	6,000,000
1300	2,000,000	1900	10,500,000
1500	1,500,000	1930	16,000,000
1650	1,750,000	1940	17,000,000
1700	2,000,000	1945	10,500,000
1800	2,500,000	1963	12,915,000

We thus see a gradual but constant decline of the Jewish population from the period of the loss of Jewish statehood in 70 C.E. to the time of its emancipation in the beginning of the 19th century. The growth of Jewish population coincides, therefore, with the advance of parliamentary government and democracy in 19th century Europe and the beginning of Jewish immigration to the New World. In the course of one century, 1840–1940, the Jewish population more than trebled itself. The year 1940 marks a turning point in Jewish history which greatly affected the numerical status of the Jewish people.

Between 1940 and 1945 the Nazi "solution of the Jewish problem" (wholesale slaughter and "production-line" extermination of defenseless Jews in crematoria and gas-chambers) reduced their number by six million. More than one half of the European Jews were destroyed by acts of atrocity unparalleled in human history. This great loss has not yet been restored.

The natural increase of the Jews in the last 16 to 18 years has brought their number up from ten and one-half million in 1945 to approximately 12,900,000 in 1962. The pre-war figure of 17 million is still a far-off goal.

The Segment of Jewry that Became Numerically Dominant

Of the two and one-half million Jews in the world in 1800, one million were Oriental Jews, that is, those living for generations in the Middle and Near East and North Africa. These Jews, predominantly Sefardim,[5] remained numerically static through the last 250 years. They lived in economically and culturally underdeveloped countries (Egypt, Morocco, Tunisia, Turkey, Bulgaria, Iraq and Palestine), ruled by colonial powers and local bands of feudal lords, kings and sheikhs who kept the masses of people in a state of serfdom. It is the other group of Jews, the Ashkenazim[6] who in 1800 numbered only one and one-half million and lived, for the main part, in central and eastern Europe, that grew numerically to over 14 million by 1930 and constituted more than 90 per cent of world Jewry. In the course of the 19th century and the first two decades of the 20th century, millions of Ashkenazim emigrated to new continents and evolved the large Jewish communities in the Americas, in Palestine (now Israel) and in the urban communities of western Europe and South Africa.

Modern Jewish Migrations

Migration (wandering from country to country) has characterized the Jewish people throughout the 2,000 years of their life in the lands of the dispersion. The Jew became known as the Wandering Jew. The Jewish people differed from the rest of the world not only because of their dispersion but also in that they were a migratory people. Though migration entailed discomfort and suffering, it played an important role in Jewish survival. A Jewish community would decline numerically and culturally in one part of the globe; another would be established and develop elsewhere.

From the time they lost their national independence (70 C.E.) to the late Middle Ages, Jews migrated from the Near East westward; from Palestine and Babylon to Spain, Italy, Germany and other western-European countries. With the rise of persecutions in and expulsions from western-European lands, the direction of migration was reversed: eastward to Poland, Turkey and North Africa. This migration, in many cases, meant moving from "civilized" lands to more primitive and backward countries. By 1700, the 2,000,000 Jews were about equally divided between western Europe and the East (Russia, Poland, Turkey, Persia and parts of North Africa).

Toward the end of the 19th century, economic depression struck many of the eastern-European countries. In Russia, the main source of Jewish emigration, the poverty of the Jewish masses was appalling. In Odessa, for example, the home of one of the "wealthiest" Jewish communities in eastern Europe at the beginning of the 20th century, 30% of the Jewish burials were financed by charitable organizations. In order to better their economic lot, many Jews began migrating westward—and re-established flourishing communities in England, France, Holland, Belgium, etc. During the last decade of the 19th century, and the first two decades of the 20th century, the Americas, especially the U.S.A. with the promise of political equality and economic opportunity, attracted several million Jews.

Only 60 years ago, most of world Jewry lived in Europe. Today European Jewry constitutes a small part of the entire Jewish population of the world. On the other hand, the American continent, which over 60 years ago harbored only 10.9 per cent of the world's Jewry,[7] is today the largest Jewish center with a Jewish population of approximately six and a half million, constituting about one-half of the world Jewish population.

Before the Second World War, when the numerical growth of the Jews reached its peak, Jewish migration became inevitable once again. The rise of Nazism marked the increased emigration

of Jews from Germany, Austria, Bulgaria, Rumania and Czecho-
slovakia and the proportionate growth of *aliyah* (literally "ascend-
ance") to Palestine. During World War II, greater emigration of
Jews from Europe would have saved many from extermination.
Unfortunately, the victims of Nazism could find no way of escape.
Very few managed to flee. Immediately after the Second World
War, Jews sailed in small numbers to Canada, Latin America,
Palestine, the Union of South Africa and Australia. Since the rise
of the Jewish State in 1948, emigration of Jews from the Arab
countries gained momentum. Most of them fled from the rising
Arab wrath to the new State of Israel.

Political and economic conditions, as well as widespread hostility to the Jew, no doubt were the most important reasons for
Jewish migration, yet there was also a strong ideological motive
behind it. "The desire to return to the soil, to build up large
settlements far removed from inhospitable Europe, to possess an
autonomous territory, a homeland of their own, gained among
the Jews." [8] Zionism intensified that desire, and the Yishuv (Jewish settlement) in Palestine in the years 1917-1948 (during the
period of the British Mandate) served as an excellent example of
the Jew's capacity to become master of his own destiny.

Jews—an Urban Population

Along with the changes in the geographic map of world Jewry
resulting from a steady Jewish migration in the last century, still
another factor became an element in Jewish transformation: the
urbanization and metropolitanization of the Jews. The Industrial
Revolution came to western Europe, setting in motion a process
of urbanization of all people which still continues. The Jews
(who were always inclined to build their homes in urban centers)
were no exception. Expanding economic opportunities, the development of educational institutions serving ever larger groups
of people, and the enriched cultural life, motivated the growth
of urban population.

The Jews, who, ever since the exile from Palestine, have been
detached from the soil, became city and town dwellers in order
to improve their political and economic status. They also flocked
to the cities for another reason: their will to survive as Jews. They
wanted to live in compact masses, to be together in larger numbers. The growing cities afforded them an opportunity not only
for the betterment of their economic status but also for the crea-

tion of Jewish communities. But living in a large city was a mixed blessing. It was an open gate to assimilation on the one hand. On the other hand, the concentration of Jews in large numbers in a given city stood not only as a barrier against assimilation but made possible the creation of spiritual centers, capable of stimulating Jewish cultural life and intellectual activity.

Even in the agrarian countries, where urbanization began only in recent years in the wake of large-scale industrialization (Russia, Poland, Rumania, etc.), Jews in the past century lived in towns and cities. In Tzarist Russia, for instance, during the period of their confinement to the Pale of Settlement[9] (1802–1917), 49 per cent of the Jewish population lived in cities, 33 per cent in towns and only 18 per cent in the rural districts.

In western Europe and the United States, the most highly industrialized areas in the world, Jews settled in the cities in large proportions, throughout the second half of the 19th century and the first three decades of the 20th century. By 1925, more than half of world Jewry lived in 166 Jewish communities; today almost 50 per cent of all Jews live in only 20 large cities of which the following have a Jewish population of 80,000 or more:

City[10]	Number of Jews
Greater New York (including Westchester, Suffolk & Nassau Counties)	2,400,000
Los Angeles (Metropolitan Area)	400,000
Moscow	400,000
Tel Aviv—Yaffo	365,000
Philadelphia (Metropolitan Area)	330,000
Chicago (Metropolitan Area)	280,000
Greater London	280,000
Buenos Aires	250,000
Paris	200,000
Haifa	160,000
Greater Boston	150,000
Jerusalem	150,000
Bucharest	130,000
Essex County, N. J.	100,000
Montreal	105,000
Cleveland	90,000
Detroit	90,000
Toronto	82,000
Greater Washington, D.C.	81,000
Baltimore	80,000
Total	6,123,000

The fact that Jews now are an urban people is to be borne in mind throughout our discussion of Jewish life in modern times. It is decisive for both their economic and their cultural lives. It is worth noting that while almost one-half of the total world Jewish population is concentrated in these 20 cities, only 2 per cent of the world's non-Jewish population is to be found there.

Notwithstanding the great tragedy of the mass murder of more than six million Jews during the Nazi reign of terror, the Jews have grown considerably in the last 60 years. From six million in 1900 to about 13 million in 1960. However, the ratio of Jews to the general population shows an appreciable drop. In 1900 the world population numbered one and one-half billion; the Jews represented 0.70 per cent of the total global population. In 1962, as we have already seen, the world population had risen to almost three billion (2,905,000,000) [11] and the percentage of Jews in the general population dropped to 0.44 per cent.

The chief reason for this numerical decline is obviously the liquidation of the large Jewish communities in central and eastern Europe. The rather small increase in the total world Jewish population as against the population explosion practically everywhere on this globe is explained by the decline of the Jewish birth rate and the rise of intermarriage.

Recent Trends in the Numerical Status of World Jewry

In the two centuries before World War II, the Jews were known as a people having large families. Strict adherence to religious teachings which counselled against self-imposed limitations upon progeny and set a premium upon fruitfulness and purity in family life, tended to uphold a system of large Jewish families. On the other hand, the Jewish parental devotion to children, the comparatively superior medical care and hygienic conditions within the Jewish communities, contributed greatly to reducing infant disease and child mortality. As a result, the birth rate of the Jews throughout the 19th century was relatively high. When the Jews showed also a remarkably good record in regard to the death rate, the natural increase of the Jewish population tripled the number of Jews in the world in a period of less than 100 years (from four and one-half million in 1840 to 16 million by 1930).

In recent decades, however, the Jewish birth rate has declined both in western and in eastern Europe. On a world scale in the period 1901 to 1914, the natural increase (births over deaths) was

19.5 per cent, but in the eight-year period 1931 to 1939, it was only 8.0 per cent.[12]

The decline of births is seen also throughout the Americas. In Canada, one of the more prosperous Jewish communities in the world, the birth rate is the lowest of any ethnic group in the country, "being only 14.0 per 1,000 as compared with 23.2 among the total population of all origins."[13] In the United States, "the Jewish fertility rate in both major age groups (women 15 to 40 years old and women 40 and older) remained constant at slightly over three-fourths of the rate—for the total population."[14] According to a recent study on a "Comparison of Major United States Religious Groups", which appeared in the *Journal of the American Statistical Association* (September, 1961), the Jews have fewer children than any other religious group. The findings indicate "that Jews have the highest percentage of two children families; the Catholics have a high percentage of their families with three or more children, and the white Baptists, Lutherans and Methodists fall between the Catholics and Jews."

In only one country Jewish natural increase does not lag behind the non-Jewish population. In Israel the birth rate exceeds the death rate by 41.0 per 1,000. While a number of sociologists point to a higher birth rate among Jews in the United States in the last few years, it is yet apparent that the Jewish population of the United States, according to the estimate of Jewish demographers, has grown only slightly in the last decade. In 1950, the *American Jewish Year Book* reported an estimated Jewish population in the United States of five million. In 1961, the same source reported five and one-quarter million. The general population in America for the same period has grown from 135 million to 180 million. In 1950 the Jewish population represented 3.70 per cent, but in the ten years following, as the general population increased by 45 million (or 33 per cent), the percentage of Jewish population, although showing a numerical increase of 250,000 (or 5 per cent), has actually decreased to 2.91 per cent.

As for intermarriage, sociologists point to a much smaller percentage in the 1950's than in the '20's and '30's. In the period 1925–1940, 25 per cent of all Jewish marriages in Vienna were mixed. In Budapest, the percentage was 28; in Berlin, 35; in Trieste, 71 and in Soviet Russia, 16.77.[15] In the period 1940–1955, with the advent of Hitlerism on the one hand and the rise of the State of Israel on the other, the Jews of large population centers in the Americas and other parts of the world have suffered little loss from mixed marriages. There is, however, sufficient evidence pointing to frequent intermarriage on the American scene in recent years. In a study of the Washington community, it was found that in every eight Jewish families there is one case of intermarriage.[16] In San Francisco, out of every 100 marriages, 17 were mixed. A very revealing analysis of the situation in a small Midwestern university town shows that mixed marriages represent 6.5 per cent of the town's Jewish community and approximately 20 per cent among the Jews on the faculty.[17] In Canada, the percentage of mixed marriages has grown from 6.2 in 1936 to 11.7 per cent in 1955.[18] In Mexico, according to reliable sources, intermarriage is a frightening phenomenon. Twenty-one couples have appeared before one Rabbi (for consultation with a view to resolving the problem) in the course of only five months.[19] In England, "While no reliable statistics are available, there was general agreement that the rate of intermarriage was well above 10 per cent, perhaps twice that high. In the light of this unprecedented high rate of mixed marriage the Orthodox religious authorities required a standard of observance on the part of converts (almost invariably women) that only a handful could achieve. . . . But it seems likely that an increasing number of candidates for mixed marriages were availing themselves of civil marriages with no concern at all for religious requirements."[20]

No matter how small the overall percentage of mixed marriages, it is another deterrent factor in the increase of the Jewish population. The loss that the Jewish people sustains from intermarriage coupled with the rather low rate of increase in Jewish births (in comparison with the rest of the population), has brought the proportional growth of the Jewish people to a standstill.

Summary

Radical changes have taken place in the Jewish world in the last few decades. Their number diminished, due in the main to the liquidation of large Jewish centers of population in central or eastern Europe, at a time when the population in the world has considerably increased. The centers of Jewish population in Diaspora have shifted from Europe to America. The American continent became the largest population center in the world in the course of half a century. The State of Israel came into being in 1948 and its gates were thrown open to all Jews in need of a secure haven. It is now the second largest Jewish population center to which there is steady immigration to this day.

Intermarriage and the low rate of Jewish birth in the Diaspora do not augur well for the continuous growth of the Jewish population. Sociologists maintain, however, that should anti-Semitism abate, greater security from fear would result in a larger birth rate and thus in further growth of the Jewish population.

TOPICS FOR DISCUSSION

1. What, in your opinion, are the clearest manifestations of "the Jewish will to survive as a people" throughout its history?

2. Which of the manifestations function in your community? Which do not?

3. How can the Jewish will to survive as a people be strengthened?

4. In what sense is it true that Jews in France and Jews in Pakistan have a common history and common hopes?

5. In what ways does the State of Israel help to ensure Jewish survival?

6. How does urbanization affect Jewish survival in the 1960's?

7. How serious a menace to Jewish survival, in your judgment, is the "population explosion"?

8. Why, in your opinion, did Jews concentrate in the large urban centers?

9. Should intermarriage be discouraged? Need it be discouraged?

10. Discuss the causes of Jewish migration in the 1960's.

NOTES TO CHAPTER 1

1. These figures were taken from: (a) United Nations Office of Public Information, (World Facts and Figures); (b) American Jewish Year Book, 1962; (c) The New Survey of Global Jewish Population, compiled by the World Jewish Congress, January, 1963.
2. Engleman, U. Z.: "The Rise of the Jew in the Western World," Behrman's Jewish Book House, New York, 1944, p. 106.
3. Ruppin, Arthur: "Ha-Sotsiologiah shel Ha-Yehudim," ("The Sociology of the Jews"), Vol. I, p. 62.
4. Levin, Dov: "Haam Ha-Yehudi Bizmaneinu," *Moladti,* Jerusalem, 5719, p. 83.
5. Sefardim—Jews of Spanish descent. A term applied especially to the descendants of the exiles and refugees from Spain and Portugal.
6. Ashkenazim—term applied to Jews who inhabited the German provinces in the Middle Ages, who subsequently migrated to eastern Europe and thence to the Americas.
7. Lestchinsky, Jacob: "Ha-Pzurah Ha-Yehudit," Jerusalem, 1959, p. 10.
8. Wischnitzer, Mark: "To Dwell in Safety," Jewish Publication Society, Philadelphia, 1948 pp. ix-x.

9. Pale of Settlement is the name for the territories in Greater Russia accessible to the Jews for settlement. The decree establishing the area of the Pale was issued in 1794.

10. American Jewish Year Book, 1961, pp. 56, 61, 387-388; also Tartakower, A.: "Ha-Hevrah Ha-Yehudit," Massadah Publishers, Tel Aviv, 1956, pp. 79-80.

11. United Nations Office of Public Information, (World Facts and Figures), p. 7.

12. Tartakower, A.: "Ha-Hevrah Ha-Yehudit," Massadah Publishers, Tel Aviv, 1956, p. 88.

13. Rosenberg, L.: "Jews in Canada," *Contemporary Jewish Record*, March-April, 1939, p. 35.

14. American Jewish Year Book, 1959, pp. 11-12.

15. Tartakower, A.: "Ha-Hevrah Ha-Yehudit," Massadah Publishers, Tel Aviv, 1956, p. 217.

16. Lestchinsky, Jacob: "Ha-Pzurah Ha-Ychudit," Jerusalem, 1959, p. 50.

17. Cohen, Henry: "Jewish Life and Thought in an Academic Community," *American Jewish Archives*, Vol. 14, New York, 1962, p. 119.

18. Rosenberg, Louis: Papers in Jewish Demography, Jerusalem, 1957, p. 22.

19. Klein, Yekutiel: *Mexicaner Leben*, Mexico, December 1, 1962.

20. Norman Cohen in American Jewish Year Book, 1962, p. 293.

2

The Rights of the Jews

A Dream Does Not Come True

"The relationship of the Jews to the outside world was, until the eighteenth century, comparatively simple—they had duties but no guaranteed rights; they fulfilled economic functions, but formed no part of the social body; they were victims of its laws but not citizens; they were human beings but condemned to be the objects on which the instincts of their environment reacted; they were the representatives of monotheism and yet were massacred in the name of monotheism."[1]

At the end of the 18th century a radical change with regard to the political status of the Jew took place. The French Revolution, the breakdown of mediaevalism, the spread of liberalism and the gradual advancement of the ideas of democracy brought political emancipation to the Jews. For the first time in their Galut[2] history, they were endowed with the rights of human beings, climaxing 1,500 years of legal disabilities and inequalities.

The first country to assert the rights and the dignity of *all men alike* was the United States of America, as provided in the Declaration of Independence of 1776. The Bill of Rights guaranteed the freedoms for which the Revolution was fought, the first article of which reads in part: "Congress shall make no law respecting an establishment of religion, or prohibiting the free exercise thereof." France followed this example, acknowledging equality of political rights for all men, including Jews, in 1791. The French influence in other European states and the enforcement of the principle of the "Rights of Man" by Napoleonic armies brought temporary emancipation to the Jews in many other countries. It is true that when the conservative reaction to the French Revolution set in after the Napoleonic Wars and the nations became once again "Christian States," the equal rights in many lands were withdrawn.

Nevertheless, the precedent had precipitated the emancipation of the Jews in central, northern and southwestern Europe in the middle of the 19th century. In the second half of the century, Jewish emancipation made remarkable progress. Jews were admitted to full rights of citizenship in an ever-increasing number of countries: Denmark—1849; Ottoman Empire—1855; England—1858; Italy —1859; Austria—1860; Sweden and Belgium—1865; Switzerland— 1866; Hungary—1867; Prussia—1869; Algiers—1870; Bavaria and Serbia—1878.

By 1900, emancipation was in vogue in many countries, except Russia, the largest center of Jewish population, and Rumania, where the state of political inequality prevailed until after the First World War.

However, in studying the records of the emancipated Jewish communities, we find that the idea of emancipation was not fully realized. In many countries where the Jews had gained political freedom, laws were deliberately misinterpreted, anti-Jewish policies adopted, various pretexts for oppression found and utterances threatening Jewish security were made by government officials as well as by private citizens. During this period of emancipation modern anti-Semitism came into being in the same countries that guaranteed freedom and equality to the Jew.

The Damascus affair in 1840,[3] the Rome Act of Baptism of the Mortara child in 1858,[4] the attacks upon the Jews in Germany in the eighties, shortly after the Franco-German War (1870–71), the Dreyfus Case in France in 1894,[5] the case of Tisca-Eszlár in Hungary in 1882[6] and the First International Anti-Jewish Congress held in Dresden, Germany in 1882,—all these incidents show that age-old prejudices against the idea of Jewish freedom still had to be overcome.

The First World War gave the Jews of Europe the hope that their struggle for equal rights on a world scale would be crowned with success. This hope was realized at the Peace Conference in 1919. The long-awaited day of political emancipation in eastern Europe came with the conclusion of the Great War. The peace treaties which were concluded both with the newly-established states (Poland, Czechoslovakia, Lithuania, Latvia) and the previously existing states (Rumania, Hungary, Greece, Turkey), contained a special minority clause guaranteeing the Jews full political freedom and complete civil equality. In the same year the revolutionary government in Russia granted its Jewish citizens equal rights, although since most of them were predominantly engaged in commerce, they could no longer maintain their status of petty traders and became impoverished. Thus, by the end of 1919, more than 90 per cent of world Jewry was legally emancipated. The League of Nations became the guarantor of the minority treaties and it looked for a while as though the Jewish dream for equal rights had come true. Moreover, the civilized world recognized the Jewish right to Palestine when the League of Nations granted the Mandate over Palestine to Great Britain, whose Balfour Declaration of November 2, 1917 promised to facilitate the establishment of a Jewish National Home in Palestine.

That Jewish hopes for equality and freedom were premature and groundless is quite obvious today. Scarcely had the ink of the signatures at the Peace Conference become dry, before many treaty provisions—in which the states provided "that all nationals shall be equal before the law and shall enjoy the same civil and political rights without distinction as to race, language and religion"— were violated. The provisions, which were regarded by the Jews as symptoms of "Athalta di-geulah" (the beginning of National Salvation) became scraps of paper. Jewish political rights were not only violated but were, in reality, restricted and nullified. Anti-Jewish outbursts and violence swept Poland and Rumania. The very lives of the "freed and emancipated" Jews were in danger. Hungary, Rumania and Poland inaugurated the "numerus clausus" (a quota system for Jews in the schools). In Lithuania, Greece, and Latvia, the Jews had to struggle to secure even partial compliance with the treaty obligations. Many became denationalized as a result of laws which required that Jews who claimed citizenship show proof of several years of continuous residence in the same region or community. In short, many states violated their pledges to their Jewish communities. Jewish rights were curtailed, guarantees for the protection of Jewish citizens were renounced, anti-Semitism was permitted to run its course. The League of Nations for fifteen years was flooded with communications from Jewish representative organizations about the infractions of Jewish rights and the violation of treaty provisions, but was too weak to deal with the defaulting governments. Jewish hopes for universal emancipation proved, therefore, illusory. In 1933 (the year of the ascendance of Hitler) the Jews of Europe were confronted with an even greater danger to their security and to their very lives than ever before in their history.

Thus, after the First World War, just at the time when, seemingly, Jews were granted equal rights in all lands of the civilized world, the forces of bigotry and Jew hatred, deeply rooted in history, became stronger and plunged European Jewry into the "Valley of Death."

The Evil of Anti-Semitism

Hatred has followed the Jewish people from antiquity. In one form or another it existed even before the rise of Christianity. Hostility toward the Jew existed in the Persian, Hellenistic and Roman Empires of ancient times.

After the annihilation of the Jewish State in 70 C.E. and with the growth of the Christian Church, the movement of anti-Judaism or anti-Jewism grew in strength and has plagued the Jewish people throughout the centuries. There is hardly a community in Europe, Asia, or Africa whose local history does not record some type of maltreatment of the Jews.

The manifestations of Jew-hatred have varied. In the wake of the Hadrian Edict of 135 C.E.[7] and the compulsory exile from Palestine, the era of systematic persecution set in, chiefly on religious grounds. Since the early 300's, when Christianity became the state religion of the Roman Empire, anti-Jewish discrimination became a permanent policy of the Church. The Jewish minority's refusal to accept Christianity prompted the Church to initiate measure after measure to "protect" the Christians against the harmful "heretics." Thus for many centuries the Jews struggled for independent religious existence in the midst of multitudes of zealous Christians. In the course of the time they were subjected to restrictions and prohibitions everywhere in the gentile world which marked them as a people set apart and inferior.

In the Dark Ages, this religious factor in organized Jew-baiting (with an additional emphasis on Jewish guilt for the tragic death of Jesus) was accompanied by an economic factor which tended to foster general dislike and distrust of Jews because they practiced a trade forbidden to Christians—that of money-lending and interest-charging. The Christian nations refused to consider the fact that the Jews were forced into money lending because of discrimination in other fields of economic life. Their usefulness as financiers and bankers was disregarded. In the eyes of the Church they were infidels and breeders of heresies. In the eyes of the people they were human parasites who should be exterminated.

Inquisitions, mass expulsions, massacres, wholesale executions were consequently heaped upon them in one period or another.

In 1290, they were barred from England; in 1306 from France, in 1492 from Spain. Crusaders, marching to redeem the Holy Land from the "unholy" Moslems, advanced on Jerusalem through streams of Jewish blood and through ruins of Jewish communities. Canonical anti-Jewish measures deprived Jews of the privilege of mingling socially with non-Jews, shut them up in ghettos, and compelled them to wear a "yellow" badge[8] in order to distinguish them from the rest of the population. The general attitude on the part of the prejudiced, agitated Christians is best illustrated in the Jew-baiting utterance of Luther (1483–1546) who said: "We know not what devil brought them into our land. We did not bring them from Jerusalem. Besides that, no one keeps them. The country and the roads are open to them. Let them return to their own land. We will gladly give them presents if we can be rid of them, for they are a heavy burden upon us, a plague, a pestilence, a sore trial."

Even during the emancipation period, anti-Semitism was not extinguished. Though the religious basis for Jew-hatred had considerably weakened in western Europe and America, nevertheless, gentile children associated the Jews with the killers of Christ. The Gospel story of Judas and the crucifixion, which is still taught to Christian children, developed in them an antagonism toward all Jews. They became prejudiced against the Jew even before setting eyes on him. Thus, in the very lands where parliamentary government was firmly established and where a modicum of democracy prevailed, and where Jews gained equal rights, anti-Semitism persisted. In the course of the last centuries, it found expression in blood accusations, anti-Jewish agitation, pogroms and discrimination. The historian Elbogen explains this paradox in the following statement: "To most of the peoples of Europe democratic rights had come as a gift. They had done little to acquire the rights they possessed. They accommodated themselves to the outward forms of democracy, but had no real appreciation of its true character. They did not realize that only that people is worthy of freedom which strives to secure freedom for others. The Jews were the first to feel this anomaly, and they felt it most keenly. They had scarcely been granted equal rights when these same rights were put into question. As long as good will, democracy, and humanity prevailed in Europe, everything seemed orderly and correct. But when ill-will, nationalism, and egoism gained dominion and baser instincts were aroused, men began to cry over the rights that had been granted the Jews as over spilt milk. Particularly if any toes were trodden on, the cry arose: *Chercher le Juif* (search for the Jew) no further cause need be sought. The Jews were a community without protection and so a convenient target for any attack."[9]

Organized Jew-baiting was practiced most effectively in eastern Europe, the habitation of the bulk of Jewry. From the bloody days of the Bogdan Chmelnitzki revolt against the Polish landlords (1646–58) when more than a quarter of a million Jews were exterminated, to the pogroms in the Ukraine in 1917–20 when tens of thousands were slaughtered and hundreds of thousands economically ruined, eastern Europe was the center of anti-Jewish activity. Until the rise of Fascism and Nazism, when the center of anti-Semitism shifted once again to the West, Russia, Poland and Rumania were the most active countries of brutal anti-Semitism beginning with economic boycotts and "numerus clausus" in the schools and ending with pogroms.

Anti-Semitism reached its peak in recent years. It became a mass movement which fostered Jew-baiting throughout the world in an organized manner, with the purpose of exterminating all the Jews. Its chief exponents were the German "National Socialists" whose racism declared "Aryans" the superior race and the Jews not simply inferior but sub-human and dangerous to human existence. Jews were considered cancerous growths which must be removed from the body of mankind.

This racial fantasy and myth was supplemented by the theory of Jewish domination of world finance and press. Whenever needed, the argument was reversed and all Jews became communists and workers for bolshevik world revolution. They were also denounced as members of an international organization which strives to subdue the Christians and rule the world.

The Nazis succeeded in exterminating most of the Jews who inhabited the territories which they conquered or occupied. Their crime against the Jewish people and against humanity is unparalled in human history. Their atrocities and cruelties are indescribable.

While the hands of Babylonians and Romans are stained with Jewish blood and while over the centuries Polish, Ukrainian and Rumanian murder corps have killed and tortured Jews in sporadic massacres, it was German minds and German might under Hitler that sent to their death six million Jews in one gigantic assassination which, for all times, should be remembered by mankind.

Why Jew-Hatred?

As already intimated, for many centuries the Jew suffered persecution because his was the religion of the minority. The Jew's persistent and even stubborn adherence to a religion unacceptable to the majority placed him in the class of the "unlike." This religious difference stimulated intolerance and incited the masses against the Jews, especially in the days of political upheavals and religious fanaticism. Hence acts of terror were committed in the name of religion and the Jewish world was plunged into bloodshed. To the fanatic Christian it was a "good deed" to rid the earth of the "non-believers," or the heretics. The Jews, by refusing to accept the religion of the majority groups, naturally typified the world-heretic.

The accusation that the Jews killed Christ became the cornerstone of Jew-baiting. It is to this day one of the outstanding causes of anti-Semitism. The hostility of the early Church and of the Dark Ages, handed down from generation to generation, orally and in writing, in church and in school, has permeated the souls of naive Christians, and is still far from being eradicated.

Even today, in an increasing faithless and unbelieving world, the "Christ-killer" motif is being fostered among young and old, embodied in religious school texts, affecting especially the hearts and minds of children.

"At the same time, as children learn to love Christ, they are naturally seized with indignation against those whom they deem to have hated, tortured and killed him. When the child hears the word, Jew, he associates this conception with the passion of Christ. In Christ he does not see a Jew who loved his people and whose being bore the stamp of religious and ethical inheritance from his forefathers . . . children who receive a non-religious education are inspired with the same anti-Semitic prejudices through scornful or spiteful utterances about the Jews from the lips of their relatives, nurses, teachers and friends. In particular, the words, 'His blood be on us and on our children,' though they must appear psychologically improbable—no angry mob thinks or speaks in this way—have contributed in a great degree to give children the idea of the Jewish people as murderers of Christ, as an incarnation of evil; not merely the generation contemporary with Christ, but all succeeding generations down to the present day."[10]

The pogroms in Russia, Poland and Rumania were instigated by exploiting the religious factor of anti-Semitism, arousing the masses to kill the Jew and avenge the blood of Christ. The fact that at various times and places there rose a Catholic Bishop, a Protestant minister or a dignitary of the Greek Orthodox Church to warn the anti-Semites repeatedly against acts of violence, declaring that Christ himself was a Jew, that his early followers were Jews and that their religion is, as any other true creed, one of brotherly love and human understanding, did not stop the Jew-baiters from using the religious motif as a tool to reach their goal. Gentiles at all times believed that the Jews killed Jesus, and this belief has been perpetuated in Christian teachings for centuries.

The masses were not told that under Roman rule the Jews had no right to pronounce a death sentence. Nor were they informed that even if the Jews had anything to do with it, only a small fraction of them could have been involved in the crucifixion. Historical and scientific explanations and unbiased insight into the truth of the incident are not feasible for the multitude. The religious leaders, on the other hand, failed to enlighten the masses about it. Thus, the Church still remains a breeding ground for anti-Jewish prejudice and, whenever the need arises for cultivating it, anti-Semitic agitators do not fail to utilize this age-long religious prejudice in inciting the public against the Jews.

Another explanation for Jew-baiting is the fact that the Jews were different not only in their religion but also in appearance, in tradition and in habits.

Jewish family life, Jewish rituals, ceremonials and customs, Jewish song and play, Jewish civic law, and even Jewish food, not to speak of inter-Jewish solidarity and relationship, all of these were until recent years quite different from the manner of life of the rest of the population. This difference bred misunderstanding, brought about an estrangement between Jews and non-Jews and gave rise to a definite dislike and distrust for the unique Jewish minority.

"There is a certain people scattered abroad and dispersed among the peoples in all the provinces of thy kingdom; and their laws are diverse from those of every people; neither keep they the King's laws; therefore it profitted not the King to suffer them." (Esther, 3:8). This passage from the Book of Esther characterizes the attitude of the Jew-baiter who tries to exploit Jewish "diverse laws" for his own anti-Jewish ends. Anti-Jewish feeling has constantly been enhanced by this factor, since people inherently develop a suspicious attitude toward the "unlike," towards the different.

"In sum, all anti-Semitism, either old or new, roots in a philosophy of life, a scheme of salvation, whose soil is the emotion imparted by Christian theology and whose intent is to make the Jew the villain of the scheme."[11] The truth of this statement is born out by Professor Jules Isaac of France who studied the persistent religious tradition of anti-Semitism in Christianity. In his monograph "Has anti-Semitism Roots in Christianity?", he says, among other things, "And today . . . Christian charity is employed in favor of the persecuted . . . But it is impossible to forget, because it is an essential factor, that Hitlerian racialism appeared on ground which previous centuries had prepared for it. Did the Nazis spring from nothing or from the bosom of a Christian people? . . . Rudolph Hess, charged with monstrous crimes for which he showed no remorse, came from a pious Catholic family and had considered taking Holy Orders. A recent inquiry has been carried out on 2,000 Roman Catholic textbooks in the French language. It has revealed that the teaching of contempt for the Jew has remained singularly alive in the vast majority of them. As examples, here are a few quotations. 'The religious life of the Jews was reduced in the time of Jesus to pure exterior formalism. The Jews had neither the fear nor the love of God . . . For more than 19 centuries, the Jewish people have been dispersed throughout the world, and have kept the stain of their deicide—that is to say, the abominable crime of which they were guilty in putting to death their God . . .Until the end of time, children of Israel will carry the curses which their fathers have called down on them.' "[12]

The nature of anti-Semitism and its danger to the free world came to light at two court trials in Nuremburg, Germany in 1946 and in Jerusalem, Israel in 1961. The civilized world has had ample opportunity to find out the truth about the Nazi atrocities and to learn that all anti-Semitic theories are false. These trials proved that the so-called Jewish problem is a Gentile problem. As Dr. Sigmund Freud put it: "Hatred for Judaism is, at the bottom, hatred for Christianity." It became apparent during these trials that any manifestations of Jew-hatred is a danger signal of a real affliction in the body of modern society.

During the last ten years many enlightened non-Jews have come to realize that the civilized world is guilty for its seeming acquiescence to the acts of violence committed against the Jew in modern times. Both these trials stirred up the conscience of the socially-minded citizenry in the world of today. They bemoan the great catastrophe which befell the Jew in this age of enlightenment and scientific progress. Many pronouncements have been made by church dignitaries and laymen to the effect that what has happened shall never happen again and that the callousness of the world during the period of horror is to be regretted. But can we be sure? "Fundamentally men have been disquieted by the Eichmann trial because it has brought them face to face with a terrible fact of recent history which poses a grim question. How was it possible that in the heart of Europe, in the full light and freedom of the 20th century, six million persons were silently murdered, without charge and without crime? The trial and sentence of Eichmann, the undoubted organizer of those murders, does not dispose of that question. Let us *not* suppose that it does," [13] And, above all, society should learn never to deform the truth. No less a spiritual and religious leader than Pope John XXIII proclaimed recently: "It is a vital principal never to deform the truth. Truth is fundamental for all responsible men. It should always prevail."

Anti-Semitism in the 1950's abated in most democratic lands, for anti-Semitism is incompatible with the democratic way of life. It threatens the freedom and the very existence of liberty-loving peoples throughout the world; consequently it undermines the foundations of civilized order. Unfortunately, even in countries that uphold the principles of the rights of man, anti-Semitism has not been completely eradicated let alone in those lands ruled by totalitarian regimes.

The following is a survey of the rights of the Jews the world over: their denial in some countries and their preservation in others.

The Decimated Jewish Communities of Europe

GERMANY

"Risking our lives for our countries
Loving our nations' flags
Hounded therefrom in repayment
Hugging our bloody rags."

(ISRAEL ZANGWILL)

With the onslaught of Nazism, Germany became the only country where a body of laws was designed with the view to annihilating the Jews.

The infamous Nazi program deprived the Jew of all his privileges as a citizen. The extent to which Nazi tyranny had abused the Jews even before the war can be gauged from the suicide of approximately 20,000 Jews in Germany within the six years, 1933 to 1939, and of 3,000 Jews in Vienna during the two months, March to May, 1938.

It is important to note that the Jews lived in the provinces which later became part of Germany since the fourth century. There were Jewish communities in Augsburg, Mainz, Cologne, and other principal cities as far back as 321 C.E. It is also worth noting that the Jews of Germany and Austria devotedly served the German culture and the German spirit with their lives, their wealth and their honor. In the First World War, approximately 100,000 out of the 500,000 Jews in Germany fought on the battlefield. The Jewish contribution to the German culture and to general European culture was so impressive that it is sufficient to indicate that of the 39 Nobel prizes awarded prior to World War II, twelve were given to German Jews. "European culture on the eve of the Second World War was thoroughly, indeed indissolubly, interpenetrated by Jewish intellect."[14]

At the time of the rise of the Nazi regime in 1933, there were 525,000 Jews in Germany. Due to the oppressive measures and overt acts of violence, Jews began to emigrate in large numbers so that at the outbreak of the Second World War, there were only 235,000 left in the country. Many of those who emigrated were subsequently annihilated by the onrushing German armies who occupied the countries of refuge.

According to unofficial estimates, the total Jewish population in West Germany in 1960 ranged between 30,000 to 40,000. Most of these Jews are senior citizens who have survived the Nazi concentration camps or who have returned to their native country from other lands to which they fled during the war.

While the West German Republic has made numerous attempts to denazify the country, anti-Semitism has not been eradicated. Anti-Jewish literature is freely distributed by the emissaries of the Arab League; neo-Nazi groups have sprung up in many provinces; anti-Semitic incidents are frequent occurrences. Though condemned in the press and by many leaders, 22 per cent of the adult population as late as 1959 maintained that "it was better that no Jews live in Germany."[15] Generally speaking, the situation in Germany is improving from year to year. While both Israel and the Federal German Republic are reluctant to establish diplomatic relations with one another, a variety of business and educational functions are carried on through the Israel Mission in Cologne, established in 1952. The West German Republic signed a reparations agreement with Israel in 1952 undertaking to pay $715,000,000 to Israel in commodities and services and an additional $107,000,000 for the Conference of Jewish Material Claims against Germany. The German Government lived up to the terms of the agreement. By 1965 it will have fulfilled its promises.

The Jewish population in East Germany is very small. The estimate for 1948 was 3,000. There was no anti-Semitism in the country until 1952, when in line with the anti-Jewish purges in the other Soviet satellites, an anti-Jewish attitude developed in East Germany. At present anti-Semitism has abated although most of the Jews still live with a feeling of insecurity.

AUSTRIA

There were 200,000 Jews in little Austria in the 1930's. Most of them, about 175,000, lived in Vienna, comprising about 6 per cent of the total population of the capital. In March 1939, German armies seized the country and annexed it to Greater Germany. This event marked the beginning of the end of Austrian Jewry. Fortunately, thousands of Jews managed to flee the country before the annexation and during the first year of Nazi rule. Those who remained were soon subjected to tortures and executions in Nazi concentration camps. By the end of the war in 1945, only 2,000 Jews survived in Austria and about another 2,000 returned immediately after the liberation, mostly from concentration camps in Bohemia. In the next few years the Jewish community was increased by a number of displaced persons as well as by infiltrees from behind the Iron Curtain. In 1959, both refugees and former members of the Austrian Jewish communities numbered about 10,000.[16]

The Austrians were deeply shaken by their experiences during the war. After the collapse of the Nazi regime, there were relatively few instances of open anti-Semitic outbreaks. But latent anti-Semitism could be felt in everyday life. The government, however, is trying to enact indemnification legislation to meet the demands of the Jews for restitution of losses during the Nazi regime. The officials resist the neo-Nazis. New life is stirring in the Austrian Jewish communities.

POLAND

More than three million Jews lived in Poland in the 1930's. The Polish Jewish community was the second largest in the world and traced its origin to the 12th century following the Crusades.

Some historians date the first colonies in Poland back to the 9th century.

Jewish immigration was encouraged by the Polish nobility who found the Jews useful in the economic development of the country. The large role played by the Jews in developing businesses and learning and in contributing to the economic growth of the land is an unquestioned historic fact. Notwithstanding restrictions and hostilities that plagued them throughout the centuries, the Jews were loyal citizens, and shed their blood for the Polish fatherland. The Jews did their share in aiding Poland regain its independence after the First World War.

With the inauguration of the Polish Independent Republic, at the end of World War I, triumphant Polish nationalism celebrated its victories by attacks on the Jews. When economic conditions became complicated (immediately after the period of rejoicing), Jew-hatred gained momentum and soon became an integral part of Polish governmental policies and Polish political activities. Nevertheless, as long as Poland was practicing at least some of the democratic principles incorporated in its constitution, Jew-baiting was under cover and in disguise.

In the years before World War II, anti-Jewish reactionary groups spread their propaganda and caused violent outbreaks and economic boycott. The Polish masses actually came to believe that the Jewish minority was responsible for all the ills of an impoverished country of more than 32,000,000 people—for the overpopulation, unemployment and a generally unhealthy economy. Anti-Jewish riots, burning of houses, periodic pogroms in towns and cities, bombing of synagogues, boycotting of businesses marked the campaign of terrorism. Jewish students were beaten and assaulted. Ghetto benches were instituted in all schools for higher learning. The Warsaw "Kehillah" Council, which for years directed all Jewish communal affairs, and which was recognized by the government as the body which had the right to supervise all Jewish activities and impose a tax upon the members for its work, was abolished. In its place the government appointed a commissar for Jewish affairs and curtailed the Jewish internal autonomy or self-government.

The maltreatment of the Jews in Greater Germany during the Nazi regime afforded an object lesson to anti-Semitic Poland. The "legitimate" confiscation of Jewish wealth and the "lawful" expulsion acts in Germany served as a stimulus for the Polish reactionary groups to redouble their terror.

When the Nazis occupied all of Poland in 1939, Polish Jewry was doomed. The Nazi plan to exterminate the Jews was executed in two stages: 1) ghettoization (the creation of special Jewish quarters in Lodz and Warsaw and other large cities), and the imposition of the death penalty for those found outside the ghetto; and 2) concentration camps to which the remnants of the ghettos, together with Jews from other lands, were deported to be murdered in crematoria and gas chambers.

Between 1939–45, nearly 3,000,000 Jews, in one of the largest Jewish communities in the world, were reduced to ashes.

Today there are 40,000 Jews in Poland, including about 11,000 repatriates from the Soviet Union. Poland is a Soviet satellite and treats its Jewish minority in much the same way Russia does. The official anti-Zionist position of the government makes Zionist activity impossible. While prior to 1957 there was continuous emigration from Poland to Israel, since 1958 it has considerably decreased. The number of repatriates from Soviet Russia is also on the decrease.

There is no official anti-Semitism in Poland, although every now and then there are acts of vandalism such as attacks on Jews in trains, desecration of cemeteries and the like. Both the leaders of the Jewish community and the spokesmen of the government acknowledge the fact that anti-Semitism is still endangering the safety of the "saving remnant" of a once prosperous, creative Jewish community in Poland.

RUMANIA

The Polish example was followed, at times with violent manifestations, in Rumania, where Jews had lived since the fourth century. There is reference to a synagogue in the year 397 in Dacia.[17] In the eighth century Jewish communities existed in many southeastern sections of the land. According to Benjamin of Tudela, who travelled through Rumania in 1179, Jews lived and suffered there as elsewhere in Europe, and were "being robbed but not killed as they do to Greeks." From the sixteenth century on, there was a continuous stream of immigrants to the provinces of Moldavia and Wallachia (at that time part of the Turkish empire) from western Europe and Poland. During all those years Jews were mistreated and, except for brief interludes, they suffered severely most of the time. The blood accusations started in the eighteenth century, which also brought frequent riots and incidental attacks. "Down to 1919, the Jews continued to exist as 'aliens', burdened

with all disabilities—and more—suggested by that status . . . ultimately the Jews of Rumania became the most wretched minority
in all of Europe. Rumanian anti-Semitism was even more patho-
logical than Russian. For it was the small, poisonous, mean-
minded anti-Semitism of a 'have-not' nation, aping and com-
pounding the vices of its larger and more powerful neighbors."[18]

The minority clause of the Peace Treaty in 1919, which Rumania was induced to sign after the culmination of World War I,
was also disregarded and Jews were robbed of their civil and political rights. Moreover, the fate of the Jews who lived in the provinces of Bessarabia (formerly part of Tzarist Russia), Transylvania,
and Bukovina (formerly Austria-Hungary) that were ceded to Rumania after the First World War, became even more tragic than
that of Jews in the old Kingdom of Rumania. The Minorities
Treaty of December 9, 1919, provided that "Rumania admits and
declares Rumanian nationals *ipso-facto* and without requirements
for any formalities, all persons habitually resident within the whole
territory of Rumania, including the extensions made by the Treaties of Peace or any extension which may thereafter be made." Yet
the Rumanian government passed laws which deprived more than
250,000 inhabitants of their citizenship. Jew-baiting manifested
itself in various forms: elimination of Jews from schools and liberal
professions, and attacks upon them in the shops, on the streets, and
in synagogues.

Even in the pre-Nazi era, Rumania was determined to free the
country "legally" of the Jewish "superfluous" population. The
frankness which accompanied such acts as Rumania's negotiations
with foreign countries about possibilities for mass exodus of Jews
is the most tragic paradox in modern diplomacy. In a country
where Jewish rights were guaranteed in official treaties, and where
Jews had lived for more than 1,500 years, the government admitted
that its policy was to exile the Jews.

With the advent of the Nazis in Germany, the Rumanian Jew-
baiters were given an object lesson in the handling of Jews. The
acts of violence became more frequent and gained in intensity.
The Jews were at the mercy of the mobs whose hatred was allowed
full expression. Finally, during World War II, "Rumanian Jewry
was subjected to pogroms, discrimination, alienation of property
and particularly in the areas outside the old kingdom, to deportation and massacres. Only a little over one-half of Rumanian Jewry
survived the ordeal."[19] The reason for this relatively large number of survivors is due to the fact that the Nazis never occupied

the old kingdom and that only the Jews of North Transylvania, Bessarabia and North Bukovina were subjected to the Nazi tyranny.

In the post-war years, many Jews left the country. In the period 1948–1956, 120,000 emigrated to Israel. Smaller groups went to other countries. The population which in 1939 numbered 800,000 was reduced to about 175,000.

In 1947, the Communist Party became the dominant political power in Rumania which gradually became a satellite of the Soviet Union. Under the communist regime life for the remaining Jews became harsher. The government nationalized factories and businesses, and thereby more than 50,000 Jews lost their economic positions. Emigration to Israel was drastically curtailed. A violent anti-Zionist campaign was launched in 1949, and a large number of Zionists were arrested and sentenced to prison terms. Emigration was suddenly suspended in 1951. In 1958, fewer than 800 Jews were permitted to leave for Israel and in 1959 two military tribunals were established to "try Jews suspected of contact with the Israeli embassy, dealing in foreign currency, or reading forbidden Zionist literature." [20] On the other hand, it was reported by American Jewish correspondents that the government did not interfere with religious activities and that synagogues are well cared for. The recent visit of Chief Rabbi Moses Rosen of Bucharest to America brought to the fore the fact that the government's attitude toward the Jews is favorable. Rabbi Rosen maintains that "no more is fear mirrored in the eyes of Rumanian Jews."

CZECHOSLOVAKIA

The 360,000 Jews of Czechoslovakia enjoyed full freedom under Presidents Masaryk and Benes (1920–1939). The Jewish communities in Prague and other cities are the oldest on the European continent. Czechoslovakia was the second oasis for the Jews in central Europe, the first being Switzerland. In government circles, there was no prejudice. Notwithstanding Nazi propaganda, the general population treated the Jews in a friendly manner, even before the dismemberment of the Republic.

The late President of the Republic, Professor Thomas G. Masaryk, was a friend of the Jewish people. The Jews were considered an autonomous group in this genuinely democratic state of central Europe. The government made every effort to check the spread of anti-Semitism. The 2,500,000 pro-Nazi German inhabitants of the Sudetenland who fostered race hatred, were not permitted to reach out to the non-German element outside the German-inhabited region.

The dismemberment of Czechoslovakia, resulting from the Munich Peace Treaty in 1939, brought into the former democracy the Third Reich. All the territories occupied by Germany had become "Juden-rein," ("free of Jews") and the two autonomous states within the Czechoslovakian boundaries, that of Slovakia and Ruthenia, were no exception. The annexation of Bohemia and Moravia by Germany in May, 1939, of Carpatho-Russia by Hungary in the same month, and the formation of the "independent" Slovakian state dealt a final blow to the Jewish community.

According to the census of 1930, there were about 350,000 Jews in the country. Between 1938 and 1940, an estimated number of 50,000 succeeded in emigrating. During the period 1941-45, 260,000 were lost. Less than 40,000 survived, most of them returnees from concentration camps, who scattered in Carpatho-Russia and in Czech lands.

After the communist coup in 1948, there were about 15,000 Jews in the land. Most of them have severed all connection with organized Jewish life and considered themselves fully assimilated in the majority groups. In 1949, the local Zionist Organization was dissolved and legal emigration stopped. The great purge of 1951-52 had an adverse effect upon the small remnant. All persons of Jewish origin were purged from prominent positions in the Communist Party and the Jews were attacked in the press as Zionists and instruments of foreign imperialism. The Jewish community, however, is retaining a semblance of Jewish life, undisturbed by government policy. The two American rabbis who visited Czechoslovakia in the summer of 1960 reported that the decreasing number of surviving Jews "endeavored to create out of the chaos and void they inherited . . . a meaningful Jewish life."[21]

HUNGARY

Records reveal the presence of Jews in the land known today as Hungary as far back as the third century. The early Jewish settlers immigrated to the land from Byzantine and Khazar Empires and founded their communities in the towns along the Danube and Tisza rivers. There is also evidence of Jewish life in the country during the Mongolian conquest in the ninth century. During the middle ages, Jews were found in every large community. Until the fourteenth century they were not menaced, though they suffered from the usual religious disabilities. From 1360 to their emancipation in 1867, throughout these centuries of political inequality, the Jews were, however, very loyal subjects and pioneered in many fields: agriculture, industry, commerce, and the arts. But since emancipation their contributions to the national life in Hungary were so outstanding that "approximately 300 Jewish families have been ennobled for outstanding services." [22] Anti-Semitic manifestations were few and insignificant up to World War I.

Hungary was one of the first states in post-World War I Europe to introduce a dictatorship. This dictatorial regime, which slowly developed into a semi-parliamentary or semi-Fascist rule, made the Jews the victims of its political adventures. Immediately after the Communist upheaval (in March, 1919) under the leadership of Bela Kun, white terror [23] activities began, which were directed against the Jews, the terrorists blaming them for the disorganized state of affairs and the Communist revolt. This white terrorism was given the aspect of a war of Magyar independence against the Jewish people, and resulted in anti-Jewish reprisals and the elimination of many Jews from the economic, social and cultural life.

The steady drift to anti-Semitism increased in 1920, despite the minority privileges granted the Jews under the Peace Treaty of 1919. All the anti-Semitic decrees and legislation were disguised under a cloak of patriotism and 100 per cent Magyarism and consequently reduced the Jews to citizens of secondary rank and robbed them of all their rights. The fact that 10,000 Jews fell in World War I in defense of Hungary was forgotten. The patriotic devotion of the Jews, who even before the war were Magyarized to the extent of drifting away from their people, was forgotten. The Jews responsible for the revival of the Magyar tongue were ignored. But the anti-Semitic arguments of old, suppplemented by the new accusations of the Hitler type, were remembered and exploited against the Jews.

The friendly attitude of Hungarian Regent Horthy toward Germany, and Hungary's joining the Berlin-Rome Axis resulted in the establishment of a Racial Bureau in Budapest, which was directed by German "specialists" and which was very symptomatic of the intentions of the Hungarian government.

The Nazi influence in Hungary and the government's systematic persecution of its Jewish citizens terrified the Jewish community to the extent that the number of suicides during 1936-39 reached enormous proportions, and the numbers of panic-stricken, fleeing Jews increased from month to month.

With the outbreak of World War II and the eventual spread of Nazism into the country, compulsory labor service for all Jews was introduced, followed by deportation to Poland. In 1942, tens of thousands of Jews were sent to work behind the Nazi battlelines, never to return alive. With the German occupation of Hungary in 1944, the Jews in the provinces were placed in ghettos. In Budapest, they were sent to special "yellow" houses and subsequently more than one-half of them were shipped to extermination camps. The infamous march on foot of 100,000 Jews from Budapest to Austria was another brutal act which brought death to more than 25,000. When the Russians occupied Hungary in January, 1945, only 143,000 Jews remained from the former community which numbered 725,000 Jews in 1939.[24] Of these remaining Jews more than 25 per cent were over 60 years old.

In the period 1945-1948 the Jews set out to rebuild their shattered lives. They endeavored to re-establish normal family lives, to rebuild their religious and cultural institutions, for they believed that the new era of democracy and liberalism would last for a long time. The belief stemmed from Hungary's prosecution of war criminals and its act of 1946, declaring anti-Semitic agitation a criminal offense. But at this very same time, anti-Semitic agitation became very strong and acts of anti-Jewish violence broke out. As a result, 108,500 Jews wanted to emigrate.[25] Only one year after their return from deportation or release from the ghettos, Hungarian Jews were seeking every means of escape from the prevalent anti-Semitism in the country. Unfortunately, only about 4,000 succeeded in fleeing the country via Czechoslovakia and Austria in 1948 and in 1949.

In 1948 the Communist party seized power. During the ensuing year, the government completed its program of nationalization, of industry and commerce, thus driving many Jews from their economic positions. The campaign of political repression of all non-Communist groups resulted in the liquidation of the Zionist movement. The nationalization of almost all schools formerly owned and operated by the Jewish community, the prohibition against teaching Hebrew and the requirement that all shops and stores be kept open on Saturdays and Jewish holidays—brought Jewish life to a standstill.

In 1951 the government decided to evict a part of the population. According to reliable sources, more than 30,000 Jews were among those evicted. Thus in the space of one decade (1945–1955) the Jewish community of Hungary decreased by nearly 30 per cent, from 140,000 in 1945 to 100,000 in 1955.

The situation somewhat improved after the anti-Communist revolt in 1956. The government abandoned class-motivated anti-Semitism. There is no discrimination in employment and the religious rights of the Jews are respected.

YUGOSLAVIA

Yugoslavian Jewry was emancipated in 1918. In the 1930's, however, the anti-Semitic movement became so violent that the government had to close temporarily the Nazi centers of anti-Semitic propaganda and arrest the party's leader. The existence of a German minority of 800,000 in the country made it much more convenient for Nazi agents and local Jew-baiters to indulge in anti-Jewish activities.

The Moslem clergy was another element of the population which stirred up anti-Jewish activities. It advocated boycott of the Jews, contending that Jews in Palestine were mistreating the Arabs. Consequently the Jews, although protected by the government, experienced discrimination and prejudice. Foreign-born Jews were naturally subjected to even more drastic persecutions.[26]

In the pre-World War II period, there were approximately 76,000 Jews in Yugoslavia. During the first year of the War the Yugoslavs resisted the German pressure for overt acts of anti-Semitism. But in March, 1941, the country became a member of the Axis. In April of the same year, the Germans occupied Yugoslavia. Anti-Jewish persecutions, mass killings and deportations became frequent occurrences.

It is estimated that eighty per cent of the Jews perished during the period 1941–45. The survivors, 13,500 of them, began to heal their wounds and reconstitute their lives.

The new constitution of Yugoslavia of 1945 guaranteed the absolute equality of all citizens. All anti-Jewish laws were abrogated. But due to the far-reaching changes in the political and economic structure of the country (the regime became Communist), the Jews turned their eyes toward Israel and in the course of one year, 1948–49, more than 8,000 emigrated to the new state.

In 1959 there were less than 6,000 Jews left in the country.

GREECE

Historians trace Jewish contact with Greece to remote times. There is sufficient evidence to show that a considerable number of Jews lived on the mainland and on the islands during the period

mans occupied the Memel region. Not only were the several thousand Jews of Memel completely ruined but the entire Jewish community of Lithuania became exposed to renewed aggression and anti-Semitic campaigns. The government circles, though still opposing anti-Jewish outbreaks, could not withstand Nazi pressure and permitted occasional anti-Jewish broadcasts and the distribution of seditious literature. Thus, the peaceful atmosphere in which Lithuanian Jews had lived from 1918 to 1935 became dense with anti-Semitism and charged with anxiety.

In the summer of 1940, the Republic of Lithuania saw the irresistible advance of the Nazi armies into Denmark, Holland, Belgium, Norway and France, and conceded to being incorporated into the Soviet Union. A year later, the Germans, at war with Russia, now gained control of this small country.

The Jews had to endure the whole barbaric program of Nazi savagery. All the sufferings which befell Polish Jewry were visited upon the Jews of Lithuania. Assault and murder were the order of the day. In 1942, the mass murder began. In Vilna alone, more than 50,000 were slaughtered. Thus, by the end of World War II, 90 per cent of the Jews had perished. The Jewish community with a population of 150,000 was reduced to less than 15,000.

There are very few Jews today in this section of Soviet Russia. Those who survived the great upheaval and remained in the formerly independent Baltic republic live there now by the grace of the Communists.

TOPICS FOR DISCUSSION

1. What conclusions must be drawn from the fact that Jewish hopes for equality and freedom after World War I proved to be premature?
    (a) Are equality and freedom less desirable goals because they were not attained?
    (b) What methods to attain them proved inadequate?

2. Do you agree with Professor Elbogen's implied identification of nationalism with ill-will and egoism?
    (a) How do you understand nationalism?
    (b) Is there an American nationalism?
    (c) Who are Jewish nationalists?
    (d) Are democracies incompatible with nationalism?

3. Must he who loves his own religion be intolerant of other religions? Are all religions intolerant of each other?

4. What forms of anti-Semitism have you encountered in your own life? What is your best explanation for them? What is your best response to them?

5. What Jewish organizations are concerned with defense against anti-Semitism?

NOTES TO CHAPTER 2

1. Kastein, Josef: "History and Destiny of the Jews," Garden City Publishing Company, Garden City, N. Y., 1934, p. 375.
2. Galut—literally means exile, it now denotes the term "dispersion."
3. A charge of ritual murder was brought against the Jews of Damascus. A Franciscan monk disappeared and the Jews were accused of murdering him for religious purposes. The local governor, by torturing a Jew, extorted a confession which implicated the leading Jews of the community. After the entire community had suffered from the bigotry of the mob, the Sultan declared the charge absurd and the accused Jews (one had been tortured to death) were released.
4. A six-year old child, Edgar Mortara, was forcibly abducted from his parents by Papal guards. The alleged basis for this act was that the child had been secretly baptized by a servant girl, and on her confession the holy office of the Inquisition ordered the abduction of the child. The incident aroused indignation, but despite appeals to the Pope, he, to use his own words, "snapped his fingers at the whole world."
5. Alfred Dreyfus was an artillery officer attached to the Intelligence Department of the French Army. Agitated by the anti-Semitic propaganda of Eduard Drumont, (the editor of a daily paper, a professed enemy of the Jews), Dreyfus' superiors accused him of turning over military secrets to German-Italian military attaches. A secret military tribunal found Dreyfus guilty and sentenced him to penal servitude for life on Devil's Island, French Guiana. Believing in Dreyfus' innocence, the famous French novelist, Emile Zola, at the risk of his life, issued the famous "J'accuse", an attack on the general staff of the French Army. He was arrested but succeeded in fleeing to England, continuing his work for a retrial of Dreyfus. In 1900 Dreyfus was pardoned and four years later he was vindicated and reinstated, serving again as an officer in the First World War.
6. In this Hungarian town, a 14-year old girl disappeared. No trace of her could be found. Rumors spread that she had been seen in the vicinity of the synagogue and that her blood had been drained for religious purposes (baking of Matzot) and the body dismembered and buried. The police could find no basis for establishing guilt. Seventy-nine days after the girl's disappearance the current of the River Theiss deposited a corpse upon the shore. The mobs in all of Central Europe raged against the Jews. After 14 months of trial of the 80 Jewish men who were accused of the murder, the court ruled that the charge could not be maintained and acquitted the prisoners.
7. The Hadrian Edict forbade the Jews to practice their religion and deprived them of all civil and political rights.
8. There were numerous signs of shame for the Jews to stamp them as a group that must be recognized by the rest of the population. It originated with the Arabs in the latter half of the 8th century, when the Jews were ordered to wear a thin rope instead of a belt and a black linen turban on the head. In the 11th century, Egyptian Jews were commanded to wear little bells upon their clothes and the emblem of a wooden calf, to remind them of their sin in the desert when Aaron molded for them a golden calf as a deity. These badges of shame were adopted in the Christian lands beginning with anti-Jewish decrees of Pope Innocent III (1190–1216). In France and Spain this shame emblem was a yellow circle upon the chest. In other countries it was half white and half red. Pope Benedict XIII

(1415) decreed that Jewish women wear this sign upon the forehead. Edward I of England set the shame-mark in the form of two tablestones. Finally Hitler introduced the yellow badge with the Star of David.

9. Elbogen, Ismar: "A Century of Jewish Life," Jewish Publication Society, Philadelphia, 1944, p. 141.

10. Valentin, Hugo: "Anti-Semitism, Historically and Critically Examined," The Viking Press, New York, 1933, pp. 13-14.

11. Kallen, Horace M.: "Of Them Which Say They Are Jews," Bloch Publishing Company, New York, 1954, p. 46.

12. Isaac, Jules: "Has Anti-Semitism Roots in Christianity?" National Conference of Christians and Jews, New York, 1961, pp. 65-68.

13. Trevor-Roper, H. R.: "Eichman is not Unique," *New York Times Magazine*, September 17, 1961, p. 13.

14. Sachar, Howard M.: "The Course of Modern Jewish History," World Publishing Company, Cleveland, 1958, p. 417.

15. American Jewish Year Book, 1960, p. 237.

16. American Jewish Year Book, 1961, p. 277.

17. Ancient Rumania was known as Dacia. It was the fertile valley inhabited by the Dacians and conquered by the Roman hordes in the 4th century.

18. Sachar, Howard M.: "The Course of Modern Jewish History," World Publishing Company, Cleveland, 1958, pp. 258-259.

19. European Jewry Ten Years After the War, World Jewish Congress, New York, 1956, p. 44.

20. American Jewish Year Book, 1961, p. 305.

21. American Jewish Year Book, 1961, p. 299.

22. Rittenberg, Louis: "The Crisis in Hungary," *Contemporary Jewish Record*, May-June, 1939.

23. The fighting units waging war against the Communists—the Reds—were designated as "Whites."

24. European Jewry Ten Years After the War, World Jewish Congress, New York, 1956, p. 60.

25. *Ibid.*, p. 67.

26. Most of the Jews in these Balkan states were of the Sephardic group.

27. "Shadlanuth" is the Hebrew term denoting intercession by means of "putting in a good word."

3

The Rights of the Jews
(Continued)

Communities that Suffered Great Losses

FRANCE

The first Jewish immigrants came to Gaul in the days of Herod, King of Judah (40 B.C.E.). Historic evidence of a Jewish community in France in the fifth century is the passage of a law which prohibited Jews and pagans from holding public office. In the sixth century, large Jewish communities existed in Marseilles, Orleans, Paris and Bordeaux. During the Middle Ages, the Jews of France were repeatedly expelled and permitted to return, depending upon the attitude of the ruling kings, dukes and clergy, and upon the need for a mercantile and artisan class to fill the treasury. The Jews were emancipated in 1791 and gained the status of full-fledged citizens. But emancipation did not result in the complete eradication of anti-Jewish prejudice or hostility.

Jew-baiting survived in the land notwithstanding all sincere attempts to uproot it. From time to time, anti-Jewish feelings became manifest.

The Dreyfus case in 1892 demonstrated the existence of a relatively strong anti-Semitic undercurrent. Since the exposé of the plot against Dreyfus, France has been very friendly to its own Jews and hospitable to those persecuted in other countries. During and after World War I, a number of Jews occupied high governmental positions and even gained Cabinet rank.[1] France became a haven for refugees from Germany, Austria, Czechoslovakia, and other countries.

Immediately after the outbreak of World War II, (1939), about 320,000 Jews were estimated to have been in France, including 70,000 German Jewish refugees. During the mobilization, the French Government ordered the internment of the refugees, and a hostility toward all Jews in France manifested itself. The population accused the Jews of war-mongering to take revenge on the Nazis. It considered the Jewish refugees from Germany potential enemies of the State, even though the French themselves were victims of German persecution, and a large number of the foreign and native-born Jews joined the French Army.

When the Nazis occupied Northern France, including Paris, a mass exodus began from the German-occupied area to the unoccupied zone. At the same time, about 30,000 Jews managed to flee the country. Nonetheless the Nazis succeeded in deporting 120,000 Jews to the East where all but 5,000 perished in the death camps. The Vichy Regime in the unoccupied zone, dominated by Nazis, was not friendly to the Jews. Many of its officials cooperated with the Nazis and inflicted untold suffering upon the Jews who sought refuge in southern France. They disfranchised many of them, interned others and made it difficult for them to escape the Nazi wrath.

It is worth noting in this connection that until 1940, the German authorities, before reaching the decision to completely destroy all Jews, considered the possibility of mass resettlement of Jews in Madagascar, a French protectorate. "The Madagascar project was designed to take care of millions of Jews. The authors of the plan wanted to empty the Reich-Protektorat area and all of occupied Poland of their Jewish population. . . . But the Madagascar plan did not materialize. It hinged on the conclusion of a peace treaty with France, and such a treaty depended on an end of hostilities with England. With no end to the hostilities there was no peace treaty, and with no peace treaty, there was no Madagascar."[2]

In the post-war period the French Government investigated the record of its tens of thousands of Nazi collaborators but only a few of those sentenced to death were executed and many of those who had been ostracized were reinstated to their former positions. This lack of interest in the prosecution of Nazi collaborators became an important factor in the organization of new anti-Semitic groups and in the revival of earlier anti-Semitic activities. After the War, the anti-Semites did not dare to profess themselves as such, yet a more or less pronounced hostility toward Jews persisted. On the whole, however, militant anti-Semitism is non-existent. Only seldom does one encounter overt acts of anti-Semitism among the common people. In 1956, the French Army cooperated with the Israelis in the Sinai Campaign against Egypt. The French attitude toward the new State is very friendly.

Only a few years ago there were in France approximately 300,000 Jews. The estimate for today is at about 500,000. The constant influx of Jewish refugees from Arab lands, especially from Algeria in the months preceeding its rise as a free Moslem state, has increased the French Jewish community by almost one-half.

BELGIUM

There was a Jewish settlement in Belgium in the early centuries of the Common Era. Its history until the emancipation in 1865 was very much the same as the history of other Jewish communities in Western Europe. During the Crusades they were subjected to physical attacks. The Black Plague resulted in a series of massacres. In the 1340's they were expelled, then resettled in the 15th century and, until their emancipation in 1865, were treated with comparative lenience. The country has, however, been a place of refuge for Jewish wanderers on numerous occasions, even prior to the complete equality granted to the Jews in 1865. Hospitality was shown to the Jews who were expelled from France in 1306 and 1321 and permission was given to Marranos in 1541 to settle in the land. In the modern period particularly, there never existed anti-Jewish immigration laws. The Jewish community which in 1891 numbered only 3,000 people was enlarged by the constant stream of refugees from Germany, Czechoslovakia and Poland, which swelled its number to 65,000 in 1937.

In the late 1930's, largely due to the influx of a few thousand immigrants from Germany, the Belgian anti-Semites raised the issue of "the overflow of the country by Jewish aliens." But the Government forbade anti-Jewish discrimination and prevented any outbreaks.

Anti-Jewish measures were introduced in Belgium immediately after the German troops invaded the country in 1940. The efforts of the Belgian Queen prevented deportations until the summer of 1942. For a short time she was able to protect the native Jews, but the others were deported. Hitler's officials however, soon overruled the Queen and the deportation of all Jews commenced. By the end of the war, 27,000 Jews had been deported to the extermination camps in the east. Only about 1,200 of these deportees survived. It is important to note that the greater part of the population was opposed to the manifestations of anti-Jewish persecution. Many of them helped the Jews to hide and to escape. Many of the Catholic clergy rescued Jews, offering refuge especially to children.

THE NETHERLANDS

Holland is one of the few countries where anti-Jewish prejudice has never existed and where Jews have never been subject to anti-Jewish legislation. Since the expulsion of Jews from Spain in 1492, when numerous Spanish exiles found a haven in Holland, persecuted and homeless Jews have always been welcomed whether they came from Germany or from Poland. In the 1930's, several thousand German refugees were admitted.

In this country, the Jews have always been treated with utmost friendliness and courtesy. In their turn they have contributed to the advancement of culture,[3] international trade and economic progress. Jews held high public office in all governmental and social institutions and gave themselves unstintingly to the country's welfare. The constitution of Holland makes a provision permitting Jews who observe the Sabbath to keep their enterprises open on Sunday. Such tolerance and such religious and civil freedom are unique in the world.

But in this country, too, where anti-Semitism was never tolerated, Hitler's hordes succeeded in inflicting great losses upon the Jews. Out of a total Jewish population of 140,000 in 1940, (of which about 30,000 were refugees), about 110,000 were deported to the Nazi death camps. Only 6,000 returned at the end of the war. The general population had been in a state of physical and economic ruin during the German occupation, but the Jews were almost completely destroyed. While the Dutch offered help and endeavored to shield their Jewish friends from the Nazi onslaught, the period of Nazi rule made them "Jew-conscious," and the Jews became more conspicious than ever in the past. Overcome by a sense of despair, the surviving Jews began to emigrate. At the end of the hostilities about 8,000 emigrated to Israel and to other countries.

The government made a concerted effort to help the survivors resume a normal life. In the ensuing year after the cessation of hostilities, about 13,000 Jews returned from Southern France, Switzerland and England, where they had found a haven during the war. By the mid-fifties their number was estimated at 35,000. The Jewish community enjoys equal rights. They live in a traditionally liberal country where anti-Semitism manifests itself only sporadically.

RUSSIA

Elsewhere in this chapter there is a discussion of the state of Jewish life in the Soviet Union. In this section of our story we must record the tragedy that befell Russian Jewry during the period of the Nazi occupation.

When the German armed forces invaded Russia in June, 1941, five million Jews were living under the Soviet regime. Four million of these Jews were to be found in territories which were later overrun by the Germans. About one and one-half million living in the affected areas fled before the Germans arrived. In order to reach as many Jews as possible, the extermination mobile units of the Nazis "had moved with such speed behind the advancing army that several hundred thousand Jews could be killed like sleeping flies. . . . During the first sweep the mobile killing units reported approximately 100,000 victims a month. . . ." [5]

The slaughter of the Jewish prisoners of war who served under the Soviet flag and the deportation into ghettos constituted the second phase of the operation. And finally the ghetto population was liquidated ruthlessly and brutally. Those who remained in hiding were found by raiding parties consisting of recruits from the civil population headed by Nazis. Thus the Germans "left behind many mass graves but few living Jews. . . . The total number of Jews killed rises to 1,400,000." [6]

This tragic phenomenon of mass graves on Russian soil prompted the famous Russian poet, a loyal communist, Yevgeny Yevtushenko, to write a poem, *Babi Yar,* in conection with the ravine in Kiev where at least 40,000 Jewish men, women and children were buried after a wholesale massacre by the Nazi killing units. This poem points to the participation of the civilian population in this act, and it is an indictment of anti-Semitism both historically and as a facet of contemporary Soviet society. [7]

Communities that Suffered Relatively Small Losses

ITALY

The Italian Jewish community is the oldest on the European continent. At the time of the Maccabees (160 B.C.E.) there were Jews in Rome, and in the days of Herod (40 B.C.E.) there must have been in Rome a Jewish population of about 50,000. After four to five centuries of Christian persecution, the Jews were treated with lenience during the Middle Ages, although they were still looked upon as aliens. From the Middle Ages until the second half of the nineteenth century, their treatment varied from occasional attacks and expulsion to resettlement, from anti-Jewish outbursts in some sections of the country to fair treatment in other parts. Their complete liberation came in 1859.

Since then the Jews lived happily in Italy, enjoying equal rights and full political freedom. They held high positions in government, in science and in business. They gave Italy poets, scientists, cabinet officers, senators and scholars. The Prime Minister, Luigi Luzzati (1909–11) and the Foreign Minister, Sannino, were Jews. In the 1920's there were more than 400 Jewish professors in the universities, Jewish officers in the army, navy and air corps and even in the Fascist Party.

There were 44,000 Jews in Italy in the decade prior to World War II out of a population of 43,000,000. There was no anti-Semitism. Jewish students from foreign countries were admitted to schools for higher learning and in the mid-thirties Jewish refugees from Germany found temporary refuge in the country.

The Fascist Government and its leader, Mussolini, had for years respected the rights of the Jews and on several occasions asserted that "the Fascist Government never thought and is not thinking of adopting political or economic measures against the Jews," and that "anti-Semitism is a product of barbarism."

However, with the formation of the Rome-Berlin Axis, anti-Semitic utterances in the press and by public officials appeared more frequently. After Hitler's visit to Italy in May, 1938, anti-Semitism became an integral part of the government's policy. The first anti-Semitic act was the expulsion from the universities of all the foreign-born Jewish students (most of the students were Polish, Rumanian and Hungarian Jews who had found a haven in the Italian universities) and the Jews who had fled from Germany. Subsequently an anti-Semitic law was enacted for a special census to determine the number of Jews in Italy, so that their participation in the armed forces, civil service and professions could be limited by the ratio of one Jew to every 1,000 non-Jewish Italians. Then followed laws expelling Jews from all government bureaus, from employment in the Cabinet of Ministers, from university chairs, from the Fascist Party. Laws also forbad intermarriage and imposed hardships upon Jews in the economic life of the country.

These decrees were patterned along the German theory of "superior" and "inferior" races, which declared all Jews to be outside the Italian-"Aryan" races and included non-Jewish families with one or more Jewish members by marriage.

The growth of anti-Semitism in Italy is seen from the anti-Jewish outbreaks in Tripoli in December, 1938, instigated by a number of Italian Fascists, the desecration of an old Jewish cemetery in Rhodes (where Jews lived ever since the Maccabean period, and whose historical records bear testimony to Jewish communal life for the last 2,000 years), and the wholesale plunder of Jewish goods. It is significant, however, to bear in mind, that the Italian people regarded Jew-baiting with much disgust. The tolerant Italians could not understand the sudden attacks but they were helpless to do anything and afraid to speak their minds.

While the government gave reluctant assent to the Nazi policy with regard to the Jewish problem, the Italians themselves endeavored to shield the Jews from the clutches of the Nazis. During the War, the Italian armies, from the moment they arrived in their zones of occupation, guarded the Jews against massacres by local Quislings and by units of German Nazis, wherever they could.

It was only when Italy herself was occopied by the armies of the Third Reich that some 10,000 of the 45,000 Italian Jews were arrested and deported to the concentration camps. It was due to the Italian attitude against genocide, and to the Jews themselves that only a small part of the Jews in Italy and in the zones of France and Croatia occupied by Italians was annihilated.

In the years after the War, approximately 58,000 Jews lived in Italy. Of them, 26,000 were displaced persons. In 1960, the Jews of Italy numbered about 32,000 natives and a few hundred refugees. Most of the 26,000 displaced persons emigrated to Israel and to other countries. There is little, if any, anti-Semitism in Italy. The Italians showed resistance to anti-Jewish measures during the War and their attitude to the Jews remains friendly to this day. A great revolution, however, has occurred in the thinking of the Italian Jews. Their enthusiasm for Israel is universal and their support of funds for the development of Israel is unprecedented.

BULGARIA

There were Jews in Bulgaria during the Roman period. When the country was absorbed by the Byzantian empire in 967 C.E. there was an influx of Jews from other parts of the empire. Ger-

man Jews settled there in 1360 and Spanish exiles found refuge
in the country in 1492. Little of importance happened to the Jews
in Bulgaria till the Russo-Turkish War of 1877–78, when they
were caught in the political cross-fire between pro-Turks and pro-
Russians. It was in that year that many of them had to flee the
country. At the culmination of the conflict, the Treaty of Berlin
of 1878 gave the Jews civil rights. They experienced no political
discrimination until the Nazi occupation save for the blood accusation in 1890.

In 1940 there were 50,000 Jews in Bulgaria. During the war,
the Jews in the old kingdom, (regions of Sofia, Phillipopoles and
Rugtchuk) escaped annihilation thanks to the determined stand
of the Bulgarian people. Anti-Jewish laws existed but were not
fully enforced. Jews were sent to centers of detention but were
not deported. The other Jewish communities (in the parts of the
country acquired from Greece and Macedonia) and Jews of foreign nationality were delivered into the hands of the Nazis and
most of them perished. The number of victims is given as 15,000.

After liberation, all anti-Jewish measures were suspended. The
Jews from the detention centers and some who had fled to other
countries returned to their homes. However, the effect of the war
left the community economically ruined, destitute and poverty-
stricken. The Bulgarian Jewish community, unlike the Jews of
other communities who survived Nazi tyranny, decided to leave
their native land and emigrate to Israel. The emigration proceeded according to plan. The Bulgarian authorities cooperated,
the Jewish Agency secured the visas which were needed to enter
Palestine during the British Mandatory Regime (prior to the rise
of the State of Israel in May, 1948) and from the day of liberation
till May 1948 there was uninterrupted emigration. With the rise
of the State, the exodus of Bulgarian Jews was intensified, and
by 1953, more than 38,000 Jews came to Israel in less than six
years. The emigration of almost the entire Jewish population is
explained in part by the Zionist traditions of Bulgarian Jewry.

The number of Jews who remained in the country is now estimated at about 7,000. The Communist Regime, which is influenced by Russian anti-Israel diplomacy, no longer views with favor
Jewish emigration to Israel, and thus potential emigrants are reluctant to take the risk of applying for an exit permit. Jewish
religious life was affected by the rapid diminution of the Jewish
population and by the Communist leaders who do not encourage

its perpetuation. Mixed marriages are frequent, and the small number of Jews remaining in Bulgaria were recently described as "gradually losing their connection with Judaism."

DENMARK

There were Jews in Denmark in the 16th century. The Jewish communities in Denmark have never been large, although during World War I there was a considerable influx of east-European Jews who found a haven in Copenhagen. The Jews of Denmark were emancipated in 1864 and lived in peace, experiencing few, if any, anti-Semitic outbursts up to the Nazi invasion in 1940. At the beginning, the Germans did not take stringent action against the Jews of Denmark because they were anxious to maintain good relations with the Danes. It is said that King Christian X issued a warning that he and his family would put on the Mogen David yellow badge of shame if the Germans compelled his Jewish subjects to wear it. It was fortunate that the Nazi Party in Denmark was very insignificant and had not a single personality of importance, as was the case in other countries. In August, 1943, an order was given to deport all Jews. A certain officer, an opponent of the persecution, advised his friends of the threat and asked them to warn the Jews. Consequently on the day before the edict was to have been issued, the Jewish population knew about the Nazi plan.

The German action against the Jews aroused a nationwide protest and gave rise to active resistance against the occupiers in wide circles of the Danish population. Until this time resistance had been confined to certain groups. Many groups were spontaneously formed with the sole purpose of rescuing Jews. Most active were those formed by doctors and the clergy but many other people participated. Jews were hidden, brought to certain places at, or near, the coast, all sorts of ships or boats were mobilized and within a week some 7,000 people were taken to Sweden. After the war, all of these Jews returned to Denmark. When the raids started the Nazis succeeded in capturing only a few elderly inhabitants of the Jewish Home for the Aged and 475 people who were caught fleeing to Sweden. These Jews were deported and sent to camps where deportees were treated as "privileged inmates." Thus the Jewish community of Denmark escaped the dreadful fate of decimation by the Nazis.

The number of Jews in Denmark in 1940 was approximately

6,000. In 1950 the estimated figure was 5,500. After the return of the refugees from Sweden, Jewish life in Denmark became normal again. There is no anti-Semitism in Denmark today.

LUXEMBOURG

In this small country there were 5,000 Jews in 1940. Before the German invasion, more than one-fifth of the Jews fled the country with the help of the retreating French troops. Another group escaped to other countries. Those remaining were deported to the Ghetto of Lodz and directly to the Auschwitz crematorium. In April, 1943 Luxembourg was practically without Jews. After the liberation in the fall of 1944, only 70 Jews emerged from hiding and 35 returned from the extermination camps. In the ensuing years other survivors returned. The community today numbers less than 1,000 persons.

NORWAY

In 1940 the total Jewish population of Norway was 1,350. During the war about 500 succeeded in escaping to Sweden and England. Some remained in hiding and the rest were deported by the German invaders. There are at present from 800 to 900 Jews, enjoying equal rights with all other citizens.

Communities Virtually Unaffected by the Nazis

GREAT BRITAIN

The history of the Jews in England begins at the end of the tenth century. Until the expulsion in 1290, there were no outstanding persecutions. From the resettlement in 1655 to the modern period, the Jews have been treated fairly well. Complete emancipation took place in 1858.

Jews in Great Britain enjoy full liberty and equality. They occupy high offices in the government and play an important part in all phases of social, economic and cultural life of the country. There are Jewish peers in the House of Lords, Jewish Members of Parliament, Jewish commissioners in the colonies and dominions, etc. The "Balfour Declaration" of November 2, 1917, pledging British support for the establishment of a Jewish national home in Palestine, is another indication of the friendly attitude toward the Jew.

However, even Great Britain is not immune to anti-Semitism. There exists a Fascist Movement, under the direction of Oswald

Mosley, which has made anti-Semitism the basis of its program. Although the activities of the Mosley group have met with strong opposition from Labour and Liberal forces, its membership is on the increase.

As a whole, Great Britain has not permitted anti-Semitism to menace the peace and welfare of the population. In the 1930's the British Isles became a refuge for thousands of Jews from Germany.

At this point, Britain's role in Palestine and the British reluctance to rescue Jews from the Nazi tyrants should be noted. The British Administration of Palestine (1919–1948), directed by the Colonial Office in London, did not act in the spirit of the Balfour Declaration. "They temporized and postponed and dallied with the application of elementary measures of foundation laying. They acted churlishly towards the Zionist commissioners. ... They wanted to hold up the show as long as possible, so that dissatisfaction and tension would rock Palestine from one end to the other. ... When that happened, the Home Government would certainly pause in its headlong drive to put the Jews into the saddle in the Near East and reconsider Balfour's utopian scheme and maybe call off the Zionists and all those Jewish zealots who were now beginning to arrive with every boat from Eastern Europe." [8]

Instead of encouraging Jewish immigration, they grudgingly doled out certificates of admission. Many a political leader maintains that had the British Mandatory power opened the gates of Palestine, the Jewish losses in Europe would not have been so great. There were masses of Jews in Poland, Rumania and Czechoslovakia waiting in vain for visas to enter Palestine. Had the Palestine Administration acted in good faith, no riots would have broken out in Palestine in 1919, 1921 or 1936. British anxiety not to quarrel with the Arabs, support for the thrones of Arab kings, over-solicitude for the so-called Arab interests—took precedence over the fulfillment of their promise to the Jews through the Balfour Declaration. Then, too, the Colonial Office did not permit the Arabs to learn that Jewish immigration would benefit the Arab population. Instead, the guardians of the Mandate issued a White Paper in 1939, on the eve of the great Jewish catastrophe, decreeing total stoppage of Jewish immigration to go into effect in 1944. Moreover, the help given by the Jews of Palestine to the Allied cause not only remained unappreciated but was "the best kept secret of the war." And finally when thousands of refugees from Hitler's persecutions crowded on ships to seek admission to the Jewish National Home, British forces denied them admission, imprisoned all "illegal" immigrants who managed to come ashore and fought Hagannah and Irgun who aided the refugees in their attempts to reach the shores.

These facts are not be ignored. It should be remembered that the British war leaders knew of the massacres perpetrated by the Nazis and did not exert pressure either upon Britain's own subjects in England or upon her compatriots in Canada, Australia and South Africa to admit Jewish refugees who could have been saved had a haven been found for them in a friendly country.[9]

Moreover, it has been established that when the brave fighters of the Warsaw Ghetto uprising negotiated with the Polish underground asking for help, several "Polish commanders expressed doubts about the desirability of active intervention. The argument ran: 'If America and Great Britain with powerful armies and air forces behind them and equipped with all the means of modern warfare are not able to stop this crime and have to look on impotently while the Germans perpetrate every kind of horror in the occupied countries, how can we hope to stop them. . .' The Polish underground thereupon contacted the Ghetto. . . . The Jews had one request which the Polish Home Army was glad to fulfill. They handed to the Poles an appeal addressed to the civilized world and to the Allied nations in particular. The Jewish leaders demanded that the German people be threatened with reprisals. The appeal was immediately transmitted to London, but the BBC maintained complete radio silence. . . . The Jews did not have many friends in London or, for that matter, in Washington."[10]

And yet Britain is a free country where Jews have equal rights. While provocative action by anti-Semites is not lacking, the Government investigates all anti-Jewish acts and punishes the instigators. During the war the Jews fought side by side with the British on all fronts and at home. The Jewish community in England numbers about 450,000 people.

SWEDEN

About 15,000 persons comprise Swedish Jewry. Anti-Semitism is in disrepute. During the war Swedish citizens helped in the rescue of orphans and refugees. One-half of the Jewish population consists of refugees who have found a secure haven in this friendly country. The 7,000 native Jews are legally required to belong to the Jewish community and the congregations possess the power to levy taxes for communal activities.

SWITZERLAND

Jewish settlement in Switzerland dates back to the end of the 12th century. During the Middle Ages the Jews, living as second-rate citizens, were mistreated. Ever since the Emancipation Act of 1866, the Jews found real hospitality in the small republic.

Beginning with the First Zionist Congress in 1897, Switzerland has been the host to many Jewish gatherings and congresses.

The Jews in Switzerland enjoy full freedom, hold many appointments in the universities and are treated very courteously and amicably. In the 1930's, German Jewish refugees were admitted to the country on transit to other lands and some of them were permitted to settle there permanently. It was only natural that Switzerland become also a breeding ground for Nazi propaganda. The government, however, made every effort to check all the anti-Semitic outbursts in the country. There are about 25,000 Jews in Switzerland today.

TURKEY

Jewish life in Turkey dates back to the days of the First Commonwealth. There is, however, ample historic evidence of Jewish communities in Asia Minor and in Constantinople during the Byzantine rule (4th century). Since the position of the Jews under the Byzantines, when they were considered a "disgraceful sect," was not a happy one, Jews welcomed the early Turkish conquerors, whose advance into Europe (end of 14th century) created for the persecuted Jewish wanderers a resting place in conquered territories. They fared well under the Turks for centuries. The Turks were sympathetic to the Jews. They granted them asylum in their empire, recognized autonomy in their internal life and permitted them to play an important part in the economic life of the country. Jewish life was comparatively free of anti-Semitic plagues until after World War I. Turkey of the 1920's and the 1930's championed a militant nationalism and culturalism, and became hostile to non-Turks, more so than in the days of the Sultans and Caliphates. This wave of nationalism naturally gave way to a new orientation with regard to all non-Turkish minorities, particulary the Jews.

The fate of the Armenian minority in Turkey during the First World War period is known to every student of modern history. Turkish nationalism actually reduced the Armenian community to a state of poverty and miserable existence. That even the Greek minority in Turkey felt the sting of Turkish nationalism is seen from the fact that about 1,200,000 Greeks have been transplanted from Turkey into Greece in the course of four years (by mutual agreement of both the Turkish and Greek governments).

It was, indeed, to be expected that the Jews would not be spared. As a matter of fact, modern Turkey's ultra-nationalistic philosophy (Turkey for the Turks) forced many Jews from their economic positions and from their active participation in the cultural life of the country.

During World War II, many Nazi agents were stationed in neutral Turkey, and exerted some influence upon Turkish officialdom. The anti-Jewish climate became conducive to an effective Arab propaganda against the Jews. The Turkish Jews felt neither safe nor secure in Turkey. Their precarious state accounts for a mass exodus.

During and after the war, especially after the creation of Israel, 35,000 Jews emigrated to the Jewish State. Smaller groups emigrated to other countries. The once prosperous Jewish community of Turkey which had numbered 155,000 Jews in 1930 diminished to 40,000 in 1960.

There is no official anti-Jewish discrimination in Turkey. The new Constitution guarantees all citizens equal rights and liberties. However, laws still exist which prevent the Jewish community from taking part in international Jewish conferences, restrict organized Zionist activities, and prohibit all ties with the Alliance Israelite Universelle. The Jews are not barred, however, from emigrating to Israel or showing their sympathy for the Jewish State.

The Situation in Soviet Russia (U.S.S.R.)

The early Jewish community in Crimea dates to 587 B.C.E., the time of the destruction of the First Temple. Jews penetrated from Poland, Lithuania and Crimea into the Russian Ukraine and Central Russia at the end of the fifteenth century.

For a long period of time, Russia had been the land of the classic pogrom. Anti-Semitism in Russia meant pogroms, the actual slaugher of the Jews. The Tzarist reactionary regime, which constantly struggled to subdue the revolutionary movement among its people, was always ready to blame the Jews for all the acute problems which perplexed the country. The government itself was, therefore, the instigator of all pogroms.

Blood accusations served as a pretext for pogroms, political upheavals for anti-Jewish agitation. Assassinations of high officials by revolutionaries, the anti-government sentiments among the intelligentsia, even strikes, were sufficient reasons for anti-Jewish riots. Ever since the days of the notorious Bogdan Chmelnitzky when hundreds of thousands of Jews were slaughtered in ten years (1648–1658) by Cossacks, and large Jewish communities reduced to ashes, Russian Jews were subjected to anti-Semitic legislation and to physical violence. Toward the end of the Tzarist regime there were 650 laws directed against the Jews. All the "academic" theories of anti-Semitic "scholars" of the West found fruitful soil in the East dominated by Russia. Every conceivable measure was adopted to make Jewish life nearly unbearable. It began with exclusion of Jews from villages and rural centers, advanced to the creation of the "Pale of Settlement" or the restriction of Jews to certain districts, and ended with acts of physical terror instigated by government officials.

In the pogroms of 1881, 1903 and 1905, organized by the "genuine Russians" with the help of terrorist bands known as the "Black Hundred," massacres occurred in more than 300 towns. During World War I, Jews suffered untold horrors from the retreating Russian armies which laid waste to many areas. Even more tragic were the pogroms in the Ukraine of 1918-1921 when almost every Jewish town suffered overt acts of violence which made the pre-war outbreaks seem no more than displays of ordinary prejudice. Between December, 1918 and April, 1921, 887 large and 342 small pogroms occurred, in which between ninety and a hundred thousand Jews were killed and seventy thousand injured. More than 700,000 lost all their worldly possessions and more than 250,000 were orphaned.[12] In the chaotic revolutionary period of 1917–1920 when the anti-Bolsheviki forces needed a national slogan to rally the peasant groups, they exploited the anti-Semitism of the masses. It was the "only way" to combat the Soviet influence and gain the sympathy of the masses. The Jews became the scapegoat.

The Soviet regime, officially banned anti-Semitism. The Soviet government regarded Jew-baiting as counter-revolutionary and punished anyone who showed signs of Jew-hatred. The Jews were given the status of an emancipated ethnic group. The government encouraged the establishment of a Jewish Republic in Biro-Bidjan, a territory in Siberia. On the other hand, the Soviet regime deprived its Jewish citizens of the cultural and spiritual freedoms enjoyed by all other ethnic groups. It is one of the paradoxes of Soviet rule which gives formal recognition to the Jews as a nationality and yet singles them out for special differential treatment. Every Jew is required by law to specify his nationality, Yevrei, ("Jew" in Russian) on his passport. This seemingly denotes formal recognition of the Jews as a distinct national group, yet it deprives them of the national prerogatives all other groups enjoy. In the 1920's the Soviets permitted the Jews to have their schools, press, theatre and similar cultural institutions, which were mostly sponsored by either Jewish Communists or loyal followers of Communism. In areas such as White Russia, the Ukraine with a large Jewish population, and in Jewish agricultural settlements in Crimea, Yiddish became the official language in courts, in government bureaus, in factories, in clubs, etc. Government agencies supported the publication of Yiddish periodicals and books. The cultural autonomy, Communist in content, Jewish in form, resulted in hastening the process of assimilation and barred any attempt to perpetuate Jewish national ideas or traditional religio-cultural life.

Religious Jews suffered greatly from the restrictions and disabilities placed on all aspects of religious life and observances. The teaching of Hebrew or the Bible was prohibited. Impatience with the adherents to traditional Judaism prevailed. Zionist organizations were held subversive. Hebrew writers, teachers and members of Zionist groups, were sent to Siberian labor camps.

But even overt acts of Judeophobia, despite the government's efforts to eradicate it, manifested themselves among the Russian people in one form or another. From the Soviet Yiddish press of the period we learn of many cases of Jew-baiting brought before the courts. Numerous forms of abuse were, of course, not recorded in the press.

In 1948, however, Stalin, with one sweeping administrative decree, "eliminated every facet of secular Jewish cultural life and physically exterminated more than 450 Jewish writers, artists and intellectuals—the cream of Soviet Jewish intelligentsia." [13] This shift of policy was the by-product of ten years of continuous anti-Jewish discrimination. For as far back as 1938, Jewish schools and newspapers were forcibly closed down and a number of Jewish communal leaders liquidated. This coincided with the purges against the old Bolsheviks, some of whom were Jews, and the growing possibility for friendly relationships with Nazi Germany. During the war, when Russia became the ally of the West against the Nazis, the anti-Jewish policy was temporarily halted (for the Soviet Regime was certain of Jewish preference for Soviet Russia over the Nazi Germans) only to be reinstated and expanded after the war.

With the rise of the State of Israel and the increasing tension between Russia and the West, the Soviet regime once again suspected Jews of disloyalty, and anti-Jewish feeling heightened. As the Soviet leaders intensified the cold war, especially against the United States, the Jews in Russia became a target of that war because they were believed to have close contacts with the West and Israel.

Gradually there developed an official discriminatory policy against all Jews. This anti-Jewish policy follows a definite pattern. The Soviet press often vilifies Jews and Judaism. The Jews are accused of "bourgeois-nationalism" and Zionism, both associated with "Western Imperialism and its Israeli puppet." Since 1957, the Soviet press has attacked the Jewish religion, the racism of the Jews and their love of Israel which is considered virtual treason to the Soviet State. The fact that 600,000 Jews including women, served in the armed forces of the Soviets during World War II was not remembered.

There is also sufficient evidence of the discriminatory policy against the Jews in government, the professions and in education. "The disappearance of Jews from leadership positions in political life has been striking and dramatic. Soviet spokesmen have tried to counter this fact by noting recently that 7,623 Jews were elected to local soviets all over the country. This seems impressive until it is realized that as of 1960, more than 1,800,000 such local deputies were elected. The 'large' number of Jews thus comes to less than one-half of one per cent. Moreover, in all but one of the Supreme Soviets of the fifteen republics, the number of Jews is far below their proportion to the population.... As for the professions, the declining number of Jews has been as much as admitted by Premier Khruschev and Culture Minister Furtseva themselves as a matter of policy. (In making such admission, they have referred to the necessity of making room for 'our own intelligentsia'—clearly giving away their feeling that the Jews are not truly indigenous).... The extent of the decline in higher education is reflected in the fact that Jews today represent 3.1 per cent of all students in higher education as compared with 13.5 per cent in 1935."[14]

The above quotation is taken from a carefully documented account of the plight of the Jews in the Soviet Union in the January, 1963 issue of Foreign Affairs. The facts present a picture of planned systematic persecution. The author concludes the article stating: "Soviet policy as a whole, then, amounts to spiritual strangulation—the deprivation of Soviet Jewry's natural right to know the Jewish past and to participate in the Jewish future. And without a past and present, the future is precarious indeed."[15]

Jewish losses in Soviet Russia during the Nazi occupation of a large part of the country in the Second World War are estimated at a million and a half. Other peoples lost heavily during the Nazi invasion of Soviet Russia, but these were primarily the soldiers who fought on the field of battle, and a considerable proportion of these were Jews. The civilian population of these nationalities (Bielo-Russians, Ukranians, Letts, Lithuanians, Russians, etc.), though greatly depleted, retained in greater part their family structure. Their communal life was not completely severed. On the other hand, the Jewish loss goes much deeper. They were practically annihilated. More than 70 per cent of the Jews of the Soviet Union who lived in the Nazi-occupied zone perished.

There are about two and a half million Jews in Soviet Russia. They are given no opportunity to develop their life as a distinct group. Their future depends upon a change in Soviet policy in any of three directions: 1) affording them an opportunity for full assimilation which necessitates a free choice of nationality through the abolition of the law requiring the Jewish identity card; 2) permitting them to emigrate, or 3) enabling them to function as an ethnic group with freedom to perpetuate their religio-cultural tradition. For the time being these alternatives are not acceptable to the authorities. The Jews of Soviet Russia therefore, continue to suffer.

Summary: The Situation in Europe

We have seen that it took the civilized world a very long time to grant the Jewish minority the elementary right of equality before the law. We have also seen that in liberal and democratic countries a climate was created which became conducive to the emancipation of Jews. Liberalism and democracy uphold the principle of the right of the individual to life, liberty and the pursuit of happiness. The growing consciousness of the Jewish problem prompts the people in free countries to suppress the age-long anti-Semitic undercurrent and to grant the Jews the rights of citizenship.

Reactionary forces, however, thrive on bigotry and incite against minority groups in order to divert the attention of the masses from the dangers inherent in an autocratic form of government.

In those countries anti-Semitic clashes occur more frequently and the seeds of hatred find rich soil for growth and fruition.

The hostility to the Jew, sown in many countries of Europe through the centuries, imbedded in the fertile soil of reactionary or semi-reactionary governments, produced the harvest of hate epitomized by the Nazi genocide.

The anti-Semitic evil was never uprooted even during the emancipation period. It existed in one form or another practically everywhere in Europe. The Nazis exploited the prevalence of anti-Semitism in Europe, and spread in their own country and among like-minded people everywhere the belief that only by launching a war against the Jews would the "Jewish Question" finally be solved.

In our survey of the fate of the Jews in Europe we have recorded the extent of the Jewish catastrophe during the Second World War and we have also pointed out that where liberalism permeated the hearts and minds of people, Jews were rescued and morality kept alive. On the other hand, we have taken note of the fact that these acts of human kindness and charity were sporadic, unorganized and few and far between. World leaders maintained a "hands off" policy. The holocaust was unopposed. The Allied Powers issued a declaration on Dec. 17, 1942, which stated that the responsible perpetrators "shall not escape retribution," but in terms of actual rescue work or retaliation, the same signatories to this document did very little, if anything.

The democracies were either too busily engaged in actual warfare against the Nazis to give special attention to the unprecedented Jewish suffering, or guarded their neutrality with such care that they could not make a concerted effort to rescue Jews from the valley of death. There were of course exceptions to this rule but the world as a whole, confronted by the threat of a great evil, did not do everything in its power to avert it.

The Jews themselves can never forget their great tragedy. They entertain the hope, however, that freedom, truth, mercy and righteousness will prevail in the affairs of all men and their dream of real emancipation will become true.

Combined TOPICS FOR DISCUSSION and NOTES TO CHAPTERS 3 & 4 will be found on pages 89 and 90.

4

The Rights of the Jews
(Continued)

Jew Hatred in Arab Lands

Anti-Semitism was not confined to Europe alone. It existed and still exists on other continents. Next to Europe, the countries dominated by Arabs in Asia and in North Africa have developed their own brand of anti-Semitism which plagued the Jews for centuries but which has gained in power and momentum in the last two decades.

When the Mohammedans (followers of the prophet Mohammed) came to power in the 7th century, they made it perfectly clear to both Jews and Christians that they could never hope to achieve equality with Moslems (believers in Islam—the new religion). They permitted the Jews, however, to maintain their own communities and to live in accordance with their own religious laws. In the Middle Ages the Jews in Moslem Spain and Egypt cooperated with the Mohammedans in scientific and philosophical studies and became the transmitters of Arabic culture to the Christian world. During the tragic days of the Spanish exile (1492), Jews found refuge in Mohammedan Turkey where they established communities in southeastern Europe and in Anatolia. They also found a haven in North Africa.

Most of the Jews of the Near East and North Africa, however, had remained in their lands of origin since the Babylonian exile. They adjusted themselves to Mohammedan rule, though in many countries they could never secure elementary human rights. They suffered various kinds of persecutions meted out to them by fanatic Moslem groups, accepting their destiny as the will of God. For many centuries they lived apart from the mainstream of Jewish history, worked chiefly in professions forbidden to Moslems, confined to their own sections and speaking a mixed Hebrew-Arabic. The refugees from Spain and Portugal (1492) augmented the numbers of the old settlers. These European Jews concentrated mostly in the urban centers, retained their Hebrew-Spanish dialect, Ladino, and formed the Sephardic group of the Oriental Jews.

The penetration of Europeans during the 19th century inspired Moslem leaders to re-examine their policies. For a number of decades Jews gained more and more privileges and were given protection by the colonial powers. But the rise of Arab nationalism at the beginning of this century brought about a resurgence of Jew-baiting. The image of the Jew as an inferior being which was held by the great masses of Arabs through the centuries made the task of the new bigots easier. The increased Jewish immigration to Palestine after the establishment of the Jewish National Home in 1917 intensified the animosity of the Arabs against the Jews. Plunder and violence became frequent occurrences. With the continuing growth of the Jewish population in Palestine and the economic development of the Jewish settlements, the entire Arab world became inflamed. The Moslem religious hierarchies initiated an anti-Zionist, anti-Jewish movement in all Arab countires, accusing the Jews of "pushing the native Palestinian Arabs out of the country." The advent of Hitlerism and the subsequent penetration of Nazi agents and German army units during the Second World War, resulted in further anti-Semitic measures. And finally the rise of the Jewish State in 1948 and the ensuing war with the Arabs brought Arab anti-Jewish bigotry to its peak. The organized Jew-baiting which resulted in acts of violence, in confiscation of Jewish properties, and in a constant threat to Jewish life, prompted most Jews of the Near East and many of North Africa to leave their native countries. In the course of a few years, almost the entire Jewish populations of Iraq, Yemen, Syria and Lebanon abandoned their homes and fled to Israel with only their lives. The Jewish community of Egypt was reduced from 75,000 in 1947 to less than 7,000 in 1960. Moroccan and Tunisian Jewries, which could no longer rely on French protection or the good will of moderate Moslems, when these two countries attained national independence, felt obliged to emigrate. Unfortunately, exit permits were granted to relatively few applicants. The exodus of Jews from Algeria which started in 1961 was intensified in 1962 during the final stage of Algeria's struggle for independence. The Algerian Jews suffered greatly from the terrorist acts of the French secret army (O.A.S.) and the violence of the Moslems. In the face of despair, in the course of six months in 1962, more than 100,000 Algerian Jews fled to France.

In the meantime the Arab League keeps fanning the religious fanaticism of the Arab masses and provoking physical assaults on Jews. Cairo established itself as the center of anti-Zionist propaganda which, to all intents and purposes, is really anti-Jewish. Anti-Semitic cartoons and hate-mongering stories appear in the press of all Arab lands, Jewish properties are being confiscated and the state of the remaining Jews in Moslem lands is becoming more and more precarious and insecure.

On the American Continent

THE UNITED STATES OF AMERICA

The United States of America was the first country in the world to afford the Jewish people freedom. The Constitution is the first document to guarantee equal rights for all citizens, barring none. It makes no distinction between the ethnic and religious origins and backgrounds of its citizens. All are equal before the law. All are entitled to the pursuit of liberty and happiness. In the history of the United States the exceptions to these rules, so far as Jews were concerned, have been few.

The American people regarded anti-Semitism with considerable contempt and on many an occasion generously supported the Jewish organizations combatting it in Europe. The United States Government at times made a special effort to combat Jew-hatred in other parts of the globe. In 1890 President Van Buren protested against the Damascus blood accusation. In 1872 and 1902 the United States intervened in Rumania on behalf of the Jews cautioning Rumania against maltreatment of its Jewish subjects. In 1912 the U.S. abrogated its trade treaty with Russia because of Jewish persecutions. In 1918 Secretary Lansing denounced mass terrorism and Jewish massacres, and in 1922 Congress approved the establishment of the Jewish National Home in Palestine. The equal treatment of the Jews may be further illustrated by the fact that in the course of the relatively brief period of American Jewish history, Jews were represented in the Presidential Cabinet, the Senate, the Congress, the Supreme Court, in the Armed Forces as well as in State and Municipal governments and administration.

In America, Jews discovered a real New World, a society without persecution, a commonwealth offering them life as their right, not on sufferance. In the course of the last 40 to 50 years, the largest Jewish community in the world had risen before our very eyes, a community which is completely integrated into the fabric of American life and which is encouraged by the very nature of America to retain its own identity. Between 1881–1929, almost two and one-half million Jews arrived. Their number today is estimated at more than five and one-half million. The Jews referred to this country as the "Goldene Medina." (The Golden State). They enjoyed security and were content with their lot. They became so loyal to America that during the First World War their percentage in the United States Armed Forces was 5.73 of their total number as compared with 3.27 of the total population. In World War II, there were 55,000 Jews, including women, who fought in the Armed Forces of the U.S.A.

With the rise of the American Jewish community, Jewish history has entered into a new phase, geographically and spiritually, the latter still in its formative stage. A special chapter will be devoted to the American Jewish community in Volume II.

In considering Jewish rights and the phenomenon of anti-Semitism, brief reference must be made to the story of Jewish bigotry in the United States, for America has not been completely free of anti-Jewish feeling.

The American brand of anti-Semitism was confined in the main to discrimination against Jews in social clubs, certain resorts, and in the purely Christian sections of a city or a suburb where the purchase of a home entailed difficulties. In some instances there was a special quota for Jewish applicants to medical schools, banks and public utilities. By and large it was the type of prejudice which was in vogue against the sons of immigrants. The Jew, of course, even after having become adjusted completely to the American pattern, was still the subject of antipathy on purely religious grounds.

In the 1930's, however, prejudice against the Jews spread with greater intensity and became the concern of some Americans. Numerous anti-Semitic organizations sprang up and poisoned the atmosphere with bigotry. In the business world, the slogans of a "Jewish domination" were frequently heard. Jews were blamed for labor's new militant stand, and the anti-Semitic charge that the Jew monopolizes all economic opportunities found an attentive ear. In the spheres of national politics, the opponents of the Roosevelt administration condemned the Jews for the New Deal policies. In the 1936 campaign, many bigots appealed to race prejudice in fighting their political opponents. Slogans like "The New Deal is the Jew Deal" and that "All Jews are Communists" were used in meetings and in election literature. In this period, anti-Semitic groups grew rapidly, spreading anti-Semitism among tens of millions of Americans. According to a study of anti-Semitic organizations in the U.S.A. by Rev. Dr. L. M. Birkher of Kansas City and submitted to the Non-Sectarian Anti-Nazi League, there existed in the U.S.A. over 100 anti-Semitic organizations[16] with a membership of over four million.

These anti-Semitic organizations distributed anti-Jewish leaflets, the *Protocols of the Elders of Zion* and Nazi literature. A number of anti-Semitic publications in the U.S.A. with large circulations appeared on the scene, and anti-Semites held annual conferences to discuss ways and means for more systematic work and united action.

Nazism influenced many Americans of German descent and became a growing concern. The German-American *Volksbund* has had a membership of tens of thousands of native Americans of German descent as well as German-born immigrants. Cells of the *Volksbund* infiltrated every community with a considerable German population and spread anti-Jewish doctrines among the American people. Their propaganda became so intensive that a special government committee was appointed to investigate.

It would, however, be untrue to fact to exaggerate the anti-Semitic activities in the U.S.A. and to infer that the U.S.A. may be classified in the category of countries where anti-Semitism was strong. There never was outright anti-Jewish persecution or active official antagonism. The Jews of the U.S. did not despair despite the existence of many reactionary groups whose scores of thousands of members fought liberalism, social reforms, social legislation and the Jews. Nevertheless, the fact remains that Jew-hatred in America gained momentum in the 1930's and constituted a threat to American democracy. The evidence for the growth of anti-Jewish prejudice appeared in the *Fortune* survey, November 1936, which asked: "Do you think that in the long run Germany will be better or worse off if it expels the Jews?" The answers were as follows: "Worse"—54.6; "don't know"—31.4 and "better"—14.0. The danger did not only lie in the 14% of the population approving of Jewish persecution but also in the 31% of the population who could not make up their minds about rights of citizens in a civilized country.

The surge of anti-Semitism was further documented before the Dies Committee in Washington, investigating un-American activities in the U.S.A. According to the committee, 135 anti-Semitic organizations disseminated anti-Jewish propaganda.

Americans began to perceive the dangers to liberty inherent in totalitarianism and sensed the connection between anti-Semitism and all anti-democratic forces within society.

The decade of anti-Semitic propaganda in the U.S.A. coincided with the period of economic depression, the struggle between the forces of liberalism and reaction which came to the fore during the Roosevelt administration and the effective functioning of the Nazi propaganda machine.

It is important in this connection to place on record the government's failure to take action in order to alleviate the Jewish disaster in Europe. As in the case of Great Britain whose leaders refused to admit refugees to Palestine at a time when such admittance would have rescued many Jews from Hitler's gas chambers, the United States government refused to enlarge the quota for Polish nationals in 1939 when Germany overran Poland. As late as August 1, 1942, at a time when about 1,500,000 Jews were already dead, the State Department insisted on verifying the reports submitted by Rabbi Stephen S. Wise, then President of American Jewish Congress, to the effect that the Nazis were committing mass murders of Jews in Russia and in Poland. The checking of the reports took more than three months. In the meantime a million more Jews perished. Finally when the reports were confirmed, the United States government joined the other Allied nations in a declaration entitled "German Policy of Extermination of the Jewish Race", issued on December 17, 1942, which stated that the "responsible perpetrators shall not escape retribution." [17]

When the United States entered the War in 1942, most of the anti-Semitic groups either curtailed their activities or completely disappeared. The Nazi terrors in Europe were instructive to the people of America. They had ample opportunity to learn the truth about the threat of Nazism to the free world and to appreciate the true meaning of Democracy. Anti-Semitism therefore abated to such a degree that in many a community it is practically non-existent. It goes without saying that bigots never fade away entirely. There are, even today, thousands of them throughout the country. Anti-Semitic literature is still freely distributed among tens of thousands of readers. Much of the literature is of Arab origin. The United States anti-Semites promote the pro-Arab line by using the terms "Zionist," "Jew" and "Communist" interchangeably. The overwhelming majority of the American public, however, accepts Jews and Judaism as an integral part of the American pattern of life.

CANADA

Jews have been living in Canada for 200 years. The first Sephardic settlers settled in Montreal in 1760. The largest part of the Jews immigrated to Canada since the '80's of the past century when the exodus of Jews from eastern Europe began.

In 1860 there were about 1,200 Jews. By 1882 the figure doubled, and by 1919 it had jumped to 120,800, largely as a result of continuous immigration from Russia and Rumania.

In the 1920's Canada limited Jewish immigration from eastern Europe as did the U.S.A. During World War II, Jewish immigration was further reduced. The post-War period, however, saw the admission of approximately 54,000 refugees and displaced persons. In 1960 the total Jewish population numbered a quarter of a million.[18]

Jews have shared in the rights and obligations of full citizenship and have participated in all realms of Canadian life. In 1871 two Jews were elected to Parliament. There are Jews in all branches of the Canadian government in our day as well.

But in Canada, too, Jews did not completely escape the evils of anti-Semitism, although for many years, discriminatory acts were infrequent and sporadic. In the 1930's, however, with the rise of anti-Semitism in other parts of the world, Canada, too, experienced a rise in Jew-hatred. At that period, the National Social Christian Party succeeded in flooding all of Canada with savage anti-Jewish and anti-democratic propaganda. Books such as *The Key to Mystery,* containing vicious anti-Jewish material, pamphlets in German, English and French patterned after Streicher's *Der Stuermer* were widely distributed. Under the pretext of war against Communism, right-wing extremists preached the gospel of "Canada for the Canadians." It was estimated that more than 10,000 organized semi-Fascists spread this doctrine throughout Canada. Then, too, the German-inspired Bund of Canada and a branch of Sir Oswald Mosley's Fascist Party of England did their share in fostering anti-Semitic feelings in the country. While it is true that on the surface there were no organized anti-Jewish outbreaks, there were, however, numerous instances of discriminatory acts in business, industry and in the professions.

During the Second World War and in the years that followed, anti-Semitism abated. The Federal government sponsored special broadcasts against discrimination and prejudice, and enacted the law of Fair Employment Practice. The Catholic Federation of

Labor included in its statement of principles a clause to the effect that "it believes in the prime dignity of the individual and the fundamental equality of all human beings." [19]

The situation in Canada resembles that in other democracies, including Great Britain and the United States.

MEXICO

The Jewish community in Mexico is the youngest in North America. It is true that there were individual Jews scattered throughout Mexico at a very early period, but due to the fact that Mexico was one of the first colonies of Spain to introduce the auto-da-fé in which Jews perished, and which existed in the country until 1820, there could not have existed a Jewish community of any considerable size in the period prior to the establishment of the republic.

The early Jewish settlers were Spanish-speaking Sephardic Jews from the Near East who easily adjusted themselves to the new land. East European Jews began to settle in Mexico after the First World War, and the stream of immigration continued until it was restricted in 1938. The Jewish community of Mexico numbered about 22,000 in 1955. Of these 61 per cent were Ashkenazim and 39 per cent Sephardim. The estimate for 1960 is placed at 28,000, about 25,000 of whom are to be found in Mexico City.

The Mexican Jewish community is young, but anti-Semitism requires little time to grow strong. Nazi agents, aided by local traders and merchants who disliked Jewish competition, engaged in anti-Semitic propaganda among the Mexican people in the late 1930's. Under the guise of concern for Mexican national interests, the bigots spread anti-Semitic propaganda in order to drive the Mexican masses into the totalitarian bloc. In the 1940's, the Sinarquist movement [20] in Central Mexico engaged publicly in anti-Semitic activity.

The Mexican Government, which recognizes that both Fascism and anti-Semitism endanger the integrity of a free republic, does not tolerate bigotry, although it is helpless to stop anti-Jewish agitation completely.

There is no official discrimination against Jews in Mexico. Jews hold important government posts. They live in complete freedom and equality but, as in many another country, they are disturbed by anti-Jewish provocation and especially by the traditional Mexican identification of all foreigners with "exploiters."

South American States

THE ARGENTINE

The largest Jewish community in South America is that of the Argentine. There were some Jews in the land immediately after its liberation from Spanish domination in 1816. These were in the main Sephardic Jews who, years later, organized the first congregation in Buenos Aires in 1862. Systematic Jewish immigration began after the Russian pogroms in 1881–82. The first group of Russian Jews, consisting of 132 families, arrived in 1899. The Jewish Colonization Association, founded by Baron Hirsch, helped them to establish agricultural settlements. This small group was augmented by larger numbers of Jews who were interested in farming. In 1931 about 30,000 people were to be found in these agricultural settlements. The majority of the immigrants who had come to the country, however, established themselves in the urban centers.

During the period 1901–1945, a total of 207,160 Jews arrived in the Argentine, 25 per cent coming in the years 1926–1935. With the rise of Nazism in the period 1934–1943, 12,126 refugees reached the land.[21]

In 1946 the dictatorial Peron government proclaimed a law permitting admittance to the country of persons who would "engage in agriculture, in the fishing industry and perform the tasks of industrial workers." This law brought Jewish immigration to a standstill, although about 6,000 refugees did enter the land illegally. Their stay in the Argentine has subsequently become legalized by a special amnesty. There are now about 400,000 to 450,000 Jews in this large country of whom 50,000 are Sephardim.

The Jews of the Argentine enjoyed freedom and equality ever since the establishment of the Republic. There were no political or economic disabilities of any consequence. But in this country too, there was a strong anti-Semitic movement in the 1930's which was supported by the Nazis. The articulate German minority and the more than a million Italians became ardent supporters of Fascism and Nazism. These elements were the chief exponents of anti-Semitic theories. The "Union Nacional Fascista," an outspokenly anti-Semitic party, distributed anti-Semitic literature, accused the Jews of Communism and fostered the Nazi pseudo-science about racially superior and inferior peoples. The government did not permit official anti-Jewish activity, but the anti-Semites found the means to engage in their activities without much hindrance. In 1942–43, when it became apparent that the Nazi war machine was about to collapse, Argentina became a safe haven for Nazi party "refugees." They came in large numbers, even before Hitler's final defeat. Many leading Nazis found sanctuary, open or covert, in Argentina, including Eichmann. *Der Weg,* a viciously anti-Semitic journal began to appear and was published regularly for several years. Anti-Semitism became a real problem and the government adopted strict measures to combat it. In 1949 a special paragraph was introduced into the revised Constitution outlawing all racial and religious discrimination. This firm stand taken by the government made it impossible for the anti-Semitic elements to engage publicly in stirring anti-Jewish feelings. But, the dissemination of anti-Jewish literature by groups headed by former Nazis and the recently organized nuclei of Arab agitators continued. "It is unofficially estimated that persons of Arabic origin in Argentina number close to 400,000 of whom close to 50,000 reside in Buenos Aires. . . . The majority of Argentine Arabs are of Syrian–Lebanese origin and many of them have converted to the Christian faith. . . . In the past, the relations between Jews and Arabs in Argentina have been exceptionally cordial. . . . However, late in 1946, all that changed. . . . Arab-Israel tensions in the Near East became a source of bitterness and animosity between the two communities. These emotions have been further inflamed by operations in Argentina of Arab League propagandists." [22]

These Arab propagandists together with the ex-Nazis have been on the alert to exploit every opportunity to stir up anti-Jewish sentiment, a deplorable fact which required the defense agencies of the Jewish community to maintain a constant vigilance.

A recent report of the American Jewish Committee on the status of the Jews in the Argentine listed several neo-Fascist organizations that are strongly anti-American and "appear to have the support of some Argentine Army officers and a number of the Roman Catholic clergy, although both the Army and the Church are officially opposed to these groups." [23] These neo-Nazi units maintain contact with similar movements in Europe and North Africa. Their anti-Semitic agitation and occasional overt acts, (defacing Jewish buildings with tar and swastikas, scattering anti-Semitic leaflets on the streets, scrawling anti-Jewish slogans on public buildings) cause a great deal of concern to both Jews and non-Jews.

The situation became more aggravated after the execution of

Eichmann, Hitler's chief agent in the annihilation of Jews, in Israel in June, 1962. Attacks by anti-Semitic hooligans on Jews both young and old, gained in intensity. Clashes between Jewish youths and members of the anti-Semitic Tecuara movement[24] became a frequent occurrence. The prevailing tense situation prompted the highest government officials to assure its Jewish citizens that the anti-Semitic "excesses" shall not be repeated. The Argentine Jewish community leaders entertain the hope that these recent outbreaks of anti-Semitism will be checked and that the traditional inter-group solidarity will not be affected by the current anti-Semitic outbursts.

BRAZIL

When, in 1548, the Jews were banished from Portugal, some of the exiles fled to Brazil. Many of them were Marranos.

When the Dutch conquered Brazil in 1624, the several thousand Jews already there were soon joined by several thousand from Holland. All were granted freedom.

With the overthrow of the Dutch regime in 1646 by the Portuguese, the dark days came back and the old community was practically wiped out. Many drifted away from the fold to vanish in the Christian population. Others suffered martyrs' deaths in the auto-da-fé. From this period to 1822, when Brazil proclaimed its independence, no information concerning the Jews in that country has come to light, although it is known that in the 1840's and 50's, Sephardic Jews from France and Germany came to Brazil and settled in Sao Paulo and Rio de Janeiro.

In 1903 the Jewish Colonization Association acquired large tracts of land for the establishment of Jewish agricultural settlements. Several thousand Jews from eastern Europe formed colonies, and by 1924, through the influx of new immigrants from eastern Europe, who settled both in the colonies and in the urban centers, the Jewish population reached the number of 38,000. During the years 1925–1933, 16,000 more entered the land. In 1938 a new law was enacted limiting immigration of all groups to 20 per cent of the total number of agricultural workers admitted, nonetheless about 30,000 refugees managed to find refuge in Brazil during the years 1933–1947.

The Brazilian Jews could not escape the plague of anti-Semitism. The German and Italian colonists inspired a great deal of Jew-baiting. At the time of the Nazi conquest of Europe there were over one million Germans in Brazil loyal to their land of origin who conducted 5,000 schools in addition to nearly two million Italians, most of whom supported Fascist Italy. These Brazilian German and Italian colonists were actively engaged in anti-Semitic activities.

The Government's policy toward the Jews was at all times favorable, and the Jews enjoyed full rights of Brazilian citizenship. Zionism, which had been prohibited during the dictatorship of Vargas during World War II, was again permitted in 1946. The powerful Fascist movement which had been outspokenly anti-Jewish during the peak of Nazi influence declined under the Constitutional Regime instituted in 1946.

Today there are between 120,000 and 140,000 Jews in Brazil. The continuing industrialization of the country requires an enterprising middle class. The Jews participate actively in the growth and development of new industries. They are also active in the cultural life of the country.

The Brazilian Government now pursues a liberal immigration policy. Recently it admitted Jewish refugees from the Arab lands, primarily from Egypt.

URUGUAY

The third largest Jewish community in South America is that of Uruguay. This small country, about half the size of Montana, has a population of only 2,700,000 but it is one of the prosperous and progressive states of Latin America.

The early Jewish settlers in this country were mostly Sephardim who arrived in the late 90's of the past century. About 26,000 east Europeans came in the period 1901–1930. Between 1933–1943 another group of about 7,000 Jews, mostly refugees from central Europe, entered Uruguay. The estimate for 1962 put the Jewish population at 48,000, 80 per cent of whom live in the city of Montevideo.

The Jews mingle freely with the native population. There is no animosity between them. The government's attitude is friendly. Uruguay's representative at the United Nations played an important role in influencing other Latin American Delegates to vote in favor of UN recognition of Israel as an independent state.

CHILE

Next in size is the Jewish community of Chile. It is one of the youngest Jewish settlements in South America, Jews having begun to come to the country as late as 1914. Their number at that time totaled about 200 out of a general population of three and one-quarter million. In 1930 there were only about 6,000 Jews in the country, mostly immigrants from eastern Europe. The largest Jewish immigration took place in 1933–1946 when more than 15,000 Jews, mostly refugees from Germany and German-occupied territories, arrived. In 1962 the Jewish population was estimated at 30,000, mostly in the capital, Santiago, and to a lesser extent in the port of Valparaiso.

There is no discrimination against the Jews. The government is steadfast in its support of democracy and does not tolerate anti-Semitism. The only group that fosters an anti-Jewish feeling is the local Arab organization. The government, however, is well disposed toward Israel and uses the services of Israeli experts in rebuilding the cities that were destroyed by the earthquake of 1959. The Chilean Jews play an important role in the economic and cultural spheres of the country's life.

OTHER COUNTRIES OF SOUTH AMERICA

There are small Jewish communities in all other countries of South America. Among the numerically stronger groups are those of Columbia (10,000), Venezuela (8,500), Cuba (1,000) Bolivia (4,000) and Peru (3,500). In the eleven smaller communities (Guatemala, Nicaragua, El Salvador, Surinam, Trinidad, Haiti, Honduras, The Dominican Republic, Curaçao, Panama and Jamaica) the number of Jews does not exceed 1,200. In most of these countries, the Jews enjoy the full rights of citizenship. Immigration, however, is practically nil. Most Latin American governments have enacted laws permitting the entry of close relatives only. According to the census of 1960 there were about 16,450 Jews in Central America and the West Indies and the figure 630,500 is given for all Jews of South America.[25]

It is worth noting that in Cuba the Jewish community dwindled from 8,000 in 1959 to approximately 1,000 in 1963. The reason for this exodus from Cuba is Jewish apprehension of the Communist regime.

The rise of Israel changed the attitude of the average person in Central South America toward the Jews. The daily reports in the press concerning the achievements in Israel, the public affairs conducted in honor of Israeli representatives have had a profound influence upon the general Central American population. The same people who previously looked upon the Jews as persons without a home have learned to see in them contributors to the establishment of the Jewish state.

Jewish Communities in Asia and Africa

THE MIDDLE EAST

We have pointed out elsewhere in this chapter that the countries of old Jewish settlements under Arab rule pursued an anti-Jewish policy which resulted in the liquidation of their Jewish communities. The Jews of Syria, Lebanon and Iraq have left those countries. There are hardly 13,000 Jews left in these Arab-dominated lands out of a total of 155,000 Jews who lived there before the rise of the State of Israel in 1948. The Yemenite Jewish population of 40,000 in 1948 has been reduced to 3,000. The remnants of the Jews in all these countries are all anxious to emigrate.

The other two large communities in Asia are in Iran and India.

IRAN (PERSIA)

The Jewish community of Iran dates back to 721 B.C.E. when Sargon, King of Assyria, conquered the Northern Kingdom of Israel and sent the Jewish captives to Media. In 537 B.C.E., Cyrus encouraged the return of the Babylonian captives to Palestine but many remained in the land. From the invasion of Alexander of Macedonia (330–323 B.C.E.) to the conquest of Persia by the Mohammedans in the seventh century, there were Jews in Persia, although much of their history is clothed in fable and myth. But it is certainly one of the oldest Jewish communities in the world.

In the modern period the Jews of Iran played an important role in bringing sugar cane, melon, rugs and other objects of art to Europe. Their number, including immigrants from Germany and Russia in the early 1940's, was estimated at more than 110,000.

The love of Zion among Iranian Jews is deep and abiding. Their Zionism is an affair of the heart; it is Bible-centered and Prayer Book oriented. As soon as the Persian Jews learned of the new colonization work of the Zionists in the 1890's, and of the Balfour Declaration in 1917, groups of Iranian Jews abandoned their homes and immigrated to Israel. By 1948, about 20,000 of them had settled in Palestine and had succeeded in integrating themselves into the life of the Yishuv. After the rise of the State, 40,000 more came to Israel. For many years the Jews of Iran were not given full citizenship rights. Many of them were confined to special sections where they lived as of old, keeping the Jewish tradition and speaking the Hebrew dialect, Gursh, peculiar to them. After the Revolution of Pahlevi in the 1940's, all Jews were given equal rights and the old ghetto walls crumbled. The Jews, however, are still emigrating to Israel and to other countries. There are now Persian Jews in London, Paris, New York, Geneva. The present population is estimated at 80,000. In Teheran alone there are 50,000 and the remainder are scattered in smaller urban centers.

INDIA

The existence of a Jewish community in India is considered an historic miracle. For a small group of Jews to retain their identity in a country whose population is 392,440,000 people is indeed little short of a miracle. Jewish association with India goes back to Solomonic times (973–933 B.C.E.) when trade with India began, which was subsequently developed by King Ahab (875-853 B.C.E.). The present Jewish settlement is divided between White and Black Jews. The latter are known as the Bene Israel, who, according to their own tradition, are descendants of Jews who fled from persecution and whose ships were wrecked on some islands in the Indian Ocean. Most of them live in Bombay. The White Jews in turn consist of two groups: the Jews of Cochin and the Baghdadi Jews. The former live in the province of Madras. They are of Sephardic descent. Their ancestors came to the land after the expulsion from Spain, married native wives, and were probably the forebears of the present-day Black Jews. The other group are the Baghdad Jews who first came to India in 1680 and were followed by Persian and other Arabian Jews.

The Jewish population, including all sects, numbers 25,000. There is no anti-Jewish discrimination in India. Many Jews occupy positions of importance in all branches of the national economy. There is small-scale emigration to Israel.

AFGHANISTAN

There is a small Jewish community in Afghanistan numbering about 4,000 souls which suffers greatly from the Arab directed anti-Israel propaganda. Most of the Jews are seeking avenues of escape.

AFRICA

We have already discussed the position of the Jews in North Africa. Their plight is becoming the concern of the world Jewish organizations. It seems that the growing tide of Arab chauvinism will force most Jews to emigrate, provided permission to leave is granted.

In Central Africa there are small communities, but the flourishing and the largest Jewish community on the continent is that of the Union of South Africa. Individual Jews settled in Capetown after the final British capture of the Cape in 1806. Shortly after the discovery of gold (1830's), Jews penetrated into the Transvaal and established small settlements in Barberton and subsequently in Johannesburg. During the Anglo-Boer War (1899–1902) Jews fought on both sides. In 1904, two years after the conflict, when South Africa became a republic attached to the British Crown, there were about 40,000 Jews in the Union of South Africa. In the ensuing years immigration from eastern Europe continued and in 1926 the Jewish population had risen to the 72,000 mark. In the 1930's, relatively few refugees from Nazi oppression succeeded in entering the country. Prior to and immediately after World War II, during the period of Jewish quest for new homes, only 2,300 were permitted to enter, just at a time when the Jewish people expected the enlightened countries to admit Jewish wanderers and displaced persons. South Africa held on strictly to its quota system. In 1960 the Jewish population numbered about 110,000, constituting a little less than 4 per cent of the total white population.

The Jews of South Africa have had freedom and security ever since they established their communities in the land. Many of them held high positions in government, commerce, industry, professions and in the academic world.

While in the late 1930's the Nationalist Party was anti-Semitic, its position changed after the war. In 1948, when their leader became Prime Minister, he assured the Jews that no discrimination against any section of the white population would be tolerated. The promise was kept. Despite the racial policies (Apartheid) of the ruling party in Parliament the status and rights of the Jews continue as in the past. South African Jewry is pro-Zionist. South African Halutzim go to Israel. It is one of the richest communities in the English speaking world and it allocates large sums of money for the development of Israel.

AUSTRALIA

A small group settled in Sydney in 1817, and in Melbourne in 1841. The official census of 1881 showed a Jewish population of 9,000. The arrival of eastern European Jews began in the first decade of the present century. In 1911, the Jewish population almost doubled. Immigration of Jews from 1911 to 1947 was very slight. As was the case in South Africa, the authorities in Australia refused Jewish refugees admission to the country at a period in Jewish history when efforts to escape European anti-Jewish measures reached alarming proportions. The largest number of immigrants came to Australia in the years 1947–1960. About 30,000 have entered the country from Poland, Germany, Egypt and Hungary. The Jewish population in 1960 was estimated at close to 70,000 out of a total general population of more than ten million.

Jews in Australia enjoyed equal rights and one of the native Jews (Sir Isaac Isaacs), became Governor General of the Commonwealth. Despite the fine attitude of the citizens towards the Jews, anti-Semitism entrenched itself even in this far-away continent.

The anti-refugee bias was strong in the late 1930's. Press agitation of an anti-Jewish character toward Israel was a frequent occurrence in 1947 [26] to 1949 and some anti-Semitic literature emanating from neo-Nazi sources in Sweden was distributed in the late 1950's. The government, however, continued to combat all anti-Semitic manifestations. It cooperated with Jewish organizations in conducting many radio broadcasts, seminars and meetings on anti-Semitism with the view to enlightening the public on this subject.

Australian Jewry enjoys full civil and political rights. It maintains contact with the Jewish communities on other continents.

Summary: The Future of Jewish Rights in the Diaspora

Inferences drawn from the survey of anti-Semitism today:
1. That Jew-hatred in one form or another existed and still exists to a larger or smaller degree wherever there are Jews.
2. That anti-Semitism is stronger in countries ruled by totalitarian governments.
3. That anti-Semitism flourishes in countries where economic distress and/or political unrest is transforming itself into hatred toward a minority and renders them objects of hostility.
4. That anti-Semitism is weaker or almost non-existent in democratic countries especially when local economic and political conditions afford no fertile soil for anti-Semitic propaganda.
5. That anti-Semitism does not parade in the open in countries influenced or guided by the democracies of the world (as in Asia and Africa).
6. That while the Jewish State redeemed the hope of all Jews, and that while most Jews in the world are attached to the new State, the existence of Israel will not bring an end to the Dispersion. Jews are loyal to their native or adopted countries.

7. That improved Jewish-Gentile relations will help the Jews, for they exist in a Gentile world.
8. That anti--Semitism is an effective weapon in the hands of skill-ful propagandists and politicians.
9. That anti-Semitism is not fully explained by reference to eco-nomic, political, or social conditions.
10. That anti-Semitism is unpredictable, irrational, and dangerous to both Jewry and democracy.
11. That Jewish martydom is not a matter of the distant past but of the near-present and the present.
12. That resistance to anti-Semitism is a requirement of Jewish honor and the Jewish will to live.
13. That the persistence of anti-Semitism is as difficult to explain as is the existence of the Jewish people itself.
14. That anti-Semitism has nothing to do with Jewish manners, ap-pearance, conduct, or speech, that no change of Jews and Juda-ism eliminates it. Anti-Semitism dogs Jewish existence in any form.
15. That, of late, Jews have begun turning on their enemies in active pursuit (Eichmann). Jewish offensive action to apprehend and try the most vicious anti-Semites is a new departure in recent Jewish history and that it is a method of responding to anti-Semites which merits close attention.

TOPICS FOR DISCUSSION

1. What do you regard as basic human rights?
   (a) Individual human rights.
   (b) Group rights.

2. What are the Jewish views (Biblical, Talmudic) on basic human rights?

3. Compare your list with the United Nations Declaration of Human Rights.

4. How would you define "the Jewish problem" or "the Jewish question?"

5. What precedents can you cite for Jewish self-defense?

6. "The existence of Israel will not bring an end to the Dispersion." Does this mean that each Jew, everywhere in the Dispersion, must not in all seri-ousness consider the possibility of Aliyah for himself and his family?

7. In the light of the great European Jewish tragedy, should Jews uphold the idea that life in the Diaspora is desirable and feasible?

8. Do you agree with those who maintain that "It cannot happen here?"

9. How do you explain the growth of anti-Semitism in Latin America?

10. Is there a Jewish problem in Soviet Russia? If so, what can be done to bring about its ultimate solution?

NOTES TO CHAPTERS 3 & 4

1. Leon Blum before the War, and Mendes France in the 1950's, served as Prime Ministers.
2. Hilberg, Raul: "The Destruction of European Jews," Quadrangle Books, Chicago, 1961, p. 261.
3. The famous philosopher, Spinoza, was a Jew.
4. On April 4, 1962, thirty memorial books containing the names of some 102,000 Jewish victims of the Nazis were presented by The Netherlands War Graves Foundation to Yad Vashem in Jerusalem, the Israeli agency devoted to memorializing the victims of the Nazi holocaust.
5. Hilberg, Raul: "The Destruction of European Jews," Quadrangle Books, Chicago, 1961, p. 192.
6. *Ibid.*, p. 256.
7. Decter, Moshe: "The Status of the Jews in the Soviet Union," *Foreign Affairs*, January, 1963, Vol. 41, No. 2.
8. Van Passen, Pierre: "The Forgotten Ally," Dial Press, New York, 1942, p. 141.
9. While Britain's record in the rescue of Jews compares not unfavorably with that of most other countries, (60,000 were admitted in the 1930's) it is now well known that many more might have been saved but for the prevalence of an anti-Semitism which the Government felt could not be ignored.
10. Hilberg, Raul: "The Destruction of European Jews," Quadrangle Books, Chicago, 1961, pp. 319-320.
11. Kastein, Josef: "History and Destiny of the Jews," p. 419.
12. In Tzeichen fun Hunger un Schchites, by Spectator, *Yiddisher Kaempfer*, December 24, 1937, p. 23.
13. *New Leader*, Special Issue, New York, September 14, 1959, p. 5.
14. Decter Moshe: "The Status of the Jews in the Soviet Union," *Foreign Affairs*, January, 1963, Vol. 41, No. 2, pp. 428, 429.
15. *Ibid.*, p. 430.
16. For a complete list of anti-Semitic organizations in the U.S.A., see *Fortune*, November, 1936.
17. Hilberg, Raul: "The Destruction of the European Jews," Quadrangle Books, Chicago, 1961, p. 719.
18. Rosenberg, Louis: American Jewish Year Book, 1961, pp. 34-35.
19. Rosenberg, Louis: American Jewish Year Book, 1953, p. 222.
20. A Mexican fascistic group.
21. Shatsky, Yakov: "Yiddishe Yishuvim in Latin America," Buenos Aires, 1952, p. 28.
22. Argentine, a Jewish Community in Jeopardy, World Jewish Congress, New York, January, 1963, p. 10.
23. *New York Times*, January 18, 1962.
24. In 1958 this neo-Fascist movement began to organize Catholic school students and alumni into effective units opposing the secularization of the schools. When the Government, in 1960, guaranteed increased privileges to the Church in the field of education, the raison d'etre for Tacuara thus evaporated and the movement was soon reconstituted as a Fascist organization. It aims at the liquidation of the middle class and curtailment of immigration of "non-assimilable" elements. The Tecuara group respects Nasser and wants to follow his example in seeking to constitute themselves as a third force in Latin America. They would like to see the Jews leave the country.
25. American Jewish Year Book, 1960, p. 282.
26. In 1947, the National Council of Jewish Women, with headquarters in New York, initiated in Sydney, a libel suit against the writer of an article in *Smith's Weekly* in which the author, Fanny Reading, accused youth aliyah of supporting terrorism and coercing Australian Jews to contribute to its campaign.

PART II
Faith

How Jews Earn A Livelihood

The Peculiarities of Jewish Economic Life in the Past

Jews have variously been called a people of traders, money lenders or profiteers. They were branded as a group which has a special aptitude or a natural tendency for bargaining, speculating, competing and haggling in business, the implication being that they shirked real work. They were referred to as an unproductive people. The fact that Jews, for many years, were not engaged in basic economic activities concerned with the production of raw materials such as agriculture, mining, fishing, forestry, and that in their struggle for economic existence they depended exclusively upon man (engaging in commerce, crafts and professional service) rather than nature, singled them out in the eyes of the world as unproductive elements of society.

Are these allegations true?

The following brief historic review of the development of Jewish economic life will answer this question.

The Jews were originally an agricultural people. When they lived on their own land in ancient times they engaged in cattle breeding, agriculture and artisanry (carpentry, pottery, spinning, etc.). These professions were held in high esteem by all the spiritual leaders of ancient Jewry. The Bible, and later the Talmud, make frequent references to manual labor, especially agriculture, as an honest and invigorating toil that spells health and happiness. Israel's literature had only praise for the toiler. Outstanding leaders themselves were either shepherds, farmers or artisans. Even after the loss of their statehood and the subsequent dispersion in many new lands, whenever opportunity presented itself, Jews engaged in tilling the soil, manual labor and handicrafts. There were Jewish farmers in Spain, France, Sicily, Egypt and Babylon, centuries after the destruction of the Jewish State. There were Jewish manual workers in all lands in every period.

That the majority of Jews engaged in non-commercial pursuits for more than a thousand years after the destruction of the Second Commonwealth is known to every student of Jewish history. The eminent scholar, Dr. Yehezkel Kaufman, points to the following:

1. The historian Josephus Flavius (37—102 c.e.) refers to the Jews as a people of workers in contrast to Egyptians and Canaanites;
2. The Talmudic sources as a whole, leave no doubt that during the period of the Talmud (100—500 C.E.) Jews were mainly engaged in agriculture and the crafts. The Jewish community of Babylon was chiefly engaged in agriculture and handiwork. Commerce only became a significant feature of their economy in the seventh century;
3. The Jews of Arabia and Arabic-speaking lands were at all times chiefly workers, farmers and artisans;
4. Until the tenth century, the Jews of Byzantium, Greece and its islands, were occupied mainly in agriculture and the crafts, and, to a lesser degree, they participated also in industry and commerce;
5. Thomas of Aquinas (1227-1274) describes the Jews as being chiefly workers;
6. From the writings of Benjamin of Tudela and Petachiah of Ratisbon, the noted Jewish travelers of the twelfth century, we learn that Jews living in the East were mainly farmers and craftsmen.

Dr. Kaufman in summarizing this historical evidence states: "Throughout the first fifteen centuries of their life in the Diaspora, the greater majority of the Jews supported themselves by the labor of their hands. And in Poland even in the beginning of the nineteenth century, the number of Jewish craftsmen was three times as large as that of Jewish merchants. In 1816 nearly all tailors, hatters and tanners of Poland were Jews, as were most of the blacksmiths and carpenters."[1]

Trade and finance began to play an increasingly important part in the economic life of the Jews, beginning with the sixteenth century, in the lands where the economic policies of the rulers deprived the Jews of the opportunity to engage in agriculture and handiwork. Transformation into a "commercial" people was the result of the endless struggle to find a place in the national economies of the lands of their habitation. Jews were forced to make economic adjustments everywhere. In order to survive they had to engage in professions that were open to them, for their opportunities in economic pursuits and their choice of vocations were always restricted. Then, too, they had also to conform to their religious laws (observance of Sabbath, Kashrut, etc.) which further restricted their vocational choices.

Four outstanding forces operated to sever the Jews from the soil, and to place them largely in vocations which yielded a livelihood derived exclusively from man:

1. Concentration of Jewry in cities, owing to insecurity of life and property outside and the prohibition against the Jews to farm the land;
2. Unfriendly attitudes of the governments towards the Jews, which resulted in their exclusion from certain trades;
3. General economic conditions in the land. The bulk of the Jews lived for the past two centuries in economically backward countries (Russia, Poland, Rumania, the Near East) where traders and "brain-labor" were needed;
4. Relative importance of the Jewish group to the economic welfare of the country. Jews were attracted to commerce and to money lending because by so doing they performed services indispensible to the general welfare of the country, especially to the ruling castes.

It is clear that the Jewish occupations in any given century depended largely upon conditions beyond their control. Their remoteness from basic industries was not a matter of choice or will. Moreover, although they did not produce the goods, their function in the distribution of raw materials into manufactured goods constituted a very significant service.

If we also bear in mind that continuous persecutions tended to drive Jews into such economic enterprises that could easily be converted into cash (in case of an impending pogrom, expulsion, or discriminating economic legislation), we can readily understand that the transformation of the Jewish people into a non-agricultural group (at a time in human history when most people were primarily farmers) was an economic necessity.

The assertion that the Jews by nature have a special inclination toward commerce is as absurd as the belief that one is born with a preference for one occupation or another. The life tasks of the Jews were not the result of inborn gifts for particular vocations, but rather of historic forces and environmental pressures which ordinarily shape the economic destinies of all men. Jewish concentration in finance, commerce, petty trading and the like was the natural outcome of the hardships of Jewish life in all lands of dispersion. Anti-Semitism, constant wanderings, forced migrations, concentration in cities and struggle for economic survival in backward countries with primitive economies removed the Jew from the major occupation of all parties—tilling of the soil—and created for him a unique economic life pattern, that of rendering a variety of services that are characteristic of city dwellers.

The other assumption that the Jewish economic occupations are "non-productive" is also untrue to historic fact.

Had Jews not performed a needed economic service in every country, the hostile majority would not have encouraged them to take up trading, money lending and artisanry. For centuries, both in Western and Eastern Europe, urban vocations, including the liberal professions, were considered undignified for the nobility and sinful to the Church. The Jews being city dwellers (not of their choice) were not only encouraged to become merchants, pawn brokers, money lenders, artisans and physicians, tailors, bakers, carpenters, blacksmiths and cobblers, but, as already stated, they were forced into these vocations because of prohibitions and discriminations in the other economic fields. With the rise of commercial capitalism,[2] the initiative, capital and business talents of some of the Jews tended to stir economic activities in the entire Western world. "The influence of the Jews on the vast extension of modern commerce has been mainly due to their international connections which enabled them to transfer goods and bullion from one country to any other with the least risk."[3] For the Jews had co-religionists and in many cases blood relations in many a country of the globe. Their wide dispersion led to their comparatively large share in country and world fairs, and in the early stages of colonial expansion. Can these be considered unproductive? "Non-productivity" is, therefore, a term that may denote remoteness from the soil or livelihoods gained from industries such as mines, forestry, fishing, etc.; it does not denote unwanted and non-serviceable activity.

A merchant or a banker, a craftsman or a petty industrialist, a peddler or a shoemaker is in no way considered a non-productive element in the economy of a given nation. Nor is a lawyer or a physician regarded non-beneficial to the life of his country, if he be a non-Jew. "Non-productivity" is therefore a term that cannot be applicable to the Jews, if any useful work is taken as the criterion.

In modern times, especially, when the economic structure of the world is undergoing a rapid change, when large-scale production and specializing tend to increase the needs of trade and commerce, and when modern mass production methods require more administrative and professional services of all kinds, the Jews (who for centuries have engaged in typical urban vocations) can utilize their skills and their dynamic force in the service of the countries where they live.

The contrast between Jews and non-Jews is less marked in occupations outside of agriculture. Thus, if we compare the occupations of the Jewish and non-Jewish urban populations of a given country (especially in Western Europe and the United States), the similarity of the economic structure of both groups will become apparent. A city population consists of groups of merchants, skilled, unskilled and white-collar workers, officials and proprietors, no matter whether of Jewish or other origins. In the modern world there is no independent or special Jewish economy.

Then, too, the Jews in modern times willingly and consciously embarked upon agricultural pursuits in Palestine (now Israel) not only as economic necessity, but primarily as an attempt to return to the soil, which is an important economic base for a people building its life anew in their old-new land. They have also established agricultural settlements in Argentina, Brazil, Canada and Russia. They produced a working class in the U.S.A. The immigrants who came to America at the end of the past century and at the beginning of the present one, flocked to the shops, primarily to the clothing industry and constituted a working class of more than one million people. In a word, the economic life of the Jews in modern times was shaped by political emancipation and the impact of the industrial revolution. These two factors transformed large numbers of Jews from a mass of petty traders and artisans into a people engaged in a wide variety of significant economic activities. The following is a brief account of this transformation.

In 1825, in Eastern Europe, the occupational distribution, according to Mr. Jacob Lestschinsky, presented the following picture:

1. Innkeepers and land agents	30%
2. Commerce and Intermediary Professions	30%
3. No definite vocations	21%
4. Intellectual professions (Rabbis, Cantors, Religious Teachers, Ritual Slaughterers)	3%
5. Handicrafts and Labor	15%
6. Agriculture	1%
Total	100%

Thus, if we compare the occupational distribution of Jews in 1825 with that of non-Jews in Eastern Europe, more than 80 per cent of whom were engaged in agriculture, the difference appears striking.

The disparity gradually decreased within the last century. On the one hand the industrialization of ever-larger sections of Europe and America resulted in the formation of a Jewish working class in both new and old Jewish centers. Participation in industry and modern commercial enterprises created classes of Jewish white-collar workers. Political emancipation opened liberal professions, public and governmental services to the Jews. In the course of the century, sizeable groups also turned to agriculture in Rumania, Carpatho-Russia and Hungary, let alone in Palestine where the pioneers considered tilling the soil a national ideal. On the other hand, the development of technology which paved the way for higher standards of living resulted in a larger proportion of personal income being spent on services which in turn afforded opportunities for many Jews to earn a livelihood in this expanding field.

At the end of World War I, the economic transformation of many Jews had already decreased the disparity between Jewish and non-Jewish economic activity, in the two largest Jewish population centers: Eastern Europe and America. Specifically, the Russian Revolution turned Jews from commerce to manual labor in industries and to agriculture with a simultaneous increase in the liberal professions. State capitalism in Poland, Hungary, the Baltic States, regulating private industry more and more, and forcing many Jews out of commercial occupations augmented the proletarian class with many former Jewish traders. The centralization of commerce and industry into trusts tended to diminish the number of Jews engaged in commerce even in America. In 1930, the Jewish economic structure on a world-scale presented the following picture: [4]

The Distribution of Jewish Occupations in 1930

Occupations	Percentage of Jews
1. Commerce and Transportation	38.6
2. Industry, Handiwork and Labor	36.4
3. Liberal Professions and Public Service	6.1
4. Agriculture	4.2
5. Domestic Service and Unskilled Labor	2.0
6. No definite vocation	12.7
Total	100.0

We thus see that history brought about a radical change in Jewish economic structure. In 1930, more than 60 per cent of the Jews were already engaged in non-mercantile professions, their economic structure becoming more similar to that of other groups who are city dwellers. It must be pointed out, however, that the environmental forces which brought changes to Jewish occupations brought also economic plight to many of them. During the period 1880–1930 virtually one-third of world Jewry was very poor. Many of them were facing starvation. Had it not been for American aid, many of the European Jews would have perished from hunger and disease. The Second World War brought further economic distress to the European Jews. Those who remained alive after the great Nazi massacre had to find new sources for earning a livlihood. Fortunately American Jewry prospered and shared its wealth with the have-nots in Europe. Israel too became helpful in rehabilitating more than a million impoverished Jews.

Soon after the culmination of the War, the economic position of most Jews improved considerably, while those inhabiting the Arab lands were subjected to discrimination and found themselves in great economic distress. The overwhelming majority of the Jewish population, especially in the democracies, attained great economic security and financial prosperity. The economic life of the Jews in the post-World War II period has been determined primarily by the general trends in the national economies of the countries of their domicile and is no longer influenced, as in the past, by other factors, such as discrimination or the so-called Jewish aptitudes for special economic pursuits.

In a word, as long as Jews were handicapped in their struggle to earn a living because they were Jews, there was apt to be a specifically Jewish pattern of economic activity. As soon as prejudice and discrimination were eliminated, Jewish economic pursuits became closer to those of the rest of the population. The well-known economist Nathan Reich has correctly observed that "the economic future of the Jews depends on the effectiveness with which access to economic opportunity will be kept open to all regardless of creed, color and national origin." [5]

Jewish Economic Life Today: Survey of Major Communities

What is the story of Jewish economic life today? We can best answer the question by surveying the situation in the largest Jewish population centers in the world.

THE UNITED STATES OF AMERICA

"It is generally known that the Jews of the United States," says Nathan Reich, "in a large measure are engaged in trade—approximately 45–50 per cent of the gainfully occupied Jews; that 15–20 per cent draw their sustenance from industry both as employers and employees. Within industry, Jews concentrate more heavily in those branches which produce finished products and not in the production of raw materials, or semi-finished products, such as iron, steel, rubber, oil, etc. We also estimate that 12 per cent are engaged in various professions and an insignificant percentage of Jews are engaged in farming."[6]

The sociologist Jacob Lestschinsky presents a similar picture based upon an intensive study of the subject. The following is his table pointing to the socio-economic structure of the Jews as of 1953, as compared with that of the general population:

Occupation	Jews	Non-Jews
1. Agriculture	1.5	15.0
2. Commerce and Finance	55.0	20.0
3. Industry and Labor	25.0	30.0
4. Liberal Professions	15.0	18.0
5. Transportation	2.1	8.5
6. Miscellaneous	1.4	8.5
Totals	100.0	100.0

If we bear in mind the fact that almost 90 per cent of all American Jews live in the 20 larger cities, where manufacturing, trade, distribution of goods, professional and white-collar services are the highest in the country, we can understand that the disparity between Jewish and non-Jewish vocations is not great. The occupation pattern has changed since the days of east-European immigration in the last decade of the past century and in the first two decades of this century. The number of self-employed Jewish traders, shop-keepers, artisans, craftsmen and the like was higher than it is today. The number of Jewish factory workers was considerably larger in the 1920's and in the 1930's than it is today. The increased proportion of the native born among the gainfully employed Jews brought to the fore a diminishing number of manual laborers, traders and self-employed, and a larger ratio of white collar workers and professionals. This change has been an inescapable phase of the national scene. Sons and daughters of factory workers and petty traders became professionals and white-collar workers. The hard working masses of immigrants, scared people in a new land, exploited by contractors and politicians, inhabiting the slums in the large cities, have given way to second and third generation Jews who built suburbia and who entered occupations more profitable and more satisfying. The education received by the natives helped greatly to attain this shift, which coincided with the tremendous developments of American economy, the rise in the standard of living, the achievements of the labor unions and the general prosperity of the American people in the last two decades. These favored the integration of Jews into the American economy and the betterment of their economic positions.

The accomplishments of the American Jews makes for a very impressive picture. While there is no adequate statistical data for a quantitative estimate of Jewish material wealth, it is known that the Jews provide hundreds of millions of dollars for welfare purposes. In the fifteen years, 1945–1960, the total raised by central Jewish community organizations for local philanthropic programs, for aid to Israel and for overseas agencies, amounted to more than two billion dollars.[7] This sum does not include the independent fund-raising sponsored by local groups primarily for synagogues, Rabbinic schools and the construction of buildings for hospitals, centers, homes for the aged, etc. Nor does it include the tremendous financial contributions made by the Jews to the welfare institutions in the general community as well as to schools for higher learning, museums and the like. Another indication of Jewish financial growth can be seen from a study that appeared in the *Journal of American Statistics*,[8] in which the total family income in 1956 for major religious groups is given. From this study we learn that the percentage of families with an annual income of $15,000 or more for the Episcopalians is 11 per cent, for the Presbyterians 6 per cent, for the Roman Catholics 2 per cent and for the Jews 11 per cent. Thus we see that the Episcopalians and the Jews rank highest in family incomes.

While the Jews of America prospered, they did their share for America. Their contributions to the growth and development of American economy are very significant. Jews played an important role in the great attainments of American labor. The names Morris Hillquit, Sidney Hillman, David Dubinsky and Jacob Potofsky are famous in American history as important labor leaders. Louis D. Brandeis, the Justice of the Supreme Court, Meyer Jacobson, the Congressman, Dr. Isaac A. Horwich, the economist, Louis

Marshall, the lawyer-statesman — are also part of the history of the American labor movement's accomplishments in all branches of American life, especially in the areas of social and economic welfare for the great masses of workers.

The Jewish share in the growth of industry is also remarkable. In the textile, shoe, lumber, furniture, fur, millinery, garment and motion-picture industries Jews displayed resourcefulness and imagination. They actually pioneered in these industries and extended their skills and talents to include a variety of other types of industry — all of which expanded the economic base of America.

They participated in the development of commerce, and the export and import trades. They established department stores everywhere in the country and helped in the development of the supermarket, drug and appliances stores. Their place in the technological growth of the country is also noteworthy. Jewish chemists, engineers, physicists and mathematicians, among them Nobel prize winners (Einstein, Rabi, Michelson) engaged in scientific research and together with their fellow Americans of other faiths and colors helped make America the greatest technologically developed country.

Of special import is Jewish philathropic endeavor which benefited all America. Julius Rosenwald (1862-1932) built hospitals and youth centers for the Negroes of the south and his heirs established the famous Rosenwald Industrial Museum; Nathan Strauss (1848-1931) won the esteem of all Americans for installing the system of pasteurized milk and for the founding of the first Tuberculosis Prevention Institute for Children; Simon Guggenheim (1867-1940) established in memory of his son the Guggenheim Memorial Foundation for aiding scientists and artists in their education. This Foundation subsequently built the Guggenheim Museum of New York. These are but a few of the Jewish philanthropists who gave generously to American institutions of learning, to hospitals, museums and social welfare agencies.

The recent study of 30,000 contributors to the U.J.A. in Essex County, N.J.[9] is very revealing. It points to the following interesting facts:

1. The contributors came predominantly from the self-employed in business and professions;

2. Half of all funds are contributed by persons with a median income of $27,000 a year. Almost 70 per cent of the top donors, i.e. those giving $2,500 or more, have an annual income of $50,000 or over. The smallest donors, giving less than $100, report a median income of $13,000.

It is worth noting that these 30,000 donors comprise almost 80 per cent of all adult Jews in the communities of Essex County, for the estimated Jewish poulation is not more than 100,000 souls.

In a word, the American Jewish community is prosperous, economically productive and charitable. No wonder that it has become the reservoir for financial aid to Jewish communities in need and that it has played an important role in the building of the National Home in Palestine, which resulted in the rise of the State of Israel in 1948.

SOVIET RUSSIA

The Soviet regime has drastically changed the entire status of Russian Jewry. Such a colossal shift in its political, economic and cultural life was not experienced by any other Jewish group. The peculiarities of Russian life, and the revolutionary displacements that took place gives Russian Jewry a unique place in the Jewish scene. This group is the only one which has become isolated, having no connection with world Jewry. It is also the only Jewish unit to undergo a complete economic and social redirection and transformation from a middle-class into a wage-earning workers' group.

Before the Revolution of 1917 the economic structure of the Jews in Russia resembled greatly that of Polish, Rumanian or Baltic Jewry. The majority was engaged in commerce, petty trades and handiwork. There were very few in agriculture and a comparatively small percentage in industry. Few were in the liberal professions, owing to Tzarist prohibitions against Jews in trade schools, universities and all other professional schools.

The Jewish masses of the pre-Revolution period, confined to the "Pale of Settlement" [10] and concentrated in the small towns (shtetl), were members of an impoverished middle-class, competed with one another in the "Luft" professions, and had little or no economic future.

By 1920 the pre-Revolution economic positions, undermined by war, pogroms, revolution and famine, were completely destroyed. The majority of Russian Jews who, until the advent of the Soviet regime, were either traders or small artisans, were deprived of their subsistence by the Soviet decrees. These decrees prohibited retail trade, nationalized all commercial and industrial undertakings, and organized co-operative retail distribution to the peasants. The problem of earning a living became so acute that masses of Jews faced starvation. In time, however, and upon the ruins of the old Jewish ghetto, arose a

new Jewish economic structure which was to a large extent similar
to that of the rest of the population.

The policy of the Soviets which forced the Jews to leave old occupations, also forced them into new areas of endeavor. The process
of change of vocations and economic adjustment lasted more than
twenty years. The transition was accompanied by great and serious difficulties. There was for a while total unemployment in
most small Jewish towns. Multitudes of people became so poor
that the acquisition of a potato was an occasion for rejoicing. It
was not easy for a people to be uprooted suddenly from an economic and a social life that had been theirs for centuries.

Russian Jews were obliged to leave not only their old professions but also their former dwelling places. The "Shtetl", the nest
of Jewish life had to be abandoned; migration to the village and
industrial city was inescapable.

At the beginning of the Soviet regime more than one-third of
the Jewish population remained without sources for a livelihood.
Many Jews became people without a trade or a profession, owing
to the elimination of commerce and middle-class occupations and
the inauguration of a new economic order. The process of adjustment brought economic despair and years of starvation to
hundreds of thousands.

However, the adjustment of Jews to the new economy was
finally achieved by 1930. Of the masses of jobless Jews at the
beginning of the economic redirection period in 1921, there
were only 75,000 without occupation by the 1930's, most of them
aged men and women, widows and sick people, and some individuals dependent upon funds from relatives in America.

Economic redirection and adjustment were conducted along
three lines: agricultural, industrial and educational.

The Agricultural Phase of the Economic Transformation:

In 1924 the *"KOMZED"* Government Committee for the
Colonization of Jews, was organized and with the aid of Jewish
agencies for the settlement of Jews on land, such as "Geserd", the
American "Agro-Joint" and the European Ort, agricultural settlements were established in White Russia, Ukraine, Crimea and
Biro-Bidjan. In 1929, 10.1 per cent of the Jewish population in
Russia were farmers. The agricultural colonization not only saved
many Jews from starvation, but created for them a "legitimate"
social status.

The Industrial Aspect of the Productivization of the Jews

The industrialization of all of Russia, the special privileges granted to industrial workers, the strengthening of industry in the city, the improvements of conditions of work in the factories, the new industrial projects throughout the country, brought about a constant flow of men and women, including Jews, to the city factory and to the industrial plant in the village or city suburb. So much were Jews attracted to industry that some of the younger people deserted the farm. In certain sections of the U.S.S.R., such as White Russia and the Ukraine, Jews formed about 80 per cent of all those engaged in industrial pursuits.

The Educational Phase of Jewish Rehabilitation

The educational phase of Jewish economic rehabilitation was of great significance in the formation of a large percentage of Jewish institutional workers. The mass education in Russia for young and old, the trade schools and evening courses for adults afforded opportunities for tens of thousands of young Jews to learn trades, attend professional schools, and enter the field of government employment.

According to official figures of the Soviet Government in 1939, at the beginning of the Second World War, the following was the economic structure of Russian Jewry:[12]

Physical laborers		21.5%
Employees in Government Institutions		37.2%
Farmers		7.1%
Artisans and Craftsmen		14.3%
Liberal professions		12.8%
Traders		—
All others		7.1%
	Total	100%

The outbreak of the Second World War already found the process of dislocation of the Jewish population in full speed. In 1939 almost two-fifths of the total Jewish population had already moved out of the Pale of Settlement. The War accelerated the process. The advancing German armies brought about the evacuation of additional hundreds of thousands. Those who remained in the old homes suffered, of course, wholesale extermination. The Germans destroyed all Jewish villages, never again to be restored. The five Jewish national districts of the Ukraine and Crimea were obliterated. The same was true in Soviet White Russia. The survivors of the Nazi holocaust and the larger groups of Jews who inhabited the regions unoccupied by the German armies, reached an estimated two and one-quarter million. Due to the creeping anti-Semitism in the Government there is little official data of the occupations of the Jewish citizens in the post-war period. From the various reports of newspaper correspondents it is possible to surmise that the Jews no longer constitute an ethnic group or a national unit with an economic, social or cultural life of their own. With the liquidation of the pre-war Jewish communities in old regions of the "Pale" and the destruction of the so-called Jewish autonomous regions, most Jews, save for some of the old men and women, have intermingled with the rest of the population economically and culturally to a large degree, the anti-Jewish feeling of the general public notwithstanding. The Jews engage in the same economic pursuits as the other citizens, but they are at a greater disadvantage in some professions due to anti-Semitism which is still plaguing the Russians.

Western Europe

ENGLAND

No definite figures are available regarding the economic pursuits of the Jews of England. They may be classified, as in the case of French Jewry, into two categories: the old settlers and those who settled in the 80's of the last century. The latter are mostly artisans, petty traders and laborers, whereas the earlier settlers form a high social bracket engaging in commerce, finance, liberal and public service professions.

The Eastern European Jews who immigrated into England, were, up to World War II, garment workers, watchmakers, furriers and peddlers. The old settlers were the merchants, the professionals, the industrialists and the men in finance.

The economic conditions of the 425,000 Jews of Great Britain after the War are similar to those of the Jews of the United States and Canada. In terms of occupations in which the Jews engage the following table gives a very concrete picture:[13]

Commerce and Trade	55%
Industry	25%
Professions	15%
Miscellaneous	5%
Total	100%

In industry the Jews are concentrated in clothing manufacture, building construction and in the chemical industry. In commerce they have a high ratio in the jewelry business, department stores. They are not represented in heavy industry nor in the public utilities. (The same is the case in America.) Generally speaking, their financial position is good. There are a few very wealthy men, heads of large business establishments, many more in the high income class and the majority in the middle income bracket. English Jewry too, contributes large sums of money for local and overseas needs as well as for the campaigns for funds to aid Israel. In 1961 over a million pounds ($2,800,000) was raised for the Joint Israeli Appeal and the Isaac Wolfson Foundation distributed during the year for all types of charity the sum of $2,800,000.[14]

The Jews of England contribute to the development of all branches of the British economy. They are represented in industry, banking, commerce, international trade and in the liberal professions.

The Jews of England have given handsome contributions to Israel educational institutions. There are a number of wealthy families (Simon Marks, Israel Sieff, A. Levenson, Isaac Wolfson, Harry Sacher, Albert Alberman) whose parents or grandparents were immigrants from Eastern Europe and who have risen to great riches and prestige. There were, of course, great Jewish philanthropists among the older settlers, the outstanding among them: Sir Anthony and Lionel Nathan Rothschild of the House of Rothschild which originated in Germany in the 16th century, and Sir Moses Montefiore. The Rothschilds financed the British participation in the Crimean War and provided cash needed by Disraeli to purchase the Suez Canal shares. Sir Montefiore was active in business, served as Sheriff of London, and took an active part in philanthropic activities in England. Outstanding in his career were his missions for Jews in distress in every part of the world. He was a pious Jew and until his death at the age of 92 he was hard at work trying to alleviate Jewish misery. His work endeared him to all Jews of the world.

FRANCE

Complete information is lacking with regard to the economic structure of the French Jewish community. The very nature of French Jewry, consisting of Sephardic Jews who resettled in France in the 17th century, German Jews who entered in the 18th century, and Oriental and East European Jews who immigrated steadily after 1880, makes it difficult to determine their social and economic status.

There is, however, some statistical data pertaining to the vocational distribution of a cross section of immigrants who became naturalized between 1924 and 1935. Since more than half of French Jewry consisted of those who immigrated since 1882, the vocational distribution of the small group of immigrants presents a rather accurate picture of a large segment of French Jewry. According to the findings of A. Menes, who studied the records of the naturalized Jews in the "Journal Official", the following was their vocational distribution: [15]

Industry and Labor	45.3%
Commerce	32.5%
Transportation	1.2%
Liberal Professions	7.9%
No definite vocations	13.1%
Total	100.0%

Jews engaged in industry and labor were mostly distributed in the clothing industry, and in the building and furniture trades. The laborers were jewelry and leather goods workers, watchmakers and metal workers. In commerce they were storekeepers, traders, peddlers, agents and salesmen. This vocational distribution is fairly representative of the gainfully employed immigrant Jews.

The economic difference between the old settlers and the new is obvious. There were fewer people among the immigrants in the liberal professions and in commerce. The reason is the lack of professional education among the newly arrived and the limited opportunities for engaging in commerce without the necessary capital.

Generally speaking, it is apparent, on the basis of Mr. Menes' study, that the immigrant Jews did not play a dominant role in any branch of the economic life of the country. The old settlers on the other hand have engaged in commerce, in colonial trading and in the field of finance. In these areas they occupied a somewhat conspicuous place in a number of cities.

In the 1930's, the vast majority of Jews belonged to the low income level. The fact that more than one-half of the naturalized Jews had no home telephone [16] is ample proof that their economic status was low. Of course, as already intimated, a small group of Jewish capitalists existed, many of whom have risen to commanding positions, in commerce and finance.

The Second World War wrought havoc with the French Jews. Many of them were deported by the Nazis to concentration camps; others managed to flee the country. Jewish economy during that period was obviously in a very precarious state.

After the War, the Jews who survived the storm returned, generally speaking, to their old professions. "Apart from the special situation of the bulk of North African Jews in the metropolis, which is the very trying one of a sub-proletariat of unskilled workers, the material lot of the majority of Jews of France is relatively good." [17] The Jewish functionaries who had been ousted by the Vichy Regime were reinstated and the despoiled Jews received restitution.

The French Jews today are engaged in wholesale and retail commerce (particularly in textiles, ready-to-wear clothes, leather goods, millinery and jewelry). Many of the sons of the immigrants are to be found in the professions as doctors, lawyers, engineers, artists and teachers. There are also many Jewish manual workers but their number is diminishing while the number of white collar workers and those in civil service and in local branches of government is increasing. Among the new Jewish immigrants from North Africa there is a considerable number of factory workers, both skilled and unskilled. On the whole, French prosperity in recent years benefited the Jews together with the rest of the population, but the Jewish community of France is seemingly not wealthy. There are many more relief cases in this country than in England, let alone America. The continuing immigration of North African Jews makes relief work an urgent necessity, but the French Jews raise barely enough money to support their own welfare institutions.

Among the wealthy Jews of France was the famous Baron Edmond de Rothschild, who was known in the non-Jewish world as banker, art collector, philanthropist, patron of science, art and literature. He was one of the most colorful personalities in Jewish life and the greatest developer of modern Palestine who helped to establish the early colonies. Another outstanding Jewish financier of France was Baron Maurice de Hirsch. His great wealth was in part inherited, but largely accumulated by banking and contracting for the Turkish railroads. Baron Hirsch was interested in the welfare of the Jews of the Near East and contributed large sums of money for the school systems of the Alliance Israelite Universelle, the agency engaged in promoting the welfare and education of Jews throughout the Middle East and North Africa. He also formed the Jewish Colonization Association to which he subscribed a capital of ten million dollars back in the 1880's for the purpose of helping East European Jews to settle in Brazil, Argentina, Canada, and the U.S.A. The total of his contributions exceeded the sum of one hundred million dollars.

ARGENTINA

As already mentioned in Chapter 4, East European Jewish immigrants who came to the Argentine in the late 80's of the past century found a small settlement of Jews from Western and Central Europe who were predominantly traders. These immigrants were aided by the Jewish Colonization Association to establish agricultural colonies. The colonists struggled very hard to remain on the land. Most of them were Russian Jews who rebelled against the conditions of life in the Pale of Settlement and who considered farming a realization of a Jewish dream to become once again rooted in the soil. The favorable climate and the abundance of uncultivated land presented wonderful opportunities for agricultural work.

In the ensuing four decades there arose in the Argentine 25 agricultural Jewish settlements, 18 of which were organized by the Jewish Colonization Association and seven by the independent homesteaders, despite the tendency of the younger men and women to prefer city life. In 1940, there were still about 28,000 Jews who earned their living from farming. [9]

While originally the east European immigrants (primarily from Russia and Rumania) were encouraged to engage in agriculture, most of the Jewish immigrants preferred the city and settled there. City life appealed to them because it offered varied opportunities for economic growth and financial advancement. These city dwellers started out as peddlers and installment dealers. Almost 90 per cent of them engaged in these occupations during and immediately after World War I (1914-1917). Twenty to twenty-five years later these peddlers became merchants and industrialists.

The new immigrants who entered the country in the intervening years (1920-45) augmented the ranks of manufacturers and traders, and also formed small groups of factory workers, small service shop owners and artisans. The sons and daughters of both the early and the late arrivals in the 40's and in the 50's became white collar workers and professionals.

According to a study in Buenos Aires in 1947, out of all gainfully employed Jews of the city, 49 per cent were engaged in commerce, 41 per cent in industry (including wage earners and administrative personnel) and 10 per cent in other vocations, including the liberal professors.[20] In the course of 15 years (1947–52) the occupational distribution changed considerably. A recent study of the records of marriages registered by the Kehillah, the new members admitted to the organization and the occupations of pupils' parents in the Jewish schools, indicated the following distribution:[21]

Occupation	
Business	28.8%
White Collar Work	27.3%
Manufacturing (Light Industry)	4.9%
Labor	3.5%
Liberal Professions	16.2%
Independent Artisans & Other occupations	19.3%
Total	100%

The Buenos Aires Jews concentrate in the textile industry, clothing, leather, fur and food.

That the financial state of the Argentine Jews (total population 450,000) is fairly good, can be seen from the budget of the Buenos Aires Kehillah (Community Council), with which all Jewish institutions are affiliated. The 1960 budget provided for the expenditures of 120 million pesos for local needs.[22]

From this brief survey it becomes apparent that the Argentine Jews constitute a middle-class group and that on the whole they are prosperous, benefitting from the dominant trends of industrialization and urbanization.

On the surface it looks as though there need be no concern with respect to the economic life of the Jewish community. Upon careful examination of the situation, however, we become aware of an important problem. As in the case of all other Latin American countries, the general population finds itself in a state of poverty, in need of economic aid from the United States of America. The masses subsist on a very low standard of living. Unlike the situation in the United States where practically the entire population has attained a high standard of living, Latin America is still divided between the large group of "have-nots" and the smaller group of "haves".

Thus, Jewish concentration in commerce, industry, petty trade and professions is more or less out of tune with the general condition in the country. The Jewish merchant and manufacturer becomes a subject of suspicion. The poor non-Jews point to him as to the foreign element whose accumulated riches are the result of "shady" business deals. Jewish predominance in certain limited occupations, although much needed in the urban economy, becomes conspicuous. In times of economic depression or political unrest, the public lends an attentive ear to the bigots and blames the Jews for their poverty.

Then too, in Argentina, as well as in other countries of Latin America, where important economic changes will inevitably occur and the state might even intervene in private business, the Jewish economy may undergo new adjustments.

The Jews are therefore eager to help those elements in Latin America who are hard at work seeking solutions to the economic problems of the countries, the chief among them being the low standard of living of the bulk of the population. The economic security of the Jews, in the long run, depends upon the social and economic welfare of the entire population.

We make no reference to the economic life of other South American Jewish communities. Most of them fall in the same category as Argentine Jewry.

ISRAEL

Ever since the early immigration of the *BILU* [23] in 1882, all through the history of the modern Jewish settlement in Palestine (since 1948 — Israel), great stress was laid on the need to build an economy on sound foundations. Since in most countries of the world the economic base (in the period 1880-1920) was agriculture, it was felt by the leaders of the Zionist enterprise in Palestine that farming should be given priority in the new venture of rebuilding the land. Moreover, the Halutzim believed that the correction of the anomalous vocational distribution of the Jews, many of whom might eventually find a home in Palestine, was of import to the entire Jewish people. The return to the soil became, at the time of the Second and Third Aliyot (1906-1908; 1917-1923) , a dominant motif in Zionist colonization. Many a young Jew was eager to prove that Jews could be good cultivators of the soil.

The idea of reconquering the land from its desolation and to make it once again flourish and bear fruit—gained many followers among the Jewish youth groups.

The Jewish National Fund, organized in 1902, as the land redeeming agency of the people, purchased land from Arabs and with the help of Jewish labor rendered it cultivable through the processes of swamp draining, afforestation, etc.[24] The motto "Kibbush HaAvodah" (Conquest of Labor) which reverberated all through the land is indicative not only of the determination to till the land with Jewish hands[25] but also of the realization of the principle of "Hagshamah Atzmit" (self-fulfilment) . This implied that in the old-new land, Jews need not continue their economic existence as "Luftmenschen",[26] but as working people engaged primarily in farming and secondarily in industry and commerce. The story of the Kibbutzim (collective settlements) which, together with Moshavim (cooperative settlements) became the frontiers in the struggle for statehood and in the war with the Arabs, is replete with this conviction. The men and women of the collective settlements, the workers' cooperatives, small holders' colonies (Moshavei Ovdim) and other types of villages, fostered the idea of self-labor on the soil and in allied branches of the agricultural economy. It was really a remarkable achievement of the Zionist undertaking that it succeeded in motivating people, who for centuries were divorced from the soil and who had never held a spade, to become farmers in the new land. It was natural, of course, that the return to the land should have been for many years the very heart of Zionism. Jewish students, workmen and traders transformed themselves into farmers, willingly and conscientiously, cultivating and guarding with their very lives the new land. This process of proletarianization (the conscious effort to do productive work as manual laborers) continued until the 1930's. The youth who came to the country sought to escape the narrowness of ghetto existence in Eastern Europe. They were also inspired by the socialist ideals of a new society with no exploiters nor exploited. These Halutzim, as Dr. Zweig points out in his study of the Israeli worker,[27] performed great things, laying the foundation for the future State, establishing the Kibbutz movement and the Histadrut (the General Federation of Labor, founded in 1920, whose members with their families constituted, in 1960, 57 per cent of the population).

With the influx of new settlers (in the pre-World War II period) who were not motivated by the Halutz ideals, and with the rise of the refugee immigration from the Nazi and hostile Arab lands, the urban centers grew and developed. In the towns and cities industrial plants sprang up offering opportunities for new economic pursuits. The government, with the aid of the Jewish Agency for Israel, made a concerted effort to find useful occupations for all newcomers in the cities, towns or villages.

The largest percentage of the more than a million immigrants who came to Israel in the last two decades settled in the towns and cities because they were absorbed in the ever-expanding industry. This large scale immigration also resulted in the rise of scores of rural settlements and in a considerable increase of agricultural workers. There are now about 700 agricultural settlements in the country, 500 of which have been founded since the rise of the State. The population of these rural settlements is nearing the half-million mark.

From May 15, 1948 (the date of the establishment of the State) to May 1959, 48.9 per cent of all immigrants were absorbed in the cities and towns and 15.5 per cent in the rural settlements. The rest were given provisional accommodations in the *ma'barot* (camps of temporary dwellings) or joined relatives.[28] Most of these newcomers who became town and city dwellers augmented the ranks of the Israeli workers. Thus began a new phase of proletarianization, which is of an entirely different character than the one in the Halutz era of 1905-1930. No longer prompted by Zionist and Socialist idealism, the new immigrants tried desperately to hold to their former trades or professions. In the new state, however, there is little or no opportunity to engage in the old-home occupations. There is planning and guidance in directing the masses of immigrants to become productive members of the new society and to do work which is beneficial to the country as well as to individual citizens. These immigrants, most of them penniless, having come to the country with the aid of Jewish public funds, formed a new class of workers, doing work for which there is a demand. Willingly or unwillingly these men and women, knowing they would starve if they did not work, became the new workers in the teeming cities and towns. Thus we find many a former merchant driving a truck or a taxi, a former salesman doing the job of a building worker, a housewife—a factory worker, and so on. Fortunately the attitude of these people to manual labor became more positive and they adjusted themselves to the new conditions in the new state.

Israel is now building a comprehensive economy, the base of which is industry rather than agriculture.

If Belgium, England or Switzerland are to be taken as criteria of the modern state with a relatively small land reserve, the nearly two million Jews of Israel, economically speaking, constitute a well balanced society. 33 per cent of the population live in the three major cities; 43 per cent in the other towns and townships and 24 per cent in the countryside.[29] An exact picture of the distribution of Israel's gainfully employed is to be seen from this table: [30]

Agriculture, Afforestation & Fishing	16.4%
Industry & Crafts	23.3%
Public Works, Public Utilities & Building	11.9%
Trade, Banking & Insurance	12.0%
Transportation & Storage	7.0%
Administration & Social Services	21.9%
Personal Services & Entertainment	7.5%
Total	100.0%

We can readily see from the above table that the so-called anomaly of Jewish economic life, which was the case in the Eastern Europe prior to World War II and which is still the case in Latin America and Western Europe, has been corrected. Only 21 per cent of the inhabitants are engaged in trade and banking; the majority of the people are workers in industry, crafts and services. The ratio of Jews in agriculture is the highest in the Jewish world, and has risen in the last few years. Many of the immigrants from North Africa, who were formerly engaged in petty commerce, have been transformed into agricultural and industrial workers. The Ministry of Labor and the unions give vocational training to the multitude of semi-skilled or unskilled workers. The ORT [31] maintains vocational schools for youth and adults, and the Ministry of Education, aided by the youth movements and by Hadassah's Youth Aliyah projects, maintains a network of training centers for all types of personnel, from agricultural and factory laborers to accountants and hotel managers.

The industry of Israel consists of the manufacture of chemical products, cutting and polishing of diamonds, metal and ceramic industries, textiles, wood, stone, cement and automobile assembly. Sixty-five per cent of the industry is privately owned. The State undertakings account for about twenty per cent, mainly devoted to the exploitation of natural resources in the Negev, and about fifteen per cent of the industry is run by cooperatives of companies controlled by the Histadrut, the General Federation of Labor. In many undertakings, there is a combination of two or more of the forms of ownership. Planned efforts in industry, as in agriculture, have greatly benefitted the entire national economy. Government loans are available to those willing to set up industries in the new areas that are yet to be developed. The same holds true for the aid given by public institutions to those who are willing to establish new agricultural settlements in the Negev and along the Arab border lines surrounding Israel.

The growth of industry has been rapid. It has more than trebled since the rise of the State. The main products that are exported are plywood, textiles, tires, chemicals, diamonds and machinery. The agricultural products for export are citrus, fresh fruits and eggs. Israel's agricultural economy today accounts for one-third of the entire export.

The Israeli economy is still not self-sufficient. While exports in 1961 reached the $240,000,000 mark, an increase of 114 per cent since 1956 [32] there are still more products imported than exported. The disparity however, is being slowly but surely reduced. The leading economists maintain that by 1968 Israel should be completely self-sufficient. In the meantime it depends on foreign investments, the tourist trade and on the funds collected in the lands of dispersion to help the country absorb the tens of thousands of immigrants who flock there every year and every month.

Summary

The world in our day is undergoing rapid change. The advance of technology which resulted in automation, the use of atomic energy for peaceful purposes, the shrinking of distances— are indications of the significant changes that are taking place in the economies of many nations. Only 20 to 30 years ago, Russia was still primarily an agrarian state. Today it is a highly industrialized country. Only little more than a century ago, the United States had seventy per cent of its gainfully employed people engaged in farming. Today only ten per cent of all Americans are engaged in agriculture and yet there is much more food in America today than ever before, even though the general population has grown considerably and despite the fact that there is a stockpile of surplus food. In England only six per cent are engaged in agriculture while more than 50 per cent are employed in professions, trade and personnel services. The illustrations of the three greatest powers in the world today point to the rapid process of a country's economic transformation. Many other countries such as Canada, Australia, France, Germany follow this pattern. Even the under-developed countries which depend on farming for their sustenance are now making great strides in the area of industrialization. Japan is a case in point. There is a remarkable economic expansion practically everywhere, and an uninterrupted shift of the center of economic gravity from the rural areas to the urban centers.

Thus, if for many, many years, the Jews (due to reasons given at the beginning of the chapter) have engaged in the so-called intermediary professions more than in manual and/or brain labor, we now find that the modern economy in the New World is leading great numbers of other peoples in the direction of non-agricultural pursuits. We have already pointed out that in America and in England the disparity between the vocations of the Jewish and the non-Jewish city dwellers is almost disappearing. The Jews in these countries are no longer an exception in an economic sense. They earn a living from much of the same sources as do all other urban people. The "isolation" of the Jewish economy is still conspicuous in South America and North Africa, where Jews are still predominantly engaged in commerce while most of the non-Jews are not. In this disparity we find a state of anomaly. The "anomaly" exists in that the Jewish economic structure differs markedly when compared with the total population within each of these countries. But should these countries follow the pattern of industrialization, the Jewish occupations will become more normal and Jewish representation in all branches of the economy will be less disproportionate.

In this respect too, Israel is the only country where the economy is planned by the Jews themselves, and where pursuit of certain occupations is encouraged or discouraged depending upon the general conditions in the land. It is again the only place where Jews are masters of their destiny in every sphere of life.

TOPICS FOR DISCUSSION

1. How do you counter the charge that most Jews were, and still are, either businessmen or professionals and that they did, and still do, shy away from hard work such as farming, mining, seagoing, soldiering?

2. What is the place of the Jew in the modern economy of the major Jewish population centers of the Free World?

3. If "Jewish occupations will become more normal," do you believe that Jews will find it easier or harder to earn a livelihood? Did the Jews derive advantages from the fact that they could enter into fields which were not occupied by the general population?

4. Do you think that the occupations of the Jews in America differ from those of all other Americans? If so, should the Jews make a special effort to engage in the same occupations as do the rank and file of the majority group?

5. Is the occupational pattern of the Jews in Israel unique? If so, why?

6. Do you accept the assumption that much of Jew-hatred is a by-product of disproportionate Jewish representation in business and in the liberal professions?

NOTES TO CHAPTER 5

1. Yehezkel Kaufman, *Contemporary Jewish Record,* New York, 1941.
2. The first stage of capitalism was the beginning of the modern credit system, international trade, colonial trade and the expansion of shipping industries.
3. Jacobs, Joseph: "Jewish Contribution to Civilization," Jewish Publication Society, 1944, p. 245.
4. See "Economishe Shriften," Vol. I, 1930, *Yiddisher Scientific Institute of Vilna.*
5. Reich, Nathan: "The Economic Structure of Modern Jewry," in *The Jews: Their History, Culture and Religion,* Edited by Louis Finkelstein, Harper Brothers, New York, 1949, Vol. II, p. 1264.
6. Reich, Nathan: *Yivo Annual of Jewish Social Science,* New York, 1950, p. 199.
7. Goldberg, S. P.: American Jewish Year Book, 1961, p. 155.
8. American Statistical Association Journal, September, 1961, p. 574.
9. Jewish Telegraphic Agency Daily News Bulletin, January 5, 1962, p. 3.
10. The provinces set aside by the Russian Government for Jewish permanent residence; other parts of the country were forbidden to them, save for merchants of the first Guild who were given special permits.
11. Literally meaning "air." Luft denotes the status of people who have no basic trade or profession and have to depend on chance for a livlihood.
12. Lestschinsky, Jacob: "Dos Sovietishe Yidentum," New York, 1941, p. 170.
13. Lestschinsky, Jacob: "Ha-Pzurah Ha-Yehudit," Tel Aviv, 1961, pp. 112-113.
14. American Jewish Year Book, 1962, p. 297.
15. Menes, A.: "Die Yiden in Frankreich," *Yivo Bletter,* May, 1937, p. 339.
16. *Ibid.,* p. 354.
17. European Jewry Ten Years After the War, World Jewish Congress, New York, 1956, p. 197.
18. The Jewish Colonization Association, established in 1891 with Baron de Hirsch funds in the sum of ten million dollars, sought to establish colonies for the Jews of Eastern Europe and Asia.

19. Lestschinsky, Jacob: "Ha-Pzurah Ha-Yehudit," Tel Aviv, 1961, p. 165.
20. Shatzky, Yaacov: Yiddishe Yishuvim in Latin America, Buenos Aires, 1952, p. 32.
21. American Jewish Year Book, 1962, p. 475.
22. American Jewish Year Book, 1961, p. 216.
23. Compounded from the initials of the sentence: Bet Ya'acov Lechu V'neilcha (House of Jacob let us rise and go). It was the name given to the first group of Russian students who in 1882 proceeded to Palestine to establish agricultural settlements.
24. J. N. F. land is held in trust for the nation and is let on 49-year leases on the principle of the Biblical Jubilee.
25. Many of the Jewish colonists employed mostly Arab labor, thus wreaking havoc with the ideal of building the land by Jews for Jews.
26. Yiddish term denoting economic insecurity; people without jobs who depend on chance (luft — air) to eke out a livelihood.
27. Zweig, Ferdynand: "The Israeli Worker," New York, 1959.
28. Facts about Israel, Israel Ministry for Foreign Affairs, Jerusalem, 1961, p. 46.
29. Ibid., p. 42.
30. Ibid., p. 114.
31. ORT is a World Jewish Organization engaged in promoting vocational education. It operates many schools in North Africa, Israel and in other countries.
32. Jewish Telegraphic Agency Daily News Bulletin, February 16, 1962, p. 2.

6

The Jew and His Religion

Introductory Statement

The word *"religion"* is of Latin origin. It was usually spelled *"rel(l)igio"* meaning an act of observing, binding together, practicing of rites. In the course of time it came to mean a relationship or a communion between the human and the super-human. In Jewish classical literature we have little reference, if any, to the word *"religion."* The word frequently used that passed for what in our day corresponds to *"religion"* was *"Torah."*[1] We find in our literature the term *"emunah,"* meaning truth, faithfulness. We have also the words *"dat,"* meaning law, edict, mandate[2] and *"Kedusha,"* meaning holiness, which, as Dr. Isidore Epstein of Jews' College in London puts it, "expresses a quality consisting negatively 'in separation from' and positively 'in dedication to.' "[3] It is the idea of separation from the debasing elements in life, the unholy, as it were, and the dedication to all that is ennobling or holy. This view implied a negative approach to idolatry in all its ramifications and a positive attitude to become "Holy unto God," an idea which calls for elevating the life of man, bringing man as near as possible to the state of perfection.

The term *"religion"* was already in vogue in the Middle Ages when our scholars engaged in polemics with Christian and Mohammedan theologians and when some of our writers employed Latin as a vehicle of literary expression. In modern times, with the intensification of secular education among Jews, the use of non-Judaic terminology to denote religious concepts became an integral part of our vernacular; for most of the Jews in the world today employ the languages of the countries of their domicile in speech and in writing.

The term used by Jews through the ages to denote the concept of Jewish religion is Judaism, *"Yahadut."* This word referred

originally to the beliefs and doctrines of the people of Judea, or
the Tribe of Judah (Yehudah) ; in the course of time it was applied to the religion of the entire Jewish people. Judaism, therefore, is a "religion" inseparably connected with the Jewish people.
It is no wonder then that most Jewish scholars assert that Judaism
is more than a religion in the sense of a creed alone. Rather it is
a way of life and a thought-world, which extends over 3,000 years
in practically all lands of the globe. Just as the Jewish people
have undergone change in the course of history, Judaism, too, did
not always retain the same form nor even the same character.
Rabbinic Judaism differed from the Judaism of prophetic times;
Helenistic Judaism differed to some extent from that of Palestine and the Judaism of modern days is different from that of the
Middle Ages.

Before we discuss the Jewish religious schools of thought in our
age, we will present, sketchily, the important changes in Jewish
history in the past century that brought about the rise of different
groupings within modern Judaism.

JEWISH RELIGIO-CULTURAL LIFE OF YESTERDAY

"The God of Israel, the People of Israel and the Torah are
one."[4] The truth of this saying becomes evident when one studies
the history of Jewish cultural life through the ages. Long centuries of wandering, entailing constant social, political and economic readjustments in all lands of dispersion, have not estranged
the Jew from the fountainhead of his being, i.e. his religious culture. It has always been the chief dynamic force in the life of
the people. It shaped their destiny; it was a constant reminder of
their Torah's call to Holiness. Judaism also represented a spiritual
fatherland and formed the basis of Jewish group existence.
While other peoples had their own countries and could draw
cultural inspiration from them, the Jews substituted religious
culture for a land and made the Torah their inspiration. They
were endowed by their faith with strength and courage to live a
Jewish life in a non-Jewish world, frequently hostile and antago-
nistic.

Religion, which became the essence of Jewish cultural life,
served therefore as a means of national self-preservation. It
served as a bond of unity for a dispersed people. As such it was
bound to motivate all social and intellectual patterns of Jewish
life. Customs, ceremonies, rituals, folk-ways,—all can be traced
directly or indirectly to the religion of the people.

Although the cultural expressions of the Jews were not purely religious in character—their scope having included poetry and drama, philosophy and history, fable and folk-lore, prose and allegory, music and art—the inspiration sprang from a Jewish religious world outlook. The Golden Age of Jewish literature in Spain is a concrete illustration of the diversity of Jewish intellectual activity. Philosophy, astronomy, medicine, philology, poetry— all these form part of the literature of the period, yet all bear the imprint of a conception of life which is rooted in, and influenced by, the religion of Israel. Amidst the many changes that characterize the history of the Jews after the golden age in Spain and until the modern period, the supremacy of religion in the life of the people remained constant. One might justly say that Jewish life was synonymous with religious life.

GRADUAL ESTRANGEMENT FROM RELIGIOUS CULTURE

At the end of the 18th century, Jewish cultural life was subjected to the stimuli of the ever-growing secularism. In many countries, Jewish life began to reflect more closely many of the environmental patterns of conduct, accepting a variety of new ideas and new world outlooks. The effect of these influences was so great that "traditionalism" began to give way to "modernism," particularly in Western and Central Europe and America where Jews mingled freely with non-Jews. Jewish literary expression absorbed the spirit of the "new age" and was no longer predominantly religious. Social life too, began to mirror the culture of the non-Jewish world, and the weakening of the religious motif in Jewish life paralleled the decline of religion in the general population. The gradual transition from ancient ways to the new scheme of things in the Diaspora was aided by two inner forces which paved the way for the gradual acceptance of secularism. The Haskalah (enlightenment) movement advocated modernization and gained many followers among the intelligentsia; and the movement of assimilationists fostered the idea of the dissolution of Jewry as a separate national entity which insists on perpetuating its distinctive traits and ways of life.

While the process of apostasy and the break with the past resulted in the flight of many Jews from Judaism, the greater part of world Jewry, then inhabiting Eastern Europe, was very little affected by the new turn of events. Moreover, cultural assimilation almost everywhere was counter-balanced by a revived and regenerated modern Judaism (Hebrew and Yiddish literatures, the new Jewish schools, the Jewish press, the ever-growing movement of Jewish nationalism, etc.); the lapse from religion by new Jewish cultural values which invigorated the modern Jew. Both forces operated in shaping the character of Jewish cultural life during the last century.

The following are the most important causes which brought about the decline of religious authority:

The Industrial Revolution

Great changes were brought about by the Industrial Revolution in the realm of economic life in the civilized world at the end of the 18th century. In the wake of these changes Jewish participation in newly-created economic spheres became possible. The Jews were thus drawn into social contact with non-Jews. These economic and social changes exposed them to new ideas and ideals which in turn resulted in the gradual abandonment of certain religious practices and unconscious neglect in perpetuating traditional and cultural institutions of their own.

The New Ideas

The evolutionary theory stresses the principle of natural selection, which comes about through "struggle for existence" and "the survival of the fittest." It is a theory applied to living things. It maintains that plants and animals have changed through generation after generation, and since this change has been going on for ages, all things that now live on earth are much changed descendants of others that lived long ago. In the process of change, a higher form evolving from a lower, those living things survived that could adapt themselves to the effects of change and thus become fit to survive. This theory conflicts with the basic religious belief of God as the creator and that man is God's creation and not a by-product of a process of evolution from a lower state.

Emancipation

Citizenship rights which were granted Jews in the United States and in western and central Europe removed the barrier which had existed for generations between them and the Gentiles. For

the first time in the Diaspora, the Jews were given the opportunity to associate freely with the non-Jews and to become an integral part of the civilization of the majority groups. In the countries where civil equality was realized, Jews willingly became assimilated. To the extent that assimilation grew, Judaic religio-
cultural values declined and the attachment to the secular culture
increased.

Secular Education and the Haskalah Movement

With the growth of general educational facilities for the masses
(democratization of education), opportunities of learning subjects,
other than Jewish studies, were opened to the emancipated Jews.
The youth flocked to the secular schools. Even in Eastern Europe
before emancipation, the demand for general education was so
great that means were devised for gaining admission to the general schools. Hence the gap between traditional Jewish learning
and the new education became deeper and wider.

Migration and the Formation of New Jewish Centers

Jewish migration from Eastern to Western Europe and to other
continents removed the immigrants from the environment of the
ghetto and made adjustments to new surroundings imperative.
The new atmosphere contributed to cultural assimilation and resulted in a constant drift from tradition. The process of westerni-
zation was thus often accompanied by a process of dejudaization.

Reawakened Nationalism and the Rise of a
Modern Jewish Culture

While all the above factors made for a retreat from Judaism,
and weakened Jewish attachment to ancestral traditions, the reawakened Jewish nationalism of the same period became a source
of conservation in Jewish cultural life. Although it did not bring
about religious revival, nor restoration of the ritual observances
as practiced throughout the centuries, it gave birth to new values,
which, based upon the essential principles of the historic Jewish
culture, revitalized and regenerated Jewish life after checking its
disintegration. The Jewish nationalist movement created new
forms of Jewish culture, which opened new avenues for social and
intellectual activity, as well as for creative imagination. Though

this movement did not emphasize religion, it had a positive effect upon religion; it arrested and prevented its complete decay.

Modern Jewish literature, music, theatre, plastic arts, education, club work, cultural societies, political organizations—all these are a direct outgrowth of the reawakened nationalism, which became an antidote to assimilation and dissolution.

JEWISH RELIGION IN OUR AGE

As already stated, the political, social and economic changes in Jewish life in the last century which were the by-product of a changed world order, seriously endangered the authority of religion in the life of the people. These changes resulted in dividing Israel into various groups, each professing a different type of Judaism. But notwithstanding these divisions in Judaism, and in spite of waning credal influence, religion is still the outstanding characteristic of the Jewish people. At present, as in earlier years, any Jew who embraces another religion is thought of as one who has deserted his people. Religion and nationality in Israel are inter-related and inter-dependent. Judaism cannot exist without Jews, nor Jews without Judaism. "For the Jews, as such, their religio-cultural heritage is all the more vital, because they have so long lacked the other basic elements of human group life, territory, state and language. Next to the blood ties of common descent, it is primarily this heritage that makes Jews Jewish; more Jewish indeed when they affirm Judaism with their conscious and voluntary allegiance, than when they accept it as a sheer accident of birth. The unity of Jews and Judaism thus has a deep meaning, and the inter-relation between the two, the interplay of the social and religious forces throughout the entire course of Jewish history, appears to be of controlling significance."[5]

Modern Jews hold varying views with regard to Judaism, yet all divisions within Judaism spring, in the main, from the historico-ethical monotheism of the Jewish religion.

Before we continue with our discussion with respect to the different religious groups in Judaism, it is important that we make a brief statement as to the fundamentals of Jewish historic religious thought.

The Idea of God

The Jews were known as the guardians of the pure monotheistic faith; for the central doctrine of Judaism is the belief in One God.

While the Jew may not fully understand the meaning of God, he believes that God exists, that He is One, Eternal, Holy, that He is Spirit, and that there is no unity that is in any manner like unto His. God is the Creator of all things. He is the Law Giver. He is the God of all mankind, transcendent[6], the ethical ruler of the world. He guides all historical events in accordance with His eternal purposes. God is just. He is the source of the moral order.

This idea of the Unity of God is the very foundation of Jewish religious teaching. The firm belief in one universal God, even though the average Jew may have only a vague notion of this idea, molded the entire history of the Jewish people.

The Idea of Torah

The Torah is divine. It is divine revelation and divine instruction. Torah promulgates a code of law. It outlines an ethic of justice and loving kindness, it prescribes rituals, it ordains institutions, it sets forth a doctrine concerning God and it propounds a conception of the Jewish people.[7] The anthropomorphic[8] terms are figurative. As the sages have put it, "Dibrah Torah B'loshon Bnei Adam"—the Torah speaks in the language of man. The study of Torah is mandatory for every Jew.

The Idea of Man's Relation to God and to His Fellow Man

To love God with one's whole soul is a primary Jewish concept. Man was created in the image of God. "He is an active co-worker with God. As a child of God, he is endowed with moral freedom and is charged with the responsibility of overcoming evil and striving after ideal ends. . . . To love God, the Father of all mankind is to love the children of God."[9] Jewish morality is thus deeply rooted in a religious principle. Man's acts of mercy, compassion, loving kindness, justice and charity are, according to the Rabbis of old, means of cleaving to the attributes of God. As for the attribute of a "jealous God," the Rabbis explained, it is to be remembered that "God can rule over jealousy, but man who has no power to rule over jealousy must rather imitate the kindness of God, not his attribute of jealousy."[10] In a word, one cannot love God unless he can love his fellow man.

The Idea of Ethical Life

As already stated, Jewish ethics stem from a religious orientation. Judaism seeks the attainment of a just society. The prophets denounced injustice and oppression, and enunciated a system of human conduct which would eliminate that type of human suffering which is a by-product of tyranny, social inequality and prejudice. Judaism makes a plea for justice and righteousness. The protection of the fatherless, the widow, the stranger, the slave and even the criminal is a precondition to being a just man. Judaism strives for a social order permeated with the spirit of human equality and freedom. It considers the ethical conduct of the individual as the will of God.

The Idea of the Land of Israel

The Land of Israel occupies a place of distinction in Jewish tradition. All of Jewish classical literature is replete with references to the Land of Israel as the Holy Land, the only propitious soil for the flowering of the Jewish religion. It is the Land of Promise. The Land of Israel and its capital, Jerusalem, are considered the holy possessions of the Jews. God promised His people through the seers, prophets and sages to restore this land to its former glory upon the realization of the messianic ideal. On the mountains of the Land of Israel God will ultimately judge all nations.

The Idea of Israel—The Chosen People

The Biblical, Talmudic and post-Talmudic literatures promulgate the conception of Israel as a chosen people. Israel has been chosen by God to declare His will to the world. It is the people to whom the revelation was made. To them God gave the Torah. This Sinaitic covenant between Israel and God makes Israel the torch bearer of God's teachings, of God's Law. Then, too, Israel is the people dedicated to serve as "a light unto the nations." While the Jews were endowed with special privileges, many responsibilities as well were placed upon them. "These responsibilities, to observe the Law, to study it, and to explain it, are expressed in the term 'The Chosen People.' "[11] When the time of Israel's service will come to an end and all mankind will be delivered, this chosen people will have discharged its duty and will partake in the universal redemption. Thus Judaism, the faith of Israel, includes, also, a faith in Israel.[12]

THE MAIMONIDES CODE

The basic Jewish beliefs were summed up by Moses Maimonides (1135-1204) in a series of thirteen principles. They are:

1. I believe with perfect faith that the Creator, blessed be His name, is the Author and Guide of everything that has been created, and that He alone has made, does make, and will make, all things.
2. I believe with perfect faith that the Creator blessed be His name, is a Unity, and that there is no unity in any manner like unto His, and that He alone is our God, Who was, is, and will be.
3. I believe with perfect faith that the Creator, blessed be His name, is not a body, and that He is free from all the accidents of matter, and that He has not any form whatsoever.
4. I believe with perfect faith that the Creator, blessed be His name, is the first and the last.
5. I believe with perfect faith that to the Creator, blessed be His name, and to him alone, it is right to pray, and it is not right to pray to any being besides Him.
6. I believe with perfect faith that all the words of the prophets are true.
7. I believe with perfect faith that the prophecy of Moses our teacher, peace be unto him, was true, and that he was the chief of the prophets, both of those that preceded and of those that followed him.
8. I believe with perfect faith that the whole Law, now in our possession, is the same that was given to Moses our teacher, peace be unto him.
9. I believe with perfect faith that this Law will not be changed, and that there will never be any other law from the Creator, blessed be His name.
10. I believe with perfect faith that the Creator, blessed be His name, knows every deed of the children of men, and all their thoughts, as it is said, 'It is He that fashioneth the hearts of them all, that giveth heed to all their deeds.'
11. I believe with perfect faith that the Creator, blessed be His name, rewards those that keep His commandments, and punishes those that transgress them.
12. I believe with perfect faith in the coming of the Messiah, and though he tarry, I will wait daily for his coming.
13. I believe with perfect faith that there will be a resurrection of the dead at the time when it shall please the Creator, blessed be His name, and exalted be the remembrance of Him for ever and ever.

These Articles of Faith, known as Ikkarim, were incorporated in the prayer-books and a rhymed version of them, known as Yigdal, was included in the liturgy in the 15th century. While they do not constitute the official credo of the Jew, and while in the course of the 13th and 14th centuries there was much discussion among scholars in favor of, and against this formulation, traditional Judaism has nonetheless unofficially accepted the Ikkarim as an important summary of basic Jewish beliefs.

Judaism and Christianity

In this connection it is important that we note the fundamental differences between Judaism and Christianity.

Judaism is God-centered; Christianity is Christ-centered. While Christians are aware of God, and in their faith in His son they also know of God the Father, in their practices and rituals they seem to be more concerned with the Lord Jesus.

"The human mind," says Dr. Leo Baeck in his book *Judaism and Christianity*, "is such that an older belief is impaired by a new one and the new belief commends the way of the future. . . . God, as it were, was removed into the background . . . the bright light, the broad glory, shines now round the Christ."[13]

Judaism is still awaiting the coming of the Messiah, the son-of-David, who will bring redemption to the world; and though he may tarry he shall come. The age of the Messiah as a reign of peace and brotherhood has not yet arrived. Christianity maintains that the Messiah has come and He was more than the human messiah of Jewish tradition. Through Him the world was already redeemed. There is to be "the second coming" which will usher in the total fulfillment of world salvation.

Judaism does not accept an intermediary to God. Every Jew has an opportunity to know God and to find Him. Man does not need a mediator between himself and God. Christianity believes in Jesus as the mediator. Man can find God through the mediation of Jesus. The gospels attest to this idea. "No one comes to Father, but by Me,"[14] said Jesus.

Judaism is not a proselytizing religion. Non-Jews may become converts to Judaism on their own accord, for Jews do not have missionaries whose function is to convince people that Judaism is the only true religion. Christianity, on the other hand, maintains that *it* is the only true faith, and that only its church leads to a communion with God.

Judaism believes that there is God in man, that man is just a "little lower than the angels" and that he is endowed with the power of being a "co-partner" with God in much of the work that is still to be done in nature and with nature. The Divine Presence is with man whenever man is worthy of it. The very words "Shekhinah" (Divine Presence) and "Shakhen" (neighbor or fellow man) suggest the relationship between God and man. Man, according to Judaism, is basically good. His soul is pure. He is, of course, tempted to do evil and very frequently does evil. There is, as the Rabbis point out, a conflict between the good and the evil *Yetser* (inclination) which helps develop character. Therefore "Judaism's primary concern was to teach man not how sin came to the world, but how to avoid sin and how to repent of sin— once having succumbed to it. All men are capable of sinning because all men are endowed with free will."[15] Hence, Judaism stresses the element of Teshuvah (repentance). Christianity maintains that man is born with sin; that he inherited the Original Sin of Adam from his ancestors. "Only those who believe in Jesus share in the atonement of his death, as previously they have shared in the guilt of Adam. They are forgiven and 'saved' for eternal life. Salvation can come to man through faith in Jesus. Judaism promises salvation to all people who fulfill the 'Seven Laws of Noah,'[16] Jews and non-Jews alike; Christianity, however, denies salvation to those who do not profess the faith of Jesus."

There are a number of common elements in Christianity and Judaism. Both share in the belief of the Fatherhood of God; both uphold the principle of redemption and both hold in common the basic laws of morality and the Golden Rule.

It goes without saying that the practices and rituals of the two religions differ widely. While originally the early Christians practiced the Jewish Law and fulfilled most of the obligations prescribed by the Torah (observance of Sabbath, dietary regulations, circumcision, laws of purity), the gulf between the two groups widened ever since Paul absolved the Gentiles from any obligation to engage in traditional Jewish rituals and practices.

With the rise of the Church as a state religion, very little of the original Jewish practices remained within Christianity. The church developed its own ceremonial laws which were codified into religious practices, such as the sacrament, baptism, the eucharist, confession, fasts, communion, etc. The Jews, on the other hand, perpetuated the old practices, although, in the course of time, some of them have been somewhat modified in accordance with Rabbinic interpretations and guidance.

These are, in the main, the major theses of historic Judaism. In the last century new interpretations of Judaism have been presented by Jewish thinkers, which resulted in the formation of four branches of Judaism. We shall now turn to a consideration of the theories of these four groups: The Orthodox, Reform, Conservative, and Reconstructionist.

Orthodox Judaism

The term "Orthodox" was first applied in connection with the Sanhedrin[17] convoked by Napoleon, and was used later to distinguish traditional Judaism from that of the Reform school. Orthodoxy is the historical religion of the Jews or the unbroken chain of traditional Judaism linking ancient and modern times. It is based on the belief in God and in His Torah. The latter came to mean the sum total of Jewish religious teachings of all ages; and it is the adherence to a code of law which defines the religious and moral duties of the individual and the group. The theoretical foundation of Orthodoxy is the doctrine that the Jewish religion is a Divine revelation. This revelation is embodied in the sacred writings of Israel. According to this doctrine, together with the Torah given on Mount Sinai, an interpretation of it was simultaneously revealed to Moses. The Torah and its interpretations were handed down from Moses to Joshua, from Joshua to the Elders, and through a succession of authorities to the rabbis, who collected this Oral Law and expounded the Torah (after the fall of the Second Temple) in the Mishna and Gemara, which together constitute the Talmud. The faith of Orthodoxy is thus based upon the principle of revelation, which is the communication of God's will to man as embodied in the Torah and codified in the Talmud. Orthodoxy maintains that the Torah and Talmud contain Divine elements and are fountainheads of our knowledge of God's will. Both of these sources, then, constitute the basic foundations of Jewish religious teachings. Orthodoxy demands strict adherence to the Torah, or written Law, and to the Talmud, or Oral Law. Each commandment of the Torah, which contains absolute truth, and each word of the Oral Law which is just as true and sacred, is designed to guide the Jew in his daily living. Judaism, according to Orthodoxy, is a way of life to be practiced and applied in everyday activity. Any reform or compromise, in so far as the underlying principles of Judaism are concerned, is considered an offense.

Orthodox or traditional Judaism implies, therefore, the obligatory fulfillment of all religious observances, the fixed belief in the 613 religious duties as specified in the *Shulhan Arukh*[18] which consists of instructions of what, or what not, to do. Consequently, the center of Orthodox life is thus religious behavior, or right conduct. The Mitzvoth (commandments or good deeds) have become the pattern of all behavior, customs, ceremonies and ideals. It is the fulfillment of these instructions or Mitzvoth by the individual that makes one an Orthodox Jew. This religious code was one of the outstanding factors in the creation of the environment which was essential to Jewish survival. Such Mitzvoth as the observance of the Sabbath, the holidays, the fasts, the study of Torah, the Dietary Law, purity in the family, education of children, prayer within, or outside the synagogue, benevolent endeavors, etc.—are ways of life of traditional Judaism. For long centuries, all of Israel fulfilled these Mitzvoth with religious fervor. The Jews sought for many years to resist the influences prevalent in the non-Jewish world, especially in the Middle Ages, which led to idolatry and impurity on the one hand and to assimilation on the other. Hence, intermarriage was strictly prohibited and active participation in festive gatherings of the Gentiles was also looked upon with disfavor. Even compulsory migration and persecution could not bring much change in this Jewish Orthodox observance. Orthodox Judaism, then, whatever the country the Jews lived in, and whoever the teacher that expounded it, was a living Judaism.

With the beginnings of the Reform movement, which coincided with political emancipation in Western Europe and America and with the spread of the Haskalah ideas among the intelligentsia, Orthodoxy could no longer remain the sole authority for guiding and motivating Jewish cultural life. The changing conditions, as previously pointed out, tended to weaken the position of the Orthodox faith and abrogated the authority of the Talmud and the Shulkan Arukh throughout the greater part of Western Jewry. The collapse of the political, social and economic ghettos which were imposed upon the Jews for centuries and which forced them to live in segregated and isolated communities, accelerated the assault upon Orthodoxy and ushered in the period of its gradual decline. The assault was given momentum by two forces: one ideological and the other social. The ideological force derived its potency from the rationalism of the 18th century which refused to reconcile revelation with reason and the social force gathered strength from all political and economic changes which lead to the disintegration of the old ghetto community. Both forces threatened the foundation of Orthodox thought and practice.

However, notwithstanding the conditions that favored the continuous withdrawal of great numbers from Orthodox practices, and the growing tide of dissenters who joined the fold of both Reform and Conservative Judaism, the bulk of the people who manifested even a minimum conformity to religious teachings and practices remained formally within the confines of Orthodox Judaism. Two vital factors were responsible for this condition. One was the people's natural attachment to the past which sprang from an age-long reverence for the Torah, and the other was the cultural segregation of the vast majority of Jews in Eastern Europe who were not exposed to the revolutionary changes in modern Jewish life, nor to the modifying effects of the non-Jewish environment. Even today, with the Jewish center of population no longer in Eastern Europe, a large percentage of world Jewry is directly or indirectly identified with what is now designated as Orthodoxy. Of course, Orthodoxy in modern times has changed much of its external manifestations. The rituals and ceremonials are no longer observed with such enthusiasm as heretofore. Many so-called Orthodox Jews, because of economic conditions and outer pressure, have abandoned many of the Mitzvoth and their ways of life are no longer Orthodox. Many work on the Sabbath and many more do not engage in prayer every day of the week, nor do all the Jews labelled Orthodox observe the dietary law strictly. But, in spite of the laxity in observance, Orthodoxy still retains its hold upon large numbers of Jews. In many countries most of the congregations are either old fashioned or modernized Orthodox. Moreover, there are to be found even today, tens of thousands of Hassidim who continue to observe their unique rites and customs, who worship God in a state of religious ecstasy and follow the minutiae of the Code of Law. Orthodox Judaism, though no longer the dominating factor in the people's lives is nevertheless the predominant religious persuasion of all Jewry.

Reform Judaism

Reform Judaism came into being as a movement (in the 1820's) with two distinct objectives: to modernize religious life in conformity with the demands of the age, and to safeguard the Jews against complete abandonment of their religion. In order to meet the needs of contemporary life and to keep the young Jew within the fold, Judaism as a whole had to reorient itself in conformity with the ideas current in the non-Jewish environment.

The real question that troubled the intellectuals of the period in Germany was: "How can one be at the same time loyally German, traditionally Jewish, and fully modern? It was not easy for everyone to harmonize the findings of science with faith in a revealed religion."[19]

Moses Mendelsohn, the renowned German Jewish philosopher, called upon German Jews to be rational in faith, orthodox in practice and German in culture. But this was no solution to the problem. The educated and the rich fled from Judaism. Many took the route of baptism. The average layman was ignorant of the real meaning of Judaism. The time was therefore ripe for a new movement to declare its loyalty to Germany and to its culture and remain at the same time loyal to Judaism. Reform tried to find the answer. It represented the first effort to adjust traditional Judaism to modern conditions.

The most interesting innovation in connection with the development of a new approach to modern Jewish life was the rise of the movement of "the science of Judaism." It came into being at a time when Germany experienced a rejuvenation of historical studies. The Jewish intellectuals felt that the investigation of the Jewish past by the methods of historical criticism would lead to a better understanding of Judaism. In the course of a few decades, great works of Jewish literature were published in Berlin which laid the foundation for an understanding of the Jewish people and their religion against the background of world history. The new generation of Reform Rabbis were given an opportunity to learn to apply the methods of historical criticism to the Jewish past and to find precedent to innovation in classical Jewish text. These studies, led by the great scholars Zunz and Geiger led to the formulation of Reform doctrine.

The theoretical basis for Reform was its interpretation of Judaism not as the tri-unity of God, Israel and Torah but as a theological doctrine of Ethical Monotheism; as a religion of truth and justice. The belief in God is singled out as the most significant aspect of Judaism. The Jews, according to early Reform, are not a nation but a religious group whose mission is to spread the moral law based upon the idea of God. According to Reform, God was revealed at Sinai, but the Torah is a composite work of many authors who lived at different times in our Biblical history. Jews should therefore give primacy to the prophetic teachings and not to the legalistic elements of the Torah. God is the world's "moral Ruler." This Ethical Monotheism means that God's kingdom of truth and justice will be universally established. Israel, to whom God revealed Himself, is therefore duty-bound to foster the prophetic teachings among all peoples on earth, and be a model of righteousness unto all nations. Jewish dispersion is a permanent condition, for Jews are part and parcel of the states of which they are citizens.

At the first assembly of Reform Rabbis in 1844, it was stated that "our spiritual religion is no longer in harmony with the external conditions of Judaism. We can no longer keep it in its traditional form." Accordingly, Reform Judaism deemed it essential not to recognize the national character of Israel, and its Messianic aspiration to return to its old homeland. A revised liturgy was therefore composed which not only introduced the vernacular instead of Hebrew as the principal language of prayer, but failed to make any reference to the return to Zion, a personal Messiah, or Israel as a people in exile.

In America, the Reform ideology, which was formulated in 1885 at the Pittsburgh session of the Central Conference of the American Rabbis, stated: "We recognize in the Mosaic legislation a system of training the Jewish people for its mission during its national life in Palestine, and today we accept as binding only its moral laws, and maintain only such ceremonies as elevate and sanctify our lives, but reject all such as are not adapted to the views and habits of modern civilization. . . . We consider ourselves no longer a nation, but a religious community and, therefore, expect neither a return to Palestine nor a sacrificial worship under the Sons of Aaron, nor the restoration of any of the laws concerning the Jewish State."

Thus, for almost a century, the Reform congregations have opposed Orthodox practices and teachings. They also resisted, and frequently fought, Jewish nationalism in all its ramifications. It was therefore natural for the vast numbers of Jews who remained outside the Reform movement, particularly in eastern Europe, to look upon the Reform Jews as heretics. A definite division emerged in the last century, barring even ordinary social contact between the Orthodox and the Reform.

In the last three decades, however, a number of changes within Reform have taken place. Reform Judaism became concerned with the building of the National Home in Palestine and subsequently with the welfare of the Jewish State in Israel. A number of traditional customs and ceremonies have found their way back into the Reform Temple. More Hebrew is being introduced into the services. The Bar Mitzvah ceremony is observed on Sabbath morning. The religious school includes the study of Hebrew in its curriculum. In some temples the congregants don prayer shawls, in others, the Rabbi, or a layman, reads the portion of the week in Hebrew. Many Reform Rabbis are Zionists. Some of them send their children to Day Schools and observe Kashrut (Dietary Laws) in their homes.

Many factors have brought about the change in Reform theory and practice. Chief among them are the following:

1. The closer social and economic ties between the descendants of the Eastern European and Western European Jews in the new Jewish centers, such as the United States of America, Canada, England and France. The native Americans, for example, whether progeny of Reform or Orthodox Jews, have been conditioned in a similar environment and have met on common ground. Most of them want to belong to their people through identification with a modern religious institution.
2. The Zionist philosophy, which penetrated the ranks of Reform Jews, changed their "world outlook" and brought them nearer to those who strive for a creative survival in the Diaspora and who affirm the centrality of Israel in Jewish religio-cultural life.
3. Some of the young Reform Rabbis, who came from Orthodox and Zionist homes, and are attached to both traditional Judaism and Zionist ideology, have exerted great influence upon their followers.
4. The rise of modern anti-Semitism especially during the Second World War era which did not distinguish between a Reform or an Orthodox Jew.

Reform Judaism in America has become an integral part of Jewish life.[20]

Conservative Judaism

The origin of the Conservative school of thought is traced back to the founding by Zachariah Frankel, in 1850, of the Jewish Theological Seminary in Breslau, Germany. This school, organized six years after the promulgation by the Reform Rabbis of their controversial platform, advanced the theory that traditionalism must be retained, but that the principle of historical development of Judaism must also be accepted. Rabbi Frankel believed that traditional Judaism through the ages was not static and unchanged, but rather, dynamic, the product of historic development. This does not imply that old practices and ideals need be surrendered for the sake of convenience or for the "love of progress." It does imply, however, that scientific research be applied to the study of Judaism which is the product of a long evolutionary process. His views were an attempt to check the extreme tendencies of Reform and to affirm the age-long reverence for Rabbinic Judaism. Frankel's ideas, expounded in Germany by students and teachers of the Seminary, gained many adherents in America in the first decades of the present century. Conservative Judaism really emerged in the U.S.A., with the appointment of Dr. Solomon Schechter in 1902 as the President of the Jewish Theological Seminary of America, founded in 1886. Dr. Schechter, like Frankel, stressed the importance of the positive values in historic Judaism—piety, scholarship, traditional observance, the divine character of the Torah, the Hebrew language, Zionism—and advocated the retention of all those practices that are generally observed by the Jewish people. He conceived of "Judaism as a divine religion, not a mere complex of racial peculiarities and tribal customs . . ." and stated that "the Jewish religion is a Weltanschauung (world outlook) and worship of God by means of holiness both in thought and in action." Dr. Schechter, in using the term "Catholic Israel" (Klal Yisrael), advanced the conception of the Jews as a universal people and not as a religious denomination. He formulated the idea of religious nationalism which became a basic precept of Conservative Judaism. The followers and students of Schechter have developed a program based on the above principles which attracted many people who could not accept Reform but who were also critical of Orthodoxy. They have adapted traditionalism to modern conditions, endeavoring to uphold all that is traditional in content rather than in form. Conservative Judaism, according to one of its present-day leaders, Dr. Robert Gordis, " . . . is *the culture or civilization of the Jewish people.* It is not merely a religion in the sense of a few articles of belief and a handful of practices, as Reform teaches, or the longer list of beliefs and practices maintained by Orthodoxy. It is a complete culture or civilization, possessing all the varied attributes of language and literature, art, music, customs and law, institutions and history. We pray in Hebrew, not because God understands no other language, but because it is our language and therefore molds the content as well as the form of our thought. . . . The practices and customs of Jewish life, our history and our traditions, are precious to us because their contents reflect the noblest aspirations of which man has yet shown himself capable, and because their forms, growing out of our own group experience, are closest to us." [21] Some deviations in Conservative practice from the old traditional pattern are the following: The synagogue service has been shortened; the vernacular has been introduced for the recitation of certain prayers; men and women are seated together; Confirmation ceremonies; late Friday evening services; the Bat Mitzvah ceremonial and the change in the wording of the marriage contract. It is an attempt to make the ritual more meaningful to the modern Jew and an excellent means to make the synagogue a house of worship as well as an institution for socialization. As a matter of fact, some of these practices, save for mixed seating, have also been introduced in many of the modern Orthodox synagogues. By and large, the Conservative leaders seek to maintain the authority of Halakha (the whole legal part of Jewish tradition), and to limit changes to those that can be made within the traditional framework.

The Conservative movement fosters the study of Hebrew as a modern language, and affirms the significance of Israel in Jewish group life. American Conservative Judaism "promotes the centrality and preeminence of the synagogue in the life of the Jewish people" in this unbelieving age and endeavors to make of it the most potent cell of the Jewish social organism.

In the last two decades Conservative synagogues have also been founded in Canada, Latin America, Europe and India.

Reconstructionism

Reconstructionism, founded by Dr. Mordecai M. Kaplan in 1934, is a new movement within American Judaism. It rejects the formulations of Jewish doctrine of all three religious groups. In order to make Judaism a vital reality, inherently interesting to the modern Jew, Reconstructionism developed the theory that Judaism is a civilization in which religion is a central element. Other elements, however, such as the legal, ethnic, literary, aesthetic and linguistic values are also important parts of Judaism. According to Dr. Kaplan, if the American Jew is to survive as a Jew, he must be at home in two civilizations, the American and the Jewish, the latter deriving much of its creative power from constant interaction with the culture of the new State of Israel.

The following is a summary of Reconstructionist ideology:

"1. Judaism is nothing less than a civilization. It consists of the group life of a people identified with a particular land, having a continuous history, a religion in common, a language and a literature of its own, and folkways, mores, laws codes and arts of its own.

2. Judaism as a religious civilization has been evolving in response to the changes in the world about it. It has passed through three stages in its evolution and is now on the threshold of a fourth stage.

3. Jewish religion is that aspect of Judaism which enables the Jew to utilize every event, act and experience of Jewish life as a means of coming to know and worship God as the Power in the universe

that impels and helps him to achieve salvation, or to make the most of life.

4. As a civilization, Judaism is the product of more than a millenium of autonomous national life of our ancestors in Eretz Yisrael, and approximately two millenia of Diaspora life outside Eretz Yisrael. With the establishment of the State of Israel, the Jewish People is now in need of being reconstituted on new structural lines.

5. Outside Eretz Yisrael, Judaism can function in the life of the Jew only as a secondary civilization, the primary one being that of the country of which he is a citizen. Outside Ertez Yisrael Jews have to live in two civilizations.

6. As a secondary civilization outside Eretz Yisreal, Judaism can flourish only through the medium of local organic communities, ethnically functioning Jewish religion, and social and cultural intercourse with the Jews in Israel.

7. The revitalization of Jewish religion, both in Israel and in the Diaspora, is indispensable as a means of giving purpose and direction to the rebirth of the Jewish People.

8. For the Jewish religion to be revitalized, it has to evolve a conception of God and of the salvation of man, which, by virtue of its greater approximation to reality than any of the conceptions thus far advanced, is bound to be more effective than they have been in impelling man to think and act with a sense of moral responsibility.

9. Jews outside Eretz Yisrael, whose primary civilization is that of the country they live in, owe it to their Jewish religion to foster the *spiritual* significance of the memorable heroes, events, texts and places of their country's civilization. They can thus fulfill their own religious vocation as well as express their loyalty to their country in terms of universal spiritual values." [22]

Reconstruction differs from all other branches of Judaism in its conception of God, in its interpretation of the nature of Jewish law and in its rejection of the doctrine of Israel as "the Chosen People." In its emphasis on Judaism as a civilization, Reconstructionism embraces all aspects of Jewish experience both individual and collective.

The work of this new movement has been conducted through the Reconstructionist Foundation, organized in 1940. The movement's forum is *The Reconstructionist*, a bi-weekly periodical. Reconstructionism gained supporters among some of the rabbis, the Jewish intellectuals and groups of laymen. A number of synagogues have recently become affiliated with the Reconstructionist Fellowship, the chief purpose of which is to arrange seminars and conferences for the discussion of Reconstructionist ideology.

The American Jewish Community—Diversity in Unity

Despite the divergence of views with regard to the nature of Judaism and despite the tendency of each of the religious groupings to strengthen its structural base, American Jewry constitutes *one community*. It is important to understand that in addition to the different current religious schools of thought, there exist, within the community a variety of groupings which represent still other interpretations of Jewish life. To begin with, there are many religiously unaffiliated Jews to whom the congregation is not the only source of Jewish identification. There are the secularists, the humanists, the Yiddish-culturalists, and the secular-Zionists (some of whom sponsor Jewish school programs for their children). Then too, there are many affiliated Jews who find religio-cultural fulfillment in civic endeavors of all kinds. They are taking an active part in the work of agencies for aid to Jews overseas, in defense against anti-Semitism, in helping their brethren in the upbuilding of the State of Israel, in looking after the sick, the aged, and underprivileged children, and in general welfare activities on behalf of Jews and non-Jews alike. Thus, despite the multiplicity of loyalties to one or another expression of Jewish life, there is a growing recognition of the oneness of the Jewish community. The tolerance and acceptance of religious views is made possible, on the one hand, by the age-old tradition that "All Jews are responsible for one another," and on the other, by the influences of the American idea, which upholds the principle of religio-cultural pluralism.

Scope of Religious Life Today

There are approximately 29,000 synagogues in the world Jewish community. The United States, constituting the largest Jewish community, maintains 23,000 synagogues [23] and in Israel, there are about 3,850. [24] These two Jewish centers account for the largest number of synagogues, a total of about 27,000. In Soviet Russia, with about 2,500,000 Jews, there are only about 100 synagogues. (It is worth noting that in the pre-Revolution period, up to 1917, there were more synagogues in Russia than we find today in the U.S.A.). For all other countries where Jews maintain their houses of worship, (the number of Jews being only two and one-half million outside the United States, Russia and Israel) the estimate is 1,657. While synagogues exist everywhere in the Jewish world, and while the vast majority of the Jews, save for those in Soviet Russia, attend services on one occasion or another (mostly on Rosh Hashanah and Yom Kippur), the attitude of many Jews in our age towards religious worship and other observances and practices is, for the most part, indifferent. Judaism is not a religion of the synagogue alone; it is rather a system of thought and practice, chief among which is the study of Torah in the broadest sense of the term. The Jews, however, do not make Jewish study and observance an essential phase of their daily lives as did most of the Jews of Eastern Europe before the great tragedy of the Second World War.

The Jews, like their non-Jewish neighbors, do not adhere strictly to their religion, and do not depend upon their faith to pilot them through the tempests of our chaotic era. Consequently many patterns of religion—such as "keeping the Sabbath holy", daily attendance in the synagogue, grace after meals, wearing the "arba kanfot" and the observance of the numerous other traditions and customs—are in this modern age, a mode of life only for certain segments of the people rather than for the majority.

In some cases, socialism and communism are taking the place of traditional religion. We also find great numbers of ardent nationalists but lukewarm religionists. Even in Europe, where religious life has been strongest in the last two centuries, the younger generation before the War stripped itself of many major religious duties, and was, to a large degree, indifferent toward Jewish religious life in all its nuances. The Jews in Soviet Russia, through no fault of their own, have almost entirely abandoned religious life and broken the link of continuity with the past. It is, therefore, difficult to determine, or to estimate with any certainty, the influence of religion upon Jewish life today. It is also impossible to ascertain the number of religious Jews, since the number of members in congregations does not necessarily indicate the extent of religious influence upon their lives. It may be stated, however, on the basis of observation, that World Jewry constitutes five "types" with regard to their religious attiudes.

1. The Jews who live a traditional life, observe the "Shulhan Arukh" and bring up their children in the spirit of traditional Judaism. These are Jews whose spiritual center is the synagogue and whose literature is the Talmud and the sacred writings. This type is represented in Israel and in small numbers in western Europe, the Americas and North Africa. They constitute about *one-eighth* of the Jews in the world.

2. There are Jews who still abide by some of the traditional rules and regulations, but do not resist the influence of the non-Jewish environment. Some of them developed a new orientation with regard to the very nature of the Jewish religion. What was considered important in the "shtetl" (east European small town) surroundings is no longer important in the urban surroundings of today. Many people have worked out a sort of compromise between the old and the new for themselves. Some religious practices are being discarded while others are observed (such as the Seder, Dietary Laws, attendance in the synagogue on the holidays). New forms of non-Jewish cultural values are being introduced while certain phases of religious life, such as daily prayer and Sabbath observance, are being neglected. Their children are given some sort of Jewish schooling. Most of them are the contributors to Jewish philanthropies, the builders of new synagogues, community centers, etc. These Jews are to be found in all lands of dispersion and, in the opinion of this writer, constitute about *three-eighths* of World Jewry.

3. The Jews who keep aloof from traditional religious life. These are the Jews who have drifted away, almost entirely, from traditional Judaism and whose observance is limited to circumcision, ritual weddings and burials, or attending the synagogue twice a year on Rosh Hashana and Yom Kippur. The most striking feature is their conscious resistance to intermarriage and baptism, their determination to remain within the fold of Israel and their sincere interest in the welfare of their fellow Jews. These Jews are in Western Europe and the Americas. They include many of the so-called "higher-income level" and many of the professionals in the large cities throughout the world. They number *one-fourth* of World Jewry.

4. Jews by birth. These are the Jews who tend to be more non-Jewish than Jewish. Their identification with Jews and Judaism is expressed in the fact that they are non-affiliates of other faiths. They are to be found in Soviet Russia, in America and Western Europe. Their number is not as small as some of our sociologists maintain. The writer ventures to estimate them at about *one-eighth* of the total number of Jews.

5. Then there are the Jews who are a-religious but who sincerely love their people and its culture, and to whom anything that is Jewish cannot be alien. Many of them are intellectuals, professionals, liberals and Jewish Nationalists. They are to be found in every land, especially in Israel. They too, constitute about *one-eighth* of the total Jewish population.

Central organizations of all Jewish synagogue groups have begun to develop new measures to meet the disintegrating forces in Jewish religious life. Besides the Reconstructionist movement in America, which attempts to offer a solution to the problem of both religious and national recession, the leaders of the synagogues have revised the functions of their institutions. The synagogues today have become not only the centers of formal worship, but social institutions which offer an incentive to every Jew to find a place of interest. Certain synagogues are also restoring the idea of study to its former state. The social and recreational activities (dances, parties, theatre performances, concerts, sports, etc.) within the temple and the synagogue, the youth clubs and women's clubs are devices to make the synagogue a community center for Jews of all shades of opinion and in all walks of life. Since the synagogue has assumed the manifold functions of a communal center, the religiously-indifferent have begun to come back to the synagogue. Should this innovation spread, embrace all denominations, and become intensified, the authority of religion may be partially restored and its decline checked.

Religion in Israel and in the Diaspora

Religious life in Israel differs greatly from that in the Diaspora. While in many countries the civil courts have jurisdiction over marriage and divorce, in Israel the Rabbinic Court exercises exclusive rights to deal with all matters pertaining to marriage and divorce. In Diaspora there are three or more religious organizations guiding the affairs of their affiliated congregations; in Israel, thus far, the institutions of Orthodox Judaism exercise full control. There are no Reform or Conservative Synagogues in Israel.* While two or three nuclei of Reconstructionist, Conservative and Reform groups conduct services and programs of adult education, the majority of citizens know of only one type of synagogue —the Orthodox shul. In Israel the Ministry of Religious Affairs is vested with the authority to designate religious functionaries who take charge of such matters as Kashrut, admittance of converts, ritual bath (Mikvah), Halitzah (a ritual signifying the release of a brother's childless widow), ritual slaughter, matzot, etrogim, circumcision, etc.

Conservative Rabbis who come to Israel either for a visit or for permanent residence have no right to perform mar-

---

* Last year one Reform and one Conservative Synagogue were established.

riages or to participate in a Bet-Din (Rabbinic Court) in granting a divorce. Then, too, Israel is the only country in the world where local governments cooperate fully with official Rabbinic authorities in the observance of the Sabbath, Festivals, and Kashrut in all public institutions.

We may understand the role of orthodoxy in Israel's public and private domains in the context of Israel's history. It was, on the one hand, the liberal groups and laboring masses of Eastern and Central European Jewry who came to Palestine in the various *aliyoth*. They tended towards secularism and their attitude towards religion was one of indifference. On the other hand, political Zionism was strongly supported by elements of Orthodox Jewry which joined the movement in the Mizrahi wing of the World Zionist Organization. For the sake of the ultimate goal of Zionism—namely the re-establishment of the Jewish State, the majority party—the Zionist-Socialists and the Zionist-Orthodox, did not engage in philosophical struggles and, as if by gentlemen's agreement, accepted each other as partners in the battle for Zionist fulfilment. With the establishment of the State of Israel came the incorporation of the Orthodox Chief Rabbinate within the system of public authority.

It remains to be seen whether, and in what form, the non-orthodox versions of Jewish religion will develop in Israel. Conservatives, Reform Jews and Reconstructionists recognize that instead of simply importing to Israel the forms of observance and the supporting body of thought as they developed in Europe and America, they will have to await the emergence of typically Israeli forms of the Jewish religion.

Summary

Jewish religious life has undergone change. It became "westernized" in the sense that many of the old customs and rituals have survived more in form than in spirit. Interaction with non-Jews influenced Jewish thought as well as Jewish practices. Most Jews of the free world live in accordance with the mores of their respective countries. The role of the religious institution is therefore to cultivate not only religious convictions, but primarily to provide social facilities for group life. Religious life in the modern setting is once again a very important factor in Jewish survival.

TOPICS FOR DISCUSSION

1. "Judaism is more than a religion."
   (a) What does "more" mean in this sentence?
   (b) Give your own definition of Judaism and explain it to others.

2. How does the theory of evolution challenge the Bible? How does it explain religion itself?

3. Conversion is a form of desertion of the Jewish people. Can you think of other forms? Is it possible to desert the Jewish people without embracing another religion?

4. Behind the differences of Orthodoxy, Conservatism, Reform and Reconstructionism—can you detect certain basic agreements?

5. Do you see merit in the popular understanding that Orthodoxy is maximal or optimal Jewishness, that Reform is minimal or "easy" Jewishness, that Conservatism is a convenient compromise between the two?

6. Why is Reconstructionism a form of Conservatism?

7. What do you think of the prediction that the four forms of religious Judaism are losing their characteristics and are gradually merging in a new "American Judaism"?

8. What strengths do you find in the "chosen people" idea? What weaknesses?

9. What does "orchestrationism" mean in Jewish life?

10. How do you understand "secularism"?

NOTES TO CHAPTER 6

1. *"Torah"* has a comprehensive meaning: It is the Bible (written law); Talmud (oral law) and also all the authoritative literature that expounds the Law.
2. In the Book of Esther we read—dat vadin (1:13) meaning law and judgment.
3. Epstein, Isidore: "Judaism," Penguin Books, London, 1959, p. 23.
4. Zohar, LV, 73 a.
5. Baron, Salo W.: "A Social and Religious History of the Jews," Vol. I, Jewish Publication Society, Philadelphia, 1952, p. 4.
6. "Transcendent" means proceeding beyond what is presented in experience.
7. From Milton Steinberg's "Basic Judaism," p. 20.
8. Described in human terms or with human attributes.
9. Finkelstein, Louis (ed.): "The Jews, Their History, Culture and Religion," Harper Brothers, New York, 1949, Vol. II, p. 1345.
10. Belkin, Samuel: "Man and His Creator," New York, 1956, p. 17.
11. Finkelstein, Louis: "The Beliefs and Practices of Judaism," p. 25.
12. Steinberg, Milton: "Basic Judaism," p. 91.
13. Baeck, Leo: "Judaism and Christianity," Philadelphia, The Jewish Publication Society of America, 1958, p. 147.
14. John 14:6.
15. Silver, Abba Hillel: "Where Judaism Differed," New York, 1957, p. 167.
16. These are the seven prohibition laws: murder, adultery, incest, robbery, eating of the flesh of living animals, idolatry and blasphemy.
17. Sanhedrin was the High Court of the Jewish State, consisting of 71 members, presided over by the Patriarch or Prince. Its origin is traced to the great assembly

of the early period of the Second Commonwealth. The Sanhedrin summoned by Napoleon in 1807 was to question Jewish leaders, rabbis and laymen on the moral character of the Mosaic code.

18. *"Shulhan Arukh"* is the code of Jewish law and life compiled by Joseph Caro in the 16th century.

19. Bamberger, Bernard: "The Story of Judaism," New York, 1956, Union of American Hebrew Congregations, p. 261.

20. At the annual conference of the American Reform Rabbis held in Chicago in 1935, resolutions were adopted calling "for intensified Jewish effort in behalf of our activities there," (meaning Palestine); and urging the congregations, religious schools and all other communal institutions to give their moral and material support to the Keren Kayemeth and Keren Hayesod.

21. Schechter, Solomon: "Studies in Judaism," Jewish Publication Society, Philadelphia, 1938, p. 180.

22. *The Reconstructionist,* June 15, 1962, pp. 23-24.

23. Yearbook of American Churches, New York, 1962, p. 248. (This number includes all places of worship for the High Holydays which are not necessarily permanent synagogues).

24. Facts About Israel, Ministry for Foreign Affairs, Jerusalem, 1961, p. 52.

7

The Jew and His Culture

Introductory Statement

The great European tragedy not only weakened considerably the numerical strength of our people but laid dry the great reservoir of Jewish learning and culture. The Jewish world is culturally no longer the same after the liquidation of the six million Jews. Israel's great strides in the realm of education and culture cannot as yet compensate for the great privation that Jews have sustained in the destruction of the great European centers of learning. And now when we record the different aspects of Jewish cultural life of contemporary Jewry, we do so with a deep feeling of pain for a *brave old world* that is no longer in existence, and with a sense of reverence and admiration for those millions of Jews who lived Jewish cultural life so intensely.

Languages Spoken by Jews

The Historical Evolution of Non-Hebraic Jewish Languages

While the original language of the Israelites was Hebrew, there were certain periods during which it gave way to foreign tongues, even prior to the loss of Palestinian independence. The first non-Hebraic language to be introduced into the Jewish state was Aramaic. As early as the Ezra period (450 B.C.E) the Jews were speaking Aramaic, not only in communities outside of Palestine, but also within the land itself. Ezra and his colleagues had to interpret the Torah to their audiences in the vernacular, namely, Aramaic. Portions in the Bible, such as Daniel and parts of Ezra, written in Aramaic, indicate the extent of its influence upon the people. Although Palestinian Jewry had once again turned to the Hebrew—particularly during the Hasmonean rule—the Aramaic had taken root so deeply that, after its decline as a spoken language, it was still used by Jewish scholars as a literary medium until the 10th century. In it was written the Gemara, the great body of traditional lore which grew up as a commentary and supplement of the Mishnah; also the Targum (translation) of the Pentateuch, the oldest Aramaic book current among the Jews. A great many rabbinic prayers are still recited in Aramaic, such as the Kaddish, Yekum Purkan, Brikh Shmey, and the like.

There were other languages, besides Aramaic, which influenced cultural patterns and served as media of expression. These were:

1. Greek, which was spoken by Jews of Alexandria and by the wealthy class in Palestine during the period of Hellenistic expansion, (167-322 B.C.E.) and used in the first translation of the Bible (Septuagint). With the destruction of Hellenistic culture in the Near East, however, this language disappeared from Jewish life.
2. Persian, which was adopted by the Jews of Persia in the 4th century before the common era, developed into a Jewish language and is still spoken in its oldest form by Persian and Bocharian Jews.
3. Arabic, which, by the end of the 10th century, was not only spoken by most of the Jews in the world, but also was used in writing the monumental works of the Jewish golden period in philosophy, poetry, and theology. The Arabic language, like Greek and Persian, did not become Judaized, as manifested by the fact that, in religious worship and in the sacred writings, Arabic, Persian and Greek were not, and are not, being used. Most of the Jewish writings in Arabic had to be translated into Hebrew in order to retain their value as Jewish works and to save them from oblivion.

At the end of the 14th century Yiddish evolved and at the beginning of the 16th century Ladino developed as a language spoken by Jews.

The expulsion from Spain and the migration from the German-speaking lands into Poland and Russia brought about the emergence of these two new Jewish languages. The exiles from Spain brought Ladino to the lands of refuge. This developed as a typical Jewish language, being an admixture of Hebrew, Spanish and Arabian-Turkish elements. Ladino has been retained as a Jewish tongue by many of the Sephardim to this day.

The emigrants from Germany used Judaeo-German, which evolved into a new Jewish language—Yiddish—consisting of old German intermingled with Hebrew and linguistic elements from the Slavic tongues. Yiddish was used until World War II by almost ten million people; and, similarly, Ladino has been preserved and used until recent years by more than a million Sephardic Jews.

Hebrew—The Historic Language

While Hebrew, as noted before, was the spoken language of all the Jews for a short historical period—during the first commonwealth and at certain intervals in the days of the second commonwealth—it has always been associated with the people as their national tongue. Throughout the ages, Hebrew was in vogue in one form or another. After it ceased to be the spoken language, it remained the "holy" tongue of the people's communion with God and the vehicle of most of their literary production. Even when the Jewish genius was productive in Aramaic and Arabic, Hebrew served as a medium of expression of Jewish thought and national cultural life. Side by side with Aramaic were literary creations in Hebrew. The Talmud is a synthesized work of both languages. In certain places the linguistic demarcation between the two disappears. The Midrashic[1] element of the Talmud, for instance, is predominantly Hebraic. During the dominance of Arabic, most of the poems, hymns and piyyutim (poetic additions to liturgy) were written in Hebrew. Almost all of the books which were composed in Arabic for general consumption were translated into Hebrew. In short, the continuity of the language was unbroken through the centuries. Hebrew kept on living. In every country of dispersion Hebrew was perpetuated, if not as a spoken tongue, then, what was equally important, as the language of spiritual expression. At almost all times, it was the language of communion with God. Most of the prayers, as well as the reading of the Pentateuch and the Haftarah (portion from the Prophets), were, and are, recited in Hebrew. Until recently, Hebrew was used in Eastern Europe in certain commercial transactions and as the language for Jewish legal documents. The fact of the matter is that "Hebrew never died: Those instrumental in the modern revival of Hebrew did not have to create a new language. They merely had to refurbish and put to modern use some of the words, expressions and idioms that have lived for centuries in literary forms, as well as in the mental patterns of the Jewish people."[2]

The people referred to Hebrew as the "L'shon Kodesh," (Holy Tongue) not only because it was the language of the Bible, the Mishnah and other sacred books, but also because it represented the national culture, because, in it there came into being a vast and varied literature in prose and poetry, covering 3,000 years, and because it served, next to religion, as the common denominator in uniting all the dispersed, and in unifying all Israel.

Broadly speaking, there have been five periods in the development of Hebrew: 1. the Biblical period; 2. the Talmudic period; 3. the Spanish period; 4. the Haskalah period, and 5. the Hebrew revival period of our day. During all the stages of its existence, Hebrew developed in word-form, syntax and vocabulary. Today it is a rich language, the living medium of expression for two million Jews in Israel and for tens of thousands more in the Diaspora. In Israel, particularly, Hebrew "no longer has the remoteness of a holy language. It has been forced from the narrow confines of exalted utterance, from the Sabbath limits of choice usage, from the atmosphere of rigid solemnity, from the resounding notes of a 'trumpet of brass'. No longer is it a cathedral of unearthly height, but a homelike cottage for daily use." [3] It is now the language of a revived modern literature, which has risen to artistic heights; it is a living, prospering language.

Yiddish—The Language of the Jewish Masses in Yester Year

The Jew's ability to transmute a non-Hebraic language to his own use and to Judaize it, is demonstrated by the evolution and development of Yiddish (written in the Hebrew script). Yiddish (derived from the German "Juedisch", meaning Jewish) originated in the 14th century in Southern Germany as a dialect spoken by Jews in all the German provinces and was carried to Eastern Europe by the early settlers coming from these regions. In Poland, Galicia, Lithuania and Russia, the Judaeo-German dialect made constant progress by employing Hebrew characters in print and script, and by the inclusion of additional Hebraic elements, thus becoming, in the 15th century, a new Jewish language.

In the 16th century, Yiddish became the spoken language of most Jews of Eastern Europe. Printed books appeared in Yiddish, generally of a religious nature, such as Teitch-Chumosh, Ivri-Teitch or Tchinoth, which were used by Jewish women who did not have the advantage of a Hebraic education. A vast oral lore of folk ballads, folk songs, and tales, as well as occasional secular books were created in Yiddish in the 17th and 18th centuries; and this literary treasure was augmented by the modern Yiddish literature of the last 80 years.

With the beginning of emigration from Eastern Europe at the end of the 19th century, Yiddish was carried to the remote corners of the globe. Thus by the end of the century there were Yiddish-speaking Jews in all the Americas, Western Europe, Asia, South Africa, and Australia.

Prior to the first World War, there were almost ten million Jews to whom Yiddish was their mother tongue. At this period, Yiddish literature, press and drama, reached their zenith, when hundreds of Yiddish books, magazines and newspapers appeared, and when the language attained the high plane of a modern tongue, becoming a medium for literary expression of great Jewish talents.

The post World War I period, having brought temporary emancipation to the Jews of Eastern Europe, marked a further advance in the growth and development of Yiddish. In many Eastern European countries as well as in other lands (United States, Canada, Argentina, etc.) Yiddish schools were established; and in regions of Soviet Russia populated by Jews, Yiddish was employed as one of the official languages until the mid-forties. In the U.S.A. Yiddish was spoken and used in daily life by masses of immigrant Jews. A rich literature was created on the American soil. There were local Yiddish dailies in all large Jewish communities. At one time, there were more than twelve Yiddish theatrical groups. Whenever the Jewish population was to be mobilized for political action, Yiddish was used as the medium.

The last three decades, however, witnessed a steady decline in the use of Yiddish. In the U.S. there were still ten Yiddish dailies in 1940. Today there are only two; in the late 1930's there were 12 weeklies; today there are only three or four. The spread of secular education and the contact of young Jews with the non-Jewish elements has increased the use of the vernacular at the expense of Yiddish. With the annihilation of East European Jewry, the stronghold of Yiddish for several centuries, and the gradual acculturation of the masses of Jews in the Americas[4] and other democracies, Yiddish as a spoken language has gradually declined.

It is estimated that there are about two and a half million Jews who speak Yiddish, although many more understand the language. Some 470,000 Jews in Russia gave Yiddish as their mother tongue in 1959 census. About half a million foreign-born Jews in the U.S. gave Yiddish as their native tongue, according to the last Federal census, taken in 1960.[5] In Canada, according to the Dominion Bureau of Statistics the number who indicated Yiddish as their mother tongue was 32.4% in 1961 as against 95.4% in 1931.[6] In total numbers, 82,448 Canadian Jews indicated Yiddish as their mother tongue. Approximately 350,000 speakers of Yiddish are to be found in Rumania, Hungary and Poland, and another million remain in other parts of the world. The younger generation, however, does not use the language. Yiddish-speaking Jews almost everywhere are mostly of the middle age and older generations.

The decline of Yiddish makes its future problematical, and several organizations are working energetically to guard its position and to check its decline. The forces of linguistic assimilation prevailing in the lands of dispersion are, however, considerably stronger, and in Israel, Hebrew has become so well entrenched that no movement has any chance of invading its position.

Ladino—The Language of the Sephardi Jews

Ladino, like Yiddish, came into being at the end of the 15th century. The Jews who were expelled from Spain carried with them the Castilian dialect, which had been radically modified by the introduction of Hebrew words and Hebrew suffixes and prefixes. The Hispano-Jewish exiles, or, as they became known, the Sephardim, spread through Southern Europe, North Africa, Palestine, the Levant and Holland. In all of these countries, they retained their Spanish dialect, which, in addition to Hebrew words, became greatly augmented by the vernacular of each country of their residence.

By the end of the 16th century, this Judaeo-Spanish, known as Ladino became another Jewish language and was spoken by all the Sephardim.

Ladino, as Yiddish, was written in the Hebrew script. Both the square form and the rabbinic characters were used in print, but only the "Ktav Rashi" was applied in writing.

The first Ladino translation of the Bible appeared in 1547, making for a closer amalgamation of Hebrew and Ladino.

In the 17th century many books relating to religious life and rituals were published as well as translations from Hebrew liturgical poetry and rabbinic literature. Sephardi rabbis and teachers in Talmudic academies addressed their audiences in Ladino. Hebrew was used as the original text followed by interpretation and translation in Ladino.

At the end of the 18th century there developed a Ladino literature, consisting of plays, folk-songs, tales and legends, biblical drama, Musar books, translations from Midrash and various other religious reading matter. The early Ladino periodicals also made their appearances in this period.

The 19th century witnessed an even greater development. The immigrants to America and Western Europe carried the language into new lands, and the ever expanding Ladino press contributed to its spread and development.

Thus, this second Jewish language became not only the spoken tongue of all Sephardim, scattered in many lands, but also a medium of literary expression.

Prior to the First World War, more than a million people spoke Ladino. Today this Judaeo-Spanish language is undergoing a steady decline. As in the case of Yiddish, the use of Ladino in daily life, particularly by the younger generation, has diminished. In Israel, of course, Hebrew is now employed not only by the young, but by many of the older people as well, and in the English-speaking lands, Ladino is not used by the native Sephardim.

Thus the number of Sephardim speaking Ladino today is estimated to be only about 200,000. There are still a number of periodicals published in Ladino in the Near East and America; their circulation, however, has dropped considerably in recent years. The only newspaper published in Ladino in Istanbul ceased publication in February, 1963, after it was first established 70 years ago.

NON-JEWISH LANGUAGES

Hardly another people on earth have spoken as many languages as the Jews: Hebrew, Aramaic, Greek, Persian, Arabic, Yiddish and Ladino. Today large groups employ the vernacular in their daily lives; non-Jewish languages have replaced the Jewish ones.

The effects of these linguistic changes resulted, on the one hand, in the spread of secular culture among all Jews. On the other hand, the sharply curtailed use of Jewish languages brought with it the gradual estrangement from Jewish cultural values, both religious and secular, and strengthened the disintegrating forces of assimilation. However, the recent tendency to introduce Judaic cultural values in the vernacular among the linguistically assimilated elements and to spread Jewish consciousness among alienated groups may prove to be yet another barrier to cultural assimilation.

The numerous publications in the vernacular, the cultural programs conducted in centers, synagogues, fraternal and labor organizations, all serve to indicate that the decline in Judaic languages may not necessarily endanger Jewish cultural survival. Then, too, the impact of modern Israel and the revival of Hebrew learning in many sections of the Diaspora tend to offset all fears of a Jewish cultural catastrophe owing to the decline of Yiddish and Ladino. On the basis of conclusions drawn from the history of Jewish languages, one may be inclined to believe that, as long as Jews continue to live in large numbers in any given locality, Jewish cultural activities, in any linguistic form, will save the Jew from complete cultural assimilation.

Jewish Literature

As in the case of speech, the linguistic adjustability of the Jew is also demonstrated in literature. All the widely-used languages of mankind were employed by the Jews in their literary work. Their literature is, therefore, unique in the annals of the history of world letters. "Its stage is the whole world and its subject matter the variegated experiences of the most dramatic career known to man, the career of the wandering Jew."[7]

Fundamentally, as already mentioned, Hebrew was the language of cultural and national continuity in which the basic literature was written (Bible, Mishna, Zohar, philosophy, poetry, liturgy, etc.). In the modern period, in addition to Hebrew, there evolved a Jewish literature in Yiddish and in the modern European languages. In the ensuing chapter, therefore, modern Jewish literature will be classified into three distinct categories: a. Hebrew literature; b. Yiddish literature; and c. Jewish literature in non-Jewish languages.

Modern Hebrew Literature

Historical Background

Even before Hebrew returned to its country of origin, the Land of Israel, where it became an organic phase of national rebirth and the only base for its cultural structure, modern Hebrew literature was already making considerable progress in the lands of the dispersion in the last decades of the 18th and throughout the 19th century.

At the end of the 18th century, the intelligentsia of the period revolted against what the Maskilim called the "rigorism" and conservatism which prevailed in Jewish life. They strove to adjust Judaism to modern conditions by introducing European cultural values. During that time, referred to as the Haskalah (enligtenment) period, the foundations of modern Hebrew literature were laid. Although the fathers of the Haskalah, Moses Mendelsohn (1729-1786), and his disciples, employed Hebrew as a means to an end, i.e., using Hebrew as a vehicle of communication with the tens of thousands of Talmudic students who were urged to have contact with European culture, the cause of Hebrew language and literature was thus indirectly promoted. The Hebrew periodicals, *Hameasef,* founded in Germany in 1785, and *Bikurei-Haitim,* published in Galicia in 1821, became a training ground for writers, poets and essayists, who implanted a love and admiration for Hebrew letters. When the German Haskalah group became absorbed in assimilation, abandoning entirely their Hebrew literary endeavors, the Eastern group, interested in the enrichment of Judaism by knowledge of universal culture, took over the literary work in the Hebrew language. These men fought assimilation and championed the idea of Haskalah within a Hebrew framework. They struggled against rabbinic dogmatism and religious superstition and injected into their writings the elements of love of Israel and its cultural heritage.

In time the literature of the Haskalah period, which was to serve the cause of enlightenment, became an end in itself. Hebrew became a true medium of literary expression.

The Development of Modern Hebrew Letters

The development of modern Hebrew letters is divided by historians into three periods: 1. The Russian Haskalah period; 2. the nationalistic period of Hibat Zion; and 3. the period of revival.

In the '40's and '50's of the last century, the Russian Haskalah which attempted to arouse within the people a love for nature, productive vocations and secular knowledge, gave rise to the romantic school in Hebrew literature. This school has marked the beginning of new literary values in the Hebrew language. While it is true that the artistic significance of the literary creativeness of the age was not great, it presented, nonetheless, an atmosphere entirely different from that of the Haskalah literature of Germany and Galicia. The lyricists of the period, A.D. Lebenson (1794-1878) and his son Mikhal (1828-1852), (the former sang songs of sun and light and fought darkness and night; the latter created poems of the biblical motif and idyl) received wide acclaim among the readers. The novelist A. Mapu (1808-1867), creator of original Hebrew prose, whose historical novel, *Ahavat Zion,* portrayed the life of Judean shepherds and farmers, and deeply stirred the hearts of the readers. It is still considered the finest and most important product of Haskalah fiction and has served as an inspiration to many a talented writer.

Kalman Shulman's (1819-1899) *History of the World* (10 vols.), *Geography* (5 vols.), bibliographical and literary essays on the Jewish writers of the Middle Ages, that were distributed in millions of copies, introduced new knowledge to the Jewish masses. His fiction, written in biblical idiom, though lacking in originality, appealed to the hearts of the multitudes. These men have made a significant contribution to the spread of Hebrew literature.

In the '60's and '70's, Hebrew literature assumed a more European character and began to display greater originality. The realistic novels of Peretz Smolenskin commanded the admiration of all readers. Smolenskin is referred to as the "Hebrew Dickens." In his novel *"Ha-to'eh Be-Darke Ha-Hayim"* (A Wanderer Astray in the Path of Life), Smolenskin denounced the depravity of the ghetto and proclaimed the revival of national dignity. In his other novel *"Am Olam"* (The Eternal People), he demonstrated the incompatibility between true nationalism and the ideal of the universal brotherhood of man. The Hebrew periodicals, which branched out in all large Jewish centers, afforded unstinted opportunity for other literary talents of the age, besides Smolenskin, to produce their works. Judah L. Gordon became known as the "Haskalah poet." In his epic poems he waged a war against superstition, medievalism and espoused the cause of Jewish womanhood. Gordon is regarded as the true forerunner of the genius of modern Hebrew literature, Bialik. S. J. Abramovitz, also known as Mendele Mocher Sepharim, appeared on the literary scene as the outstanding literary artist in narrative style. His works attest to a keen psychological insight into the lives and works of the "shtetl" characters that he depicted, the ruthless and the defenseless, peddlers and middlemen. M. Lilenblum, the publicist, skillfully discussed the tragedy of Jewish homelessness and the hopelessness of life in the Galut. These men paved the way to a more diversified and more comprehensive literature.

The creative genius of the modern Jew found its redemption in the '80's, with the spread of the idea of nationalism. It was a transition period in Jewish life generally, and particularly so in the field of Jewish letters. Anti-Semitism reigned in Eastern Europe. Assimilation and Judaic degeneration reached a high peak in Western Europe. There was need for something new to kindle a genuine desire, in the hearts of the people, for cultural regeneration and, above all, for the renewal of national life in Palestine. Gifted writers made their appearance, expressing in poetry and prose the Jewish passion for liberation. These men of letters widened the scope of Jewish literary activity to include all aspects of modern literature. Nahum Sokolow stands out as a gifted essayist, journalistic and critic, who advocated the theory of Zionism by pointing to the illusory optimism of solving the Jewish problem through emancipation. Ahad Haam, the great philosopher, stylist and father of spiritual Zionism, who argued that the problem of Judaism, like the problem of Jews, requires an environment all its own, free from foreign influences and domination. Chaim Nachman Bialik, the genius of modern Hebrew poetry, who bewailed the plight of his people under the yoke of Tzardom, bemoaned the fate of Jewish youth living a cruel, bitter and helpless life in the ghetto environment, and sang with a burning passion the song of Jewish liberation. These men of letters as well as other poets, novelists and essayists made Hebrew literature compatible to that of the modern civilized peoples.

The last decade of the 19th century and the first two of the present—known as the revival period—witnessed a further development. Poetry was enriched by a number of great talents in addition to Bialik, outstanding among whom were: Saul Tchernichovsky; Jacob Cohen; Z. Shneur; J. Fichman; and D. Shimonovitz.

Saul Tchernichovsky "is a pantheist",—writes Harry Fain, the English translator of some of Tchernichovsky's poetry, "seeing magical harmony reigning over all. There are no isolated and contending forces in the universe, one unity includes them all. He is an asthete, and does not concern himself with the problems and questions of the purpose of life and the world. Love is his goddess, in his love there is no sadness or grief, no philosophizing or theorizing, but intoxication of life and virile passion. He has introduced a variety of graceful and tuneful rhythms hitherto unknown in Hebrew poetry."[8] But this poet of love and beauty cannot accept his people's misery and calls upon them to revolt. In the Halutz effort in Israel and in his attempt to rebuild his country and his people, the poet finds a partial realization of his dreams.

Jacob Cohen elevates to sainthood the victims of the pogroms and admires their idealism in sanctifying the name of God. A spirit of mysticism pervades his songs. "His pantheistic union with the world of nature makes him love the sun, the sky, the woods and the mountains. . . . He sings the song of enchanting beauty and divine harmony in the world."[9]

Zalmen Shneur typifies the poet of man. "Deep as his interest in nature is, he cannot take refuge in her recesses from the hounding pursuit of man. . . . And because he was always haunted by man, he often suspected man, yet always reverted to man. It was he, apprehensive of man's wiles, who even before the World War foretold the return of the Middle Ages in his poem, 'The Middle Ages are Approaching,' a poem which will remain for all time an unequalled example of sheer prophecy in a poet of the 20th century." [10]

In the poetry of Jacob Fichman expression is given to the contemplative mood of the individual who stands out alone, for he is a world all to himself.

David Shiminovitz (Shimoni) is best known for his Israel idyls in which he glorifies the courage and the sincerity of the Second Aliyah pioneers.

Then there are the story writers, Gnessin and Schoffman, who portray "not merely individuals, but entire generations and they seem always to emphasize that the distress of one person is an inevitable consequence of the anomalous life of society." [11] A. Z. Rabinowitz, who sees in the man his innate goodness and tells of characters who quietly sacrifice their lives for others, M. Y. Berdichevsky, who describes the struggles and passions of the ordinary folk and whose style is a mixture of realism and fable, and I. Ch. Brenner who became part of Israeli folklore. "His was an individualism of moral awareness, of responsibility for ones deeds, thoughts and relationships . . ." [12] Finally Judah Steinberg who tells the Hassidic tale, S. Ben Zion who describes the poverty and despair of the East European town, and D. Frishman whose literary criticism, and short stories convey a mood which is strong and colorful and significantly modern.

This period produced many scholarly works. Hebrew scientific studies developed to a high degree of modern research. Some of the scholarly writers were Dr. J. Klauzner, author of *"Jesus of Nazareth"* and *"The History of Hebrew Literature"*; Dr. J. Klatzkin, the biographer of Spinoza, author of a dictionary of philosophy and philosopher who negated Jewish life in the Diaspora; Dr. S. Horodetzky and Hillel Zeitlin the historian and philosophic essayist of the Hassidic movement; and A. D. Gordon the advocate of close association with nature as the only basis for a just and healthy society. This period also marked the development of Hebrew literature in the U.S.A. and the rise of American-trained young Hebrew writers.

Thus we see that prior to World War II Hebrew literature had already become of age.

HEBREW LITERATURE TODAY

The development of the Jewish center in Palestine and the subsequent rise of the State of Israel resulted in the emergence of a modern Jew whose complete cultural needs must be satisfied through the medium of the Hebrew language. It necessitated a newly specialized and scientific literature for school and home, stores and offices, hospitals and social centers; and created a demand for greater variety in the field of belles-lettres. A great deal of pioneering produced literary works to meet the needs of the community. The achievements of the pioneers of Hebrew literature in Palestine—Israel constituted a phenomenon unparalleled in Jewish history. Hebrew literature flourished alongside the young national life in Israel and unfolded in all directions. It also stimulated similar achievement in the Diaspora between the two World Wars.

Contemporary productions in Hebrew literature may be classified as follows:

Hokhmat Yisrael or the Science of Judaism

For eighty years until the rise of Israel, a great many works in the field of the science of Judaism were written in the language of the countries where Jewish scholars lived. A great deal of it was in German and English. In recent years, however, scholars have turned to Hebrew for research in Judaica. Studies in Bible, Talmud, Kaballah, Messianism, great Jewish personalities, Hasidism, old customs, Jewish philosophy, medieval literature, archeology and sociology have been published in Hebrew. Many of these works have been translated into European languages. This field is continuously being tilled by many a talented scholar. The list of works is too large to be recorded in this brief survey. Suffice it to point out that more than one hundred scholars have produced, in the course of two decades, an estimated six hundred important works, including concordances of Bible and Mishnah, the Talmudic Encyclopedia, histories of Jewish religious thought, voluminous works in history, linguistics, dictionaries, archeology and the like.

Literary Criticism

The field of analysis and evaluation of Hebrew literature has become a highly specialized branch of creative effort. Histories of

Jewish literature, and criticisms of contemporary writers, present a picture of a living, growing literature, highly diversified and in need of proper critical evaluation have been written, and more of it is being published currently.

Poetry

Contemporary poetry is perhaps the most significant accomplishment of Hebrew literature. Whether the Hebrew language lends itself to poetic expression, or whether poetry generally possesses qualities which speak to the soul of the Jew, bestowing upon him poetic talents, the fact remains that modern Hebrew poetry has surpassed all expectations. Besides the great poets Bialik, Tchernichovsky, Shneur, Shimonovitz, Fichman, Kahan, a new generation of Hebrew poets has appeared who contribute to the enhancement of this remarkable cultural creativity. Some of the outstanding poets of the generation following that of the Bailik group are: Yaacov Steinberg, known as the "Ecclesiastes of modern Hebrew literature" whose poems ask the old question "What is life?" and "Why are we here?"; Nathan Alterman, the popular poet of whom it was said, "If one can imagine a single writer who is capable of combining some of the functions of say, a Saggitarious (the political satirist of the New Statesman and Nation), an Ogden Nash and song writing Noel Coward on the one hand—and a Jewish Longfellow and W. B. Yeats on the other—some notion may be grasped of the mercurial significances of Alterman for the Hebrew reading public in Israel"; [13] Sh. Shalom in whose poetry "man tries to unravel the mystery of his own being and to trace the ties that bind him to other individuals . . . and to mankind of the past and future;" [14] Abraham Shlonsky who sings the song of the redeemed soil of Israel and who considers the act of redemption an act of consecrated worship; Yitzhak Lamdan whose poem "*Massada*" is considered as one of the most challenging works of modern Hebrew poetry, "Against a background of pogromized Russian Jewish communities after the First World War, there juts out in all its sublimity and melancholy loneliness the modern '*Massada*,' [15] last citadel of Jewry. Its defenders are refugees of horror forging faith out of frustration." [16]; Yehudah Karni, one of the most colorful poets of the City of Jerusalem, who finds the element of majesty in the landscapes that are desolate and in ruin; U. Z. Greenberg, whose outcry of grief over the Nazi slaughter turned into a curse upon the head of the civilized world for its complacency and who has finally found in the new Jerusalem the symbol of Jewish greatness.

And the other poets, Broides and Meltzer, Temkin, Meitus and Shalev, diverse in character but all transforming into song and ballad the exploits of the builders and defenders of the new State. The group of poetesses: Bat Miriam, Rachel, Pinkerfeld and Lea Goldberg, each leaving a distinctive mark on Hebrew poetry.

And finally the American group of Hebrew poets, all of whom were influenced by the American environment. E. Lisitsky, who draws from the rich folklore of the American Indians and Negroes. Israel Efros, who writes on a variety of themes, from the struggle of the Indians and the frontier life of the Gold Rush, to the Jewish tragedy in World War II and the new generation in the new Israel. Hillel Bavli, whose poetry is permeated with a great love for his old home in Lithuania and whose verses express a great yearning for Israel, on the one hand, and an exaltation of the grandeur of the New World on the other; Sh. Halkin, whose poetry "embodies the constant struggle between conscience and desire and which reveals the gap between wish and fulfillment."[17] E. Silberschlag, the contemplative, intellectual poet; A. Regelson— the poet-philosopher; A. S. Schwartz; Simon Ginzburg and N. Silkner; H. Friedland; A. Halevi; M. Feinstein; G. Preil; T. Carmi; and A. Zeitlin. All have had an infinite appeal to the Hebrew reading public the world over.

Fiction

Colorful and many-sided is contemporary Hebrew fiction. Next to poetry, it occupies a most prominent place in Hebrew literature. Its domain covers several millenia of history, from the days of the Patriarchs to frontier life in present-day Israel. Upon such a broad canvas, Hebrew writers depict life, personalities, events, impressions and adventure. From this reservoir they draw their inspiration and their subject matter.

In the not too distant past, David Frishman told Biblical tales; Vladimir (Zev) Jabotinsky described the heroic Judge Samson; A. Kabak recreated the life of Jesus in the Jewish environment of the Second Commonwealth, as well as the life of pseudo-Messiah Shlomo Molcho of the 16th century (1585-1640); M. Shoam probed into the roots of Jewish faith and destiny in both his dramas and poems; Yochanan Twersky delineated the lives of Uriel Acosta and Ahad Haam; Nathan Bistritsky dramatized the false Messiah, Shabatai Zvi; Harry Sackler produced a variety of historical novels, while Sh. Agnon depicted the folk ways of 18th century Galicia and Austria. Avigdor Hameiri, Rachel Feigenberg, A. Friman, A. Steinman and Hayim Hazaz dwelled upon the First World War and the post-World War conditions in Central and Eastern Europe. Sh. L. Blank, Sh. Halkin, R. Wallenrod, I. Rabinowitz, L. Arieli and J. D. Berkowitz dealt with the American-Jewish environment and M. Smilansky, D. Kimchi, R. Hadani, A. Reubeni, Sh. Zemach, Y. Zarchi, A. Barasch, E. Smoli and David Maletz portrayed the Palestine Yishub in the pre-Statehood period with its tribulations, struggles, triumphs and joys. The characterizations of oriental Jews were artistically done by J. Burla, Y. Shami, M. Tabib and Hazaz.

Thus in the period between the two world wars about 80 novelists and short story writers poured forth their creative energies in the Hebrew language.

And in the post-World War II period some of the older writers in both Israel and Diaspora, and especially the new generation of literati in Israel, displayed their creative powers in new works. Among them are A. Shamir, whose historical novel *"Melekh Basar V'dam,"* gained the admiration of all critics; S. Yizhar, who skillfully recorded in numerous stories and novels the events during the War of Liberation; Aharon Meged, whose dramatization of the mission and execution of Hannah Senesh has drawn world-wide attention; Yigal Mosinson whose stories of the life and thought of the Israeli Sabra (native) constitute a contribution to the history of modern Israel; A. Tabkar's stories of life in the kibbutzim are of the highest quality; Nathan Shacham's novels, short stories and plays have been acclaimed by the reading public; Bar Yosef's trilogy *"Ir Kesuma"* (A Magic City) deals with life in his native city at various periods in the last four centuries; and I. Shenberg's *"The Seven Who Left,"* describing the seven men and women who left a refugee camp in Europe and went to Israel, grips the heart of the reader.

In surveying the growth and development of modern Hebrew literature in the confines of a brief chapter, the writer realizes the encyclopaedic aspect of his statements, which cannot do justice to the men and women who tilled the vineyard of Hebrew letters. We trust that the reader will avail himself of the bibliographies appended to the chapters of this volume.

The Role of Hebrew in Israel

The following is a quotation on the development of Hebrew language and literature in Israel today: [18]

"The consolidation and continued development of modern Hebrew are of basic importance for Israel's cultural life. Two generations of scholars and educators have succeeded in transforming the ancient tongue into an instrument of daily speech, scholarship and science.

The Hebrew Language Academy was established by law in 1953 "to direct the development of the language on the basis of research into its various periods and branches." The Academy's decisions in matters of grammar, terminology and transliteration, published in the Official Gazette, are binding on educational and research institutions, as well as on Government departments and local authorities.

It publishes a research journal called *"Leshonenu"* (Our Language), and is preparing a Historical Dictionary of the Hebrew Language, which will take many years to complete.

Israel takes second place in the world for the number of titles published in proportion to the population, according to recent UNESCO figures. In 1959, 1,280 different books were published, of which about three-quarters were original works and the rest translations, including world classics and outstanding contemporary works.

A new generation of writers has arisen, with Hebrew as their mother tongue, who naturally express the experience of contemporary Israel in that constantly developing medium. Some of their works have been widely translated and well received.

New editions of the Bible, the Talmud and the outstanding works of rabbinic literature, incorporating the latest results of Israel scholarship, have been issued. Encyclopedias of various types are in course of publication, notably the comprehensive Hebrew Encyclopedia, which has over 40,000 subscribers.

Israel Prizes are awarded once a year by the Government on Independence Day to distinguished scholars, artists, scientists and men of letters. More than 15 literary awards besides are made each year by local authorities and other institutions.

The Hebrew Authors' Association, founded in 1921, has some three hundred members. It looks after the professional interests of authors (fees, copyrights, etc.), represents authors at home and abroad, and fosters the development of Hebrew literature and cultural life. It publishes a literary monthly, *"Moznayim"* (The Balance), and maintains a bibliographical institute, a fund for encouraging Hebrew literature, and a writers' club (Beit Tchernichosvsky).

The Bialik Institute (Mosad Bialik), an autonomous department of the Jewish Agency, is named after Hayim Nachman Bialik, the greatest of modern Hebrew poets. It was founded in 1935. In addition to original works of scholarship and literature, it publishes translations of outstanding books by Jewish scholars who molded European and world thought, and Hebrew versions of world classics and modern works of universal literary, scientific and artistic appeal.

The Institute is publishing the Historical Dictionary of the Hebrew Language for the Hebrew Language Academy, and an Encyclopedia of Education in conjunction with the Ministry of Education and Culture.

Interest in the study of the Bible, which is the basis of Jewish nationhood, religion and culture, is widespread among all sections of the population. It takes up 20-30 per cent of the school curriculum. The annual Bible Contests are followed with intense interest by almost the entire population. Jerusalem is now one of the most important international centers for Bible study and research, which are conducted there by the Hebrew University, the Rabbi Kook Institute, and many individual scholars, as well as the Pontifical Biblical Institute and other Christian institutions. Outstanding publications include the Encyclopedia of the Bible, The History of the Israelite Faith by Professor Y. Kaufmann, a new Bible Concordance, The New Biblical Dictionary, and Views of the Biblical World in several languages.

The Hebrew Reading Public in the Diaspora

An ever-growing supply of Hebrew reading matter enjoys a relatively small demand for it in the lands outside Israel. While some Hebrew books are being published in the Diaspora and while many more are being received from Israel, the number of readers on a world-wide scale has not grown. Scarcely sixty years ago, almost every Jew in Eastern Europe who knew Hebrew also read its literature. Non-Jewish reading matter was secondary in importance. Today the situation is reversed. Hundreds of thousands of readers of Hebrew literature together with hundreds of creative writers of Europe have perished alongside the multitudes of the Yiddish reading public. Russian Jewry, as already stated elsewhere, has become estranged from its literary sources both in Hebrew and in Yiddish. (A quarterly, entitled *"Sovietshe Heimland,"* has recently made its appearance in Moscow). Only few among the younger Jews who were born since the liquidation of the Yiddish school system and the disappearance of the Yiddish press in the late thirties have any access to Jewish literature. The number of people in the Diaspora who know enough Hebrew to appreciate reading the output of its modern literati is not too great; and many of those who do know enough Hebrew to enjoy it, must read, of necessity, literature in the non-Jewish languages. Consequently, the Hebrew-reading public in the Diaspora has dwindled.

Organizations for the advancement of Hebrew in the Diaspora, which exist in many countries (as the Histadrut Ivrit in the U.S.A.) and are linked internationally to the "Brith Ivrith Olamith" (World Federation for Hebrew Culture) make a concerted effort in promoting the study of Hebrew among youth and adults. Jewish educational agencies do their share in spreading Hebrew among children. The new State of Israel kindled a warm feeling toward the language. There is much more study of the language today than in the years before the rise of the State. Hebrew is studied in many of the American colleges and universities, in some of the public high schools, and naturally, in the synagogue schools for adults. It is to be hoped that in the future there will be more people in the Diaspora who will be ready to read Hebrew literature.

Yiddish Literature

Although books in the Yiddish language appeared in print as far back as the 16th century, and old Yiddish poetry dates back to the 15th century, Yiddish literature did not develop until the middle of the 19th century. The earlier Yiddish books were largely of a devotional character and of an "oral" folk-lore which was collected and put into print only in recent years.

The first literary works in Yiddish made their appearance with the publication of the writings of Isaac M. Dick (1807–1893), the father of Yiddish literature, whose stories, essays, sketches gained a large following. With the rise of Yiddish periodicals[19] (the Yiddish supplement to the Hebrew weekly *Hamelitz* called *Kol Mevaser*, (1862) followed by *Warshawer Yiddishe Zeitung*, (1867) and the *Judishes Volks-Blatt*, (1881)), writers who had previously regarded the language as unsuitable for literary expression, began to write in Yiddish. The famous Mendele (S. J. Abramovitz) who produced works of lasting value, made his debut in the early Yiddish periodicals in Russia. The popular folk-lorist, Eliokum Zunser, the dramatist, Goldfaden, and the essayist M. L. Lilenblum, also published much of their work in the Yiddish press of the period.

Thus, these early Yiddish periodicals, that were intended to disseminate Haskalah ideas, became, as did the Hebrew periodicals, a stimulus for writing, and provided an opportunity for many talented writers to express themselves in the language of the Jewish masses—Yiddish. The press became a training school for many of the poets, novelists and essayists, who enriched Yiddish in form and in vocabulary. By the beginning of the 20th century, Yiddish literature flourished everywhere in Europe. The classics of Mendele, Peretz and Sholem Aleichem had already established Yiddish as a literary medium. Mendele, who combined irony and humor, satirized Jewish life in the Pale, attacking the squalor, ignorance and uncouthness of ghetto life. Peretz, the master of the short story, portrayed the piety of the simple people, explored the life and faith of the ghetto dwellers, blending sarcasm with kindliness in all of his wondrous and supernatural folk tales. Sholem Aleichem sketched the small town characters, wrapped in gloom, but aglow with hope and faith. He reproduced the shtetl life in such a way that he taught his people to laugh at themselves, and at their sufferings. The popularity of these men was wide-spread and their works were translated into all European languages. This period (beginning with the 1880's) saw the beginning of the Yiddish theatre pioneered by Abraham Goldfaden, a playwright and an artist whose plays became classics of the Yiddish stage. Yiddish literature soon developed on the Western Hemisphere.

Between the two world wars, Yiddish literature was thriving in all Jewish population centers and had reached an enviable position. Sholem Asch, the prolific writer and expert stylist produced a number of masterpieces, among them *"The Tehilim Jew"* and *"The Three Cities."* David Pinsky and Sh. Ansky were bringing out plays of note, the most prominent among them Pinsky's *"The Eternal Jew"* and Ansky's *"The Dybbuk"* which appeared continually on the boards of European and American theatres. Joseph Opatoshu, a master of prose, had already produced a number of novels, the outstanding among them *"In die Polishe Welder,"* a dramatic account of Hasidic characters in a realistic setting of the Rebbe's Court. Morris Rosenfeld portrayed, in poetic form, life of the sweat-shop worker in New York. Zalmen Shneur was making conquests both as a Hebrew poet and as a Yiddish novelist of great ability. His Yiddish novels gained the admiration of literary critics for their direct and vigorous style, and the uncompromisingly realistic depiction of characters. I. J. Singer utilized his mastery of psychological insight in describing human relationships, and in the gradual unfolding of events, and David Bergelson made use of empathy in the treatment of inanimate objects.

As for the American Yiddish literati, consisting mostly of emigrants from eastern Europe, the following deserve special note: Abraham Reisen, poet and short story writer who wrote on a variety of themes with great charm and with much kindness; Abraham Liessen, the poet who glorified the past of the Jewish people and whose poetry conveyed his attachment to the ideals of Jewish nationalism and universal socialism; Mani Leib, the Yiddish balladist; Yehoash, the poet and the translator of the Bible into Yiddish; M. Boraisha, whose odyssey of a Jewish intellectual seeking a solution to the problem of individual existence was widely acclaimed as a work of great merit; Peretz Hirshbein, the playwright; Sh. Niger and A. Mokdoni, the literary critics; A. Raboy, who portrayed rural life in America; Bashevis, the author of *"Yoshe Kalb"* and *"Brothers Ashkenazi,"* depicting the life of Polish Jewry; I. J. Schwartz, the poet and translator of Medieval and modern Hebrew poetry; H. Leivik, the author of the Golem trilogy and one of the greatest Yiddish poets of our generation; Chaim Grade the lyricist; J. Gladstein, prolific writer of prose and poetry, and scores of others who have made notable contributions to Yiddish literature, and who have gained admiration in the literary circles of the civilized world.

There are also active groups of Yiddish writers in Canada, Latin America, Western Europe, and in Israel—among them Abraham Sutzkever, a partisan leader during the Nazi occupation of Vilna, now a prominent literary figure in Israel; Itzig Manger an original and skillfull master of verse, now in France; Abraham Zak and Mark Turoff of The Argentine, who depicted the tragic occurrences during the Second World War; and Jacob Pilowsky who portrayed Jewish life in Chile. In Canada the writers are Melech Ravitch and Rachel Coran, poets of distinction. In this connection it is important that we take note of the group of twenty-two Yiddish writers in the Soviet Union, who were executed on false accusations during the Stalin purges in 1952, among them Leib Kwitko,

David Bergelson, Der Nister, Itsik Pfeffer, G. Hofstein and Izi Charik—men of great stature in the Yiddish literary field.

In addition to the field of belles-lettres there were, and still are today, many literary analysts and critics, historians, publicists, bibliographers, etc. who produced scholarly works, school texts, dictionaries and translations from the world's classics as well as from the ancient and medieval Hebrew, to say nothing of original works in philosophy, biography, sociology, pedagogy, linguistics, and the like.

A most significant accomplishment was the establishment in Vilna in 1925 of the Yiddish Visenshaflicher Institut (Y.I.V.O.), or the Jewish Scientific Institute for the development of the Yiddish language and literature. The Institute which is composed of four sections—historical, philological, economic-statistical and phychologico-pedagogic—became the center for all the scholars and scientists who write in Yiddish. It still exists today, its headquarters being in New York City. Its library of 170,000 volumes, in all areas of Jewish scholarship, is one of the largest in the Jewish world.

The index of Yiddish literature and press, compiled by Z. Reisen in 1929, shows that, during the First World War period, there were about 500 Yiddish writers. In the 1950's the number is estimated to have risen to approximately 1,000,[20] notwithstanding the fact that the number of speakers of the Yiddish tongue, and the readers of its literature, has considerably declined.

It seems that the great decline in the use of Yiddish, especially since the tragic loss of the East European Jewry, and the growing generation's inability to use Yiddish, has failed to produce the anticipated negative effect upon the further development of Yiddish literature. There is evident a courageous effort to advance the cause of Yiddish literature. Although Yiddish literature is exposed to the unequal competition of non-Jewish literature, it continues to occupy a significant place in Jewish cultural life.

Jewish Literature in Non-Jewish Languages

Besides Jewish literary activity in Yiddish and Hebrew, a great deal of creative effort has gone into non-Jewish languages. There are today hundreds of writers who hold a prominent place in the realm of Jewish letters, but whose medium of expression is one of the European languages. Their works constitute an integral part of Jewish literature, not only because the writers are Jews (many contribute to the general field of world literature), but because they convey Jewish ideas and portray the life of the Jewish people.

Since the largest Jewish communities are situated in English-speaking countries, English is the leading medium for most of the Jewish literature in non-Jewish languages, and the major language for the literary productions of the writers who do not employ Yiddish or Hebrew. Of course, there are many Jewish authors who write in German, Russian, Polish, French, Spanish and other languages; their number however, is considerably smaller than the Anglo-Jewish groups.

The books in non-Jewish languages may be divided into three outstanding branches: Scholarship, fiction and essay.

Scholarly Works

Until recent years, most of the writings in the so-called field of "Science of Judaism" were in non-Jewish tongues. Historical treatises, studies of the Bible, the Talmud, social problems, theology, etc. were compiled in German, English and other languages. Today a great deal of that work is being done in Hebrew, particularly in Israel. Outside of Israel, however, most of the Jewish scholars publish their works in the European tongues. In recent years, hundreds of valuable books have been written in the field of Jewish scholarship.[21]

Then too, there are important scholarly journals in the Diaspora which publish studies of important research. The annual American publications of the Hebrew Union College—Jewish Institute of Religion, YIVO Social Studies, publications of the American Academy for Jewish Research, the American Jewish Year Book, Jewish Social Studies, Jewish Quarterly Review—all contain significant studies in every field of Jewish learning.

Fiction

In fiction numerous works of importance have appeared in all European languages, especially in English, portraying life of Jews as well as non-Jews. To name but a few Americans: Ludwig Lewisohn, an avowed Zionist and a violent anti-assimilationist, whose novels deal with characters who find in the Jewish tradition a source of strength and a real solace in their confused and frustrated lives; Herman Wouk, whose heroes live the lives of marginal Jews; Irving Feinman, depicting the life of the East European immigrants; Bernard Malamud, who deals with the first generation inhabitants of the American ghettos; Meyer Levin who draws upon his experiences in America and in Israel; Philip Roth, working on the theme of the complex relationships between Jews and Gentiles; Chayim Zeldis, an American writer of poetry who became a member of a kibbutz in Israel; Charles Reznikoff, novelist, historian and poet; Charles Angoff, short story writer and literary critic. In England, Israel Zangwill, the distinguished English novelist, poet, playwright and critic, who became strongly identified with Jewish causes and Jewish literary themes; Louis Goldberg, a popular English writer of short stories. In South Africa, Meir Davidson, writing short stories in the style of an O. Henry; Arthur Markowitz, who portrays urban Jewish life and Albert Segal whose *"Johannesburg Friday"* constitutes a sincere and moving study of a Jewish family and Olga Kirsh, who introduced the Hebrew experience into Afrikaans poetry. Boris Pilniak and Isaac Babel produced significant works in Russian; Edmund Fleg, poet, dramatist and critic, whose Hebraic "looking within" set him apart as an original writer; André Schwartz-Bart, whose novel *"Last of the Just"* deals with the recent Jewish tragedy in Europe against the background of a "Lamed-Vovnik," a current best seller on a Jewish theme which appeared in French.

Essays and Translations from Yiddish and Hebrew

Translations from the Yiddish and Hebrew are becoming a specialized field. Maurice Samuel has rendered a great service in pioneering the studies of Yiddish classics and translations of the great classicists Bialik, J. L. Peretz, Sholem Aleichem and Sholem Asch. There followed translations by other gifted translators of Hebrew poetry and prose such as I. M. Lask, Moshe Spiegel, V. Snowman, Sholom J. Kahn, J. Leftwich, S. Katz. These translations acquaint the Jewish public with the celebrated writers and their works written in the original Judaic languages. In short, books on Jewish topics appear almost every month in all the large communities.

As for essay writing, it may be safely stated that it embraces a growing array of works which reflect Jewish thought everywhere. The articles that appear in the scores of journals are indicative of the remarkable developments in this field of literary endeavor.

Whether or not Jewish literature in the vernacular will replace Jewish literary works in Hebrew or Yiddish, cannot be predicted. It seems, however, that just as in the case of the Jews themselves, who struggle to live and retain their identity, Hebrew and Yiddish letters will live on in Diaspora, notwithstanding the operation of all factors that indicate their natural decline. Hebrew, especially, having come to life again, has shown symptoms of normal growth in its native soil, and will, no doubt, follow its course of development for many generations to come.

Thus, while it is true that to a great many Jews their literature in Hebrew and Yiddish is a closed book, Jewish culture is conserved and furthered by creativeness in the vernacular, which has become a striking feature of Jewish cultural life in the Diaspora.

Jewish Contributions to General Culture

"For two-thousand years the Jews have formed part of Europe. They have, throughout that period—though more intensively during the past century, since the gates of the ghetto were broken down—made their contribution to the common heritage: sometimes as intermediaries, sometimes as pioneers, more often (so far as their activities were not curtailed) as participants. In the long run their contribution has become interwoven with the common stock by a thousand different strands."[22]

It was not until the end of the 18th century that the Jew was able to leave the ghetto and freely interact with the non-Jewish scholar. A study of original Jewish contributions to civilization in the last 150 to 200 years brings to light the remarkable fact that among the men who have advanced all branches of knowledge, many were Jews. From Baruch Spinoza (1632-1677) of Amsterdam, who influenced modern philosophy and modern political science, to Joshua Lederberg, one of three winners of the Nobel Prize in Physiology in 1958, Jews have made significant contributions to modern thought. The extent of Jewish intellectual attainments is attested to by the large proportion of recipients of the Nobel Prize. "Among the 313 Nobel Prize winners from 1901 to 1959, there have been 40 Jews. . . . This constitutes 12 per cent of the total winners. . . . The proportion of Jews in the world population is less than one-half of one per cent."[23] Of equal significance is the collective contribution of the thousands of scientists, teachers, artists, writers, philosophers, mathematicians and the like, whose names are not recorded on the pages of modern history as leaders in the particular field of their specialized studies.

But is is also difficult to list the men who have excelled in their respective fields of endeavor. It would take us far afield from our general theme. However, some of the outstanding men whose Jewish origin and traditions moulded their genius may be named: Leon Blum (1872-1950), Premier of France and friend of Labor Israel; Louis D. Brandeis (1856-1926), the eminent Justice of the Supreme Court, who steered a course for American Zionism; Martin Buber of our own day, the acclaimed religious thinker, whose writings have a profound influence upon Jew and Gentile alike; Herman Cohen (1842-1918) the philosopher to whom Judaism was a "Religion of Reason," which encouraged its adherents to strive for a society of moral perfection; Albert Einstein (1879-1955) the famed scientist, the author of the Theory of Relativity and the great humanist; Sigmund Freud (1856-1939) the master-mind who penetrated the world of the unconscious as Einstein rediscovered space; Harold J. Laski (1893-1955) the political thinker who formulated the blueprint of a welfare state (the concept of cradle to grave security); Herbert Samuel (1870-1963) of England, distinguished statesman; Professor Selman A. Waksman (1888-   ) a former Yeshiva student, the discoverer of streptomycin; Chaim Weizmann (1874-1954) the creative chemist and the first President of the State of Israel; Harry Wolfson (1887-   ) the interpreter of Hellenistic and Medieval Jewish philosophy, and Lazarus L. Zamenhof (1859-1917) the inventer of Esperanto, the international language—all of whom were contributing to human progress and at the same time carrying their Jewishness with dignity. A far greater number of leading men are to be found in the fields of literature, music, theatre and the plastic arts. To mention but a few who attained distinction during the last half-century: Israel Zangwill, the eminent dramatist of England; Max Nordau of Hungary and France, the fearless social critic, novelist, dramatist, thinker—and, with Theodor Herzl, co-founder of the World Zionist Organization; Georg Brandes of Denmark, the eminent literary critic; Jacob Wasserman, Arnold Zweig and Leon Fuchtwanger, the novelists of Germany; Franz Kafka and Franz Werfel of Austria; and Waldo Frank, Louis Untermeyer, Fanny Hurst, Howard Fast, Robert Nathan, Karl Shapiro, the novelists and poets of the United States. As for the composers, artists and performers, it will suffice to name the more prominent among them: Ernst Bloch, the composer of Switzerland; Jean de Bloch and Leopold Auer of Russia; George Gershwin, David Diamond and Leonard Bernstein of United States. In the field of plastic arts, the sculptors Antokolski and Chaim Gross of Russia; Boris Schatz of Bulgaria and Israel; Jo Davidson and William Zorach of the United States; Jacob Epstein of England. These are leading artists whose works gained universal recognition. The great painters whose works were displayed in art galleries: Camille Pissaro of France; Max Lieberman and Herman Struck of Germany; Lesser Ury and Marc Chagal of Poland-France; Joseph Budko and Jacob Steinhardt of Israel and Max Weber and Elias Neuman of the United States. Some of the famous instrumentalists are Vladimir Horowitz, Artur Rubinstein (piano); Mischa Elman, Jascha Heifetz, Nathan Milstein, Isaac Stern, Yehudi Menuhin, David Oistrakh (violin); Georg Piatigorsky and Emanuel Feuermen (cello).

Most of these artists drew inspiration from the Jewish tradition; some of them express subconsciously, perhaps, the experiences of their people.

We have omitted from the list the Israeli group of leaders in the various fields of cultural endeavor. Special consideration will be given to them in Volume II.

To quote from Norman Bentwich of England, the author of *"The Jew of Our Time,"* who says: "The contribution of Israel is, and will be, not only of individuals, but of a community living freely according to its own genius. Israel may make another indirect contribution: to reinvigorate the Jewish consciousness of writers and artists of all kinds in the other communities of Jewry. Jewish dissimilation is as important for the well-being of the whole society as Jewish assimilation."[24]

Jewish Education

THE ROLE OF LEARNING IN JEWISH LIFE

Teaching the young the tenets of Judaism was paramount among all other social and cultural functions of the Jew at all times. The command, "Thou shalt teach . . . diligently unto thy children" (Deut. 6:7), has been a holy task for every father in Israel throughout history. For centuries Jews studied Torah with great zeal and devotion. To the average Jew study was more than pursuit of knowledge; it was the fulfillment of a religious duty. The Jews considered religious education a lifelong process, and learning for learning's sake was an important pattern of Jewish conduct.

TRANSITION FROM RELIGIOUS TO SECULAR LEARNING

The major goal of Jewish education, until the end of the eighteenth century was to impart to the young a knowledge of the sacred literature, and to bring up good and pious Jews. The curriculum, therefore, consisted of instruction in the reading of the Hebrew prayers, the Pentateuch, the Psalms, portions of the Prophets, the Talmud, and the Commentaries. This sort of education was uniform for all Jews in the world. Secular knowledge, such as natural sciences, art, history and allied branches, was neglected, except for small groups in Spain and Italy.

With the beginning of emancipation and with the increasing social intercourse between Jew and non-Jew, secular education became a necessity. A strong urge for modern learning became manifest. The transition between religious training as the sole type of education, and instruction in secular subjects, was accompanied by great difficulties. Not only were the people generally reluctant to change an age-old tradition, but many orthodox rabbis manifested great resentment, fearing that secular studies would lead to the abandonment of traditional Judaism. The new environment, however, overwhelmed the opposition.

Simultaneous with the advent of universal and compulsory education in a number of lands of Jewish domicile, the Jews exhibited great devotion for secular learning and an understanding of its need and utility. In the period before World War I, most Jewish children were attending either the public schools or Jewish educational institutions where secular subjects were taught alongside the Jewish studies. In the post-war period, all resistance to secular education was broken.

JEWISH RELIGIOUS EDUCATION BECOMES SUPPLEMENTARY EDUCATION

Indeed secular education has been espoused by the Jews to such a degree that Jewish religious education has been relegated to a secondary place. The chief concern of the Jew today is to afford opportunities for his children to acquire a secular and professional education. Modern conditions have, perhaps, necessitated such a change in educational orientation, which has made for such a wide gap between the Jewish educational standards of only a century ago and those of today. But this thirst for knowledge of secular subjects has not estranged the Jew from his Torah. While intensive Jewish studies are pursued by a minority, a curriculum of extensive Jewish learning has been devised to meet the needs of children and adolescents. Some knowledge of Jewish religio-cultural values is being transmitted in one form or another to a major portion of children everywhere in the Jewish world.

The overwhelming majority of Jewish children in the Diaspora who acquire some type of a Jewish education are to be found in schools that operate on weekday afternoons, on Sunday and/or Saturday. Most of the children of these Jewish schools attend the educational institutions of the general community such as the public schools in the United States. Thus, Jewish education for these children is primarily supplementary to the general education that they receive in the Government schools. Only a minority of the Jewish children in the Diaspora attend Jewish "complete" schools where a combined program of Jewish and general studies is offered. Quite different is the situation in Israel, as we shall see in another section of this chapter.

Jewish schools in the Diaspora differ from each other in form, content and operation. The following is a brief description of the types of Jewish education in the lands of the Diaspora.

TYPES OF JEWISH EDUCATION

The Most Intensive Education—the Day School

The Jewish day school or the Jewish "complete" school, generally defined, is an institution in which a combined program of Jewish and general studies is offered. There are three types of institutions that are included in the category of Jewish day schools. These are the Talmudic day school, the modern day school and the integrated school. While educational approaches among these schools vary, they, nevertheless, approximate the designation of a school which provides the most intensive Jewish education in modern times.

The Talmudic day school, also known as Yeshiva, makes provision for the study of the Pentateuch together with the commentary by Rashi, major portions of the Prophets and Scriptures in the original Hebrew and places great stress on teaching of Talmud and the Code of Laws (Shulhan Arukh).[25] Hebrew language and modern literature are not taught, nor does the curriculum include the teaching of Jewish history. The general studies meet the requirements of the city and state authorities. The school day ranges from eight to ten hours. About twenty hours per week are given to Jewish studies.

The modern day school stresses the study of Hebrew language and literature. In addition to Hebrew, there is the study of Bible, Jewish history, prayers and selected portions from the Talmud. All instruction in Jewish studies is in the Hebrew language. The general studies are given equal attention and equal time. In most schools of this type, fifteen hours per week are scheduled for Jewish studies.

The integrated day school aims to integrate the general and Jewish cultures, and to achieve a blending of Judaism and Westernism. The pupil may begin the school day with the study of Bible, go next to a lesson in arithmetic, then proceed to the study of the Hebrew language, then to geography, and so on. The idea of integration is also incorporated into the subject matter of instruction. The subjects taught are the same as in the modern day school, but with more stress on the mutual relationships between general and Hebrew studies. From fifteen to sixteen hours per week are devoted to Jewish studies.

In recent years a number of day schools were also sponsored by Yiddish-culture groups. The program of these schools differs from the modern day school in that Yiddish language and literature are included as basic subjects of instruction and that there is little stress on religious subject matter.

The Most Intensive Supplementary Education— the Talmud Torah

Next to the day school, the Talmud Torah offers an intensive Jewish education. Its program is geared to an appreciation on a child's level of the totality of the Jewish cultural heritage, including religion—in many cases, especially religion. It meets daily after public-school hours for seven and a half to ten hours of instruction per week. The Talmud Torah is either affiliated with a synagogue—or conducted by an association of laymen. Its program is based on a six-year curriculum which includes the following areas of study: The Hebrew prayerbook, the Bible (a knowledge of the narrative and legalistic portions of the Pentateuch, and selections from the early Prophets), the Hebrew language (an ability to understand, read, and write simple Hebrew), Jewish history, customs, and ceremonies and Jewish music. In the post-World War I period the Talmud Torah, or community Hebrew School functioned very effectively as the only type of intensive supplementary Jewish education. It was considered the best type of school in the Diaspora, especially in America. In the post-World War II period, this type of school gave way to the congregational Hebrew school. Only few community Hebrew schools have remained in operation to this day.

The Congregational Weekday School

The weekday congregational school is the prevailing type of institution for supplementary Jewish education. Its pupils attend classes generally for an hour and a half or two hours a day, two days during the week and on Sunday. While there are variations in the pattern, in many of these schools the children concentrate on Hebraic studies during the week, and on Sundays, join pupils who come only once a week, for the study of those subjects that are taught in the vernacular. Among these are Jewish history, customs and ceremonies; Jewish civics; Israel; and the Jewish arts.

The curriculum of most three-day programs is based upon five years of attendance. The children enter at the age of eight and graduate at thirteen, upon becoming Bar-Mitzvah. They study selections of the Pentateuch in Hebrew, the prayerbook, the Hebrew language (as preparation for the study of Bible as well as for an understanding of the prayerbook), Jewish history, religious practices in home and synagogue, and Jewish music.

Almost 35 per cent of all enrollees in the Jewish schools in the United States are to be found in this type of school.

The One-Day-A-Week Type of Education

These schools are frequently referred to as Sunday schools because they conduct their classes on Sunday mornings. The time of instruction in these schools averages two hours a week. The Sunday schools usually meet between thirty-two and thirty-five Sundays a year, and provide a total of sixty-four to seventy hours of instruction. Their course of study is based on six to eight years of attendance. In the United States, 45 per cent of the enrollees attend Sunday schools. The curriculum includes Bible stories for the very young, Jewish history, and synagogue practices.

The Yiddish Supplementary Schools

The basic elements of their curriculums are Yiddish language and literature and Jewish history. The orientation of these schools has undergone a considerable change in the last decade. Their programs now include the study of Hebrew language, selections from the Bible, and the observance of Jewish festivals. The number of Yiddish schools has declined considerably in recent years.

In the U.S.A. they constitute less than 3 per cent of the entire Jewish school population.

Programs of Jewish Education in Government Schools

Another type of supplementary instruction in Judaism is that which is conducted in government schools for one or more hours a week. Such programs are maintained in Belgium, Switzerland, West Germany, Great Britain, Luxembourg, Austria, and Australia. The religious classes reach relatively large numbers of Jewish children, because in some countries attendance is compulsory. However, parents may make written requests that their children be excused from these classes.

Enrollment by Type of School

The following table shows enrollment by type of school.

Country	Number of Children of School Age (5-17)	Children Attending Supplementary Schools		Children Attending Day School		Total
		No.	%	No.	%	
Western Europe	163,235	38,998	72.2	15,062	27.8	24,024
Central and South America	128,386	23,005	67.4	11,108	32.6	34,113
Arabic Speaking Countries	73,935			46,975		46,975
Iran	16,000			12,830		12,830
South Africa	23,000	6,000	50.0	6,000	50.0	12,000
Australia	13,460	5,122	75.0	1,707	25.0	6,829
Canada	50,000	14,297	66.6	7,149	33.3	21,446
Total	468,016	87,422	46.4	100,795	53.6	188,217
% of Children of School Age		18.7		21.5		
United States	1,106,300	547,323	91.6	50,000	8.4	597,323

From the figures in the above table we learn that in countries of the Diaspora other than the United States, more than one-half of all the children enrolled in Jewish schools attend the day schools.[26] In the United States, however, only a little more than 8 per cent of all enrollees are to be found in the day school. In the past twenty years, the day schools have grown both quantitatively and qualitatively on a world scale. Almost 20 per cent of all Jewish children who receive some type of Jewish education attend the day schools where studies of Jewish subject matter are equal to those in the field of general education.

SECONDARY SCHOOLS FOR JEWISH EDUCATION

Graduates from the elementary schools are directed to central high schools, where they continue their Judaic studies on a higher level. Regrettably, the secondary schools attract only about 7 to 10 per cent of these graduates. The courses of study in the one-day a week high schools are conducted in the students' spoken language. In the more intensive high schools where students attend three times a week, the course of study is more comprehensive and the language of instruction is Hebrew. In both types of high schools the program calls for the continuation of study of basic subjects taught in the higher grades of the elementary school.

The relatively small number of Jewish youth who continue their studies beyond the elementary level is due, primarily, to parental lack of understanding of the principle that education is a life-long process, and that a real appreciation of Jewish life and thought requires the maturing mind of an adolescent. While on the elementary level children can acquire the rudiments of Jewish learning, their knowledge and understanding of Jewish concepts and values is very shallow indeed. Hence the cry of Jewish educational leadership to build this second rung in the Jewish educational ladder—the high school.

THE JEWISH SCHOOL ENROLLMENT IN THE DIASPORA

It is estimated that approximately eleven million Jews live in the Diaspora (outside the State of Israel). If we deduct the 2¾-million residing in the Soviet Union and its Satellites, where Jewish education is practically non-existent or severely curtailed, we find that, insofar as the figures for Jewish school enrollment are concerned, we must reckon with a Jewish population in the Diaspora numbering only 8¼-million. Taking the estimate of demographers, that children of elementary and high school age in the age bracket 5-17 constitute one-fifth of the total population, we will arrive at a figure of 1½-million for the potential Jewish school population in the Diaspora (outside the USSR and its Satellites). Of these, as pointed out in the following table, almost 800,000 are to be found in Jewish schools in a given year. Thus we readily see that one-half of the Jewish children in the Diaspora do not receive any kind of Jewish education. No matter how shallow the Jewish educational program may be for those who do attend, they nontheless are exposed to some Jewish religio-cultural stimuli. The problem, therefore, is not only that of intensifying the education already given, but also that of attracting the non-enrolled children to a Jewish educational institution.

Jewish School Enrollment

Country	Jewish Population	Jewish School Population (5-17)	Number of Children Enrolled in Jewish Schools	Proportion Attending Jewish Schools
Western Europe	985,404	163,235	54,024	33.1
U.S.A.	5,531,500	1,106,300	597,323	54.0
Canada	250,000	50,000	26,351	25.7
South & Central America	673,850	127,386	34,113	26.8
Arabic Speaking Countries	341,250	73,935	46,975	63.5
Iran	80,000	16,000	9,891	61.8
Union of South Africa	113,000	23,000	12,000	52.2
Australia	67,000	13,460	6,829	50.7
Total	8,042,004	1,573,316	787,506	50.1
USSR and its Satellites	2,695,300			

SCHOOLS FOR HIGHER LEARNING

For many centuries the Yeshivot constituted the fort of advanced Jewish learning. Tens of thousands of young men studied for study's sake (mostly Talmud). Some of these students prepared for the Rabbinate. With the annihilation of the large Jewish communities in Europe, the old type of Yeshivot were reduced to ashes, together with their students and teachers, by the Nazi hordes. Fortunately, some were transplanted to the United States and Israel. In Israel, many of the old type Yeshivot that offer a program of Talmudic studies to thousands of young men, function to this day. A number of new Yeshivot have been organized with the large influx of immigration in the last twenty years.

In modern times other institutions for higher Jewish learning have arisen. Their curricula include, in addition to Talmudic and Biblical studies, other branches of Jewish learning such as philosophy, sociology, rhetorics, history and literature. The modern schools for higher learning may be classified into three categories: Rabbinical seminaries; colleges or institutes for Jewish studies and departments in Judaica in colleges and universities.

The oldest modern Rabbinical seminaries which originated in Germany had to close their doors with the advent of Hitlerism. The other Rabbinical schools which existed in Western Europe at the outbreak of the Second World War and which are in operation today are: The Netherlands Israelitische Seminarum in Amsterdam; the Institute d'Etudes Hebraïques in Paris (for the training of Rabbis and teachers to service Reform educational institutions and temples) and the Seminarie Israëlite de France (for the training of Orthodox Rabbis); the Rabbinical School in Rome and the Jews' College (for the training of Orthodox Rabbis) and the Leo Baeck College for the preparation of Rabbis for Liberal congregations in England.

In the United States the following Rabbinical schools exist: (a) the Hebrew Union College—Jewish Institute of Religion, the only school in America designed to meet the needs of Reform Congregations. The college has one of the finest Jewish libraries in the United States and publishes a scientific journal, "The Hebrew Union College Annual." (b) The Jewish Theological Seminary of America and its branch, the University of Judaism in Los Angeles for the training of rabbis, cantors, teachers and lay leaders to service the Conservative congregations in the United States, Canada and Latin America. This Seminary, too, has a fine collection of books and some rare Jewish manuscripts. (c) The Rabbi Isaac Elchanan Theological Seminary of the Yeshiva University is the largest Orthodox theological school for the training of Orthodox Rabbis. Other Orthodox Rabbinic schools are the Hebrew Theological College of Chicago, which in recent years became an integral part of the Jewish University of Chicago; the Mesifta Rabbi Chaim Berlin, Yavneh Theological Seminary, the Mesifta Rabbinical Seminary of Torah Vodaat—all in New York; the Ner Israel Rabbinical College in Baltimore and the Rabbinical Colleges in Cleveland (organized in 1875 in Telshe, Lithuania and transferred to Cleveland in 1941) and Lakewood, N. J.

JEWISH COLLEGES AND ADULT INSTITUTES

Far greater in number are the institutions which provide opportunities for systematic study on an adult level under the guidance of expert teachers and scholars to those who do not necessarily prepare for the Rabbinate. These schools for adult Jewish education are designed for the men and women who wish to acquire a knowledge of Jewish sources on a college level, and for hundreds of younger people who want to qualify as teachers for all types of Jewish schools. There are twenty-one such colleges in the United States and Canada, where special teacher-training courses are offered as well as general subjects in all aspects of Jewish life and culture. In addition to these institutions, the larger rabbinical schools maintain departments for teacher training and departments in advanced Jewish studies for the laity. In Western Europe there are thirteen teacher education institutions, seven of which are to be found in England.[26a] In Central and South America there are only three teacher training schools (Mexico, Argentina and Brazil). While the enrollment in the teacher colleges is relatively small, a larger registration is reported in the adult education classes that function either as adjuncts to teacher education schools, or as independent entities. Adult education classes for the laity are also to be found in many synagogues as well as non-synagogal organizations, such as the Jewish community centers, B'nai B'rith study groups, Young Israel adult classes, Hadassah education circles, and the like.

There are no statistics on the enrollees in adult education groups, nor is there an authoritative study on the qualitative aspects of the educational program. It is known, however, that the numbers of attendees in adult education classes is growing from year to year, but that it constitutes a very small ratio of the adult Jewish population.

ADVANCED JEWISH STUDIES IN UNIVERSITIES

In addition to Rabbinical Seminaries, the colleges for teacher education and Institutes for Adult Jewish Studies, there are now many universities in the United States that offer courses in Judaica. The same holds true to a smaller extent in Canada, Western Europe and Latin America. Thus, Jewish university students can choose one or more courses in Judaica toward their academic degrees. There are, in addition, four universities in the United States under Jewish auspices, where courses in Judaica constitute a major phase of their programs. They are: Yeshiva University in New York; Brandeis University in Waltham, Mass.; the Jewish University in Chicago and the Dropsie College for Hebrew and Cognate Learning in Philadelphia, a non-sectarian post-graduate institution for Hebrew learning and other branches of Semitic culture. The last has been in operation since 1907.

COORDINATION, OF LOCAL JEWISH EDUCATIONAL ENDEAVORS

In the U.S.A., local central agencies for Jewish education, known by the name of Bureaus, were organized in the past three decades in all major communities. The function of these community agencies is to render service to every element in the community with a positive attitude toward Judaism and Jewish life, and "to help each element carry on its work in terms of its own ideology, in accordance with the highest standards which conditions permit, and to encourage each element to engage in experimentation, and to seek new ways, and new means, for implementing its objectives." There are forty-two such local agencies in the United States.

NATIONAL IDEOLOGICAL COMMISSIONS ON JEWISH EDUCATION IN THE U.S.A.

The schools of the three major religious groups are being serviced nationally by their own ideological mentors—the national commissions on Jewish education. There are four such commissions for the Orthodox groups, one for the Reform, one for the Conservative, and two for the Yiddish schools. Each commission prepares curricula and syllabi for their affiliated schools, reflecting the aims of Jewish education of their particular ideologies. They also publish textbooks and audio-visual aids and sponsor workshops for the teachers in service. These commissions have also organized the professional-school personnel into five associations corresponding to their counter-parts among the lay groups.

"UMBRELLA" AGENCIES FOR JEWISH EDUCATION

The American Association for Jewish Education (organized in 1939) is the over-all national service agency in the U.S.A. It relates itself to all elements of the American Jewish community, irrespective of ideological differences. It is dedicated to the principle of community responsibility for Jewish education, and strives to stimulate, promote, extend and improve the status of Jewish education on all age levels, and among all ideological groups. The A.A.J.E. offers services in the fields of educational research, community organization for Jewish education, pedagogics and curricula, promotion and interpretation, personnel and teacher-training. It sponsors the National Board of License for the certification of full-time professional teachers, conducts a department on Jewish audio-visual materials, and cooperates with all national and local organizations in the advancement of the cause of Jewish education for children, youth and adults. It is the parent agency of all local bureaus of Jewish education.

The National Council for Jewish Education organized in 1931, is a professional fellowship of leading Jewish educators. The N.C.J.E. publishes *Jewish Education* and *Shvilei Hahinuch,* two periodicals in English and Hebrew respectively. It also arranges regional and national conferences for its membership and in cooperation with other agencies engages in the promotion of Jewish education in the country.

In other countries, too, there are coordinating agencies whose task is to advance the cause of Jewish education and to help local schools raise educational standards. In England, it is the Central Council of Jewish Religious Education and the London Board of Jewish Religious Education; in Canada it is the Education Department of the Canadian Jewish Congress, the Keren Hatarbut and the local Bureaus in Toronto and Winnipeg; in Argentina it is the Organizacion Central de Escuelas Israelitas, supervising all schools in Buenos Aires, and in France it is the Education Department of the J.D.C. (American Joint Distribution Committee) and the local Council for Jewish Education and Culture in France. The J.D.C. extends its educational services to most European communities not under Communist rule. The Alliance Israelite Universelle (headquarters in Paris), conducts schools in North Africa and in a number of other countries and Ozar Hatorah operates schools in Iran.

Education in Israel[27]

Historical Background—Molding a nation out of a multitude of immigrants, arriving from a myriad of different countries and civilizations, and speaking a Babel of languages, was one of the most important tasks facing the State of Israel. The main instruments for its realization have been the school system and the adult education programs. Fortunately, in 1948, the reborn State did not have to start from the beginning. It inherited from the self-governed Jewish community in the country an established and autonomous school system which had been developing along with agriculture, industry and commerce for about sixty years.

During the period from 1882 to 1948 the Jewish school system in Palestine grew from a few hundred to nearly 100,000 students, attending a large variety of schools, ranging from kindergartens to the Hebrew University in Jerusalem and the Israel Institute of Technology—Technion in Haifa. Hand in hand with this expansion went the revival and enrichment of the Hebrew language as a living instrument of expression in all fields of human endeavor. The Hebrew school has been both the workshop and the disseminating agent for Hebrew as a language of instruction and as a vernacular.

From Ideological Trends to a Unified School System

Within the framework of administrative unity under the Department of Education of the National Council (Vaad Leumi), the highest autonomous authority of Palestinian Jewry, the school system had been divided into three ideological trends, the General, Mizrahi, and Labor. The Mizrahi or Religious trend represented a distinctly religious approach while the Labor schools attempted to educate their students towards a pioneering and cooperative society. The General schools put the stress on liberal education. The Compulsory Education Law of 1949 recognized these trends as well as an additional one, that of Agudat Israel, which is of a religious—orthodox character. Parents could freely select for their children a school belonging to any one of the four recognized "trends." There were also a few schools outside any "trend."

To a Unified School System

It became increasingly evident, however, that the trends had outgrown their usefulness and should be replaced by a unified state educational system. The acute shortage of teachers that resulted from the rapid expansion of the school system, and the wastefulness of maintaining three to four different schools in small communities, provided an additional incentive for doing away with the "trend" system. In August, 1953, the Knesset passed the State Education Law, which abolished the "trend" system and set up a unified system of state education in kindergartens and elementary schools subject to the supervision of the Ministry of Education and Culture. In addition, the Government provides for state religious education. Institutions in this category are religious with respect to curriculum, way of life, teachers and inspectors. Private schools may operate outside the network of State schools, provided that the curricula, teaching standards and buildings are approved by the Ministry of Education. Such schools

are eligible for financial assistance. Some schools previously belonging to the Agudat Israel "trend" have taken advantage of this
leeway and have formed a separate school network.

Educational Philosophy Defined

The educational philosophy of the unified public school system,
as stipulated in the Law, derives from a common denominator of
the basic elements in all the trends. This philosophy is defined
in the following terms: "The state educational system aims to
establish primary education in the state on the values of the heritage of Israel and the achievements of science, on love for the
homeland and loyalty to the State of Israel and the Jewish people,
on training in agriculture and manual labor, on pioneering and
on striving for the creation of a society built on freedom, mutual
help and love of humanity."

Structure of School System

Israel's School System provides a continuous education from
Kindergarten to University. Universal, compulsory and free education for all children from the age of 5 to 13 (last year of kindergarten and eight years of elementary school) was established by
the Compulsory Education Law of 1949 and is being fully imple-
mented. Youth between the ages of 14 and 17, who for any reason
have not completed an 8-year elementary school education, must
attend special classes until they either complete the required curriculum, or reach the age of 17.

The majority of schools are co-educational.

Freedom of Language and Education

In addition to the traditional freedoms of religion and conscience, the Israel Declaration of Independence guarantees "freedom of language, education and culture." Most Arab citizens have
availed themselves of this right. The Government thus provides
for schools where Arabic is the language of instruction, with Hebrew as a second language, and where special emphasis is
placed on Arab history and literature. These schools constitute a
separate entity within the framework of State education maintained by the Government.

Kindergartens

A unique feature of Israel education is the prevalence of kindergartens covering the ages from 3 to 6.

The kindergarten plays a significant role in Israel society. It is of primary importance in the cultural integration of masses of immigrants from diversified backgrounds. In a country where many women work outside their homes and where domestic help is scarce—the kindergarten relieves the mother for her other duties for part, or all, of the day.

Elementary Schools

The elementary school provides an eight-year education. Attendance of Jewish children in the age group 6 to 13 (provided for in the Compulsory Education Law), is virtually complete. Arab school attendance increased from 48 per cent of the total Arab school age population before 1948 to about 90 percent in 1960. It is not yet complete because many Arab girls are prevented from attending school by their parents. A concerned educational effort is under way to persuade Arab parents of the importance of primary education for both boys and girls.

The Curriculum

In 1954/55 the Ministry of Education and Culture introduced for the first time a comprehensive and detailed obligatory curriculum for the elementary schools. After a trial period of a few years the curriculum will be subject to review and evaluation. The curriculum comprises two parts—one for the state schools and the other for the state religious schools. The difference between them, however, lies almost exclusively in the greater emphasis on religious studies in the state religious schools. A similar curriculum for Arab schools is in the final stages of preparation.

In subject matter and pedagogy the elementary school follows the pattern of primary and elementary education developed in Europe and the United States, as adapted to the ideals and particular needs of the renascent nation.

Educating a Pioneer

The school aims not only at preparing the pupil for his future life as an individual and as a good citizen but also at shaping him in the image of a pioneer—selfless, courageous and constructive. Farming, manual labor and home economics are given special attention as subjects of instruction. Most schools in villages as well as in the cities have plots of land available for farming and workshops for woodwork and metal work. A great many schools are equipped with kitchens in which the pupils themselves, boys and girls, by way of training in cooking, prepare a hot lunch for the entire school.

Extra-curricular activities, such as farm clubs, nature study, etc., are encouraged.

Secondary Education

The high school consists of a four-year course of studies following the eight-year elementary school. Some vocational high schools have a three-year course of studies.

Secondary education is provided by private schools deriving their income from tuition or by schools sponsored by local Government and civic organizations. Many schools are subsidized by the Government. The Government also offers scholarships to capable students who are financially in need. The Jewish Agency grants scholarships to students from oriental countries in order to encourage immigrant youth from those countries to continue their education.

High school students account for only a little more than one-third of the youth between the ages of 14 and 18.

Integration of Youth in the Schools

The picture of education in Israel cannot be complete unless reference is made to the problem of integration. The children of Israel come from homes of different social, religious and cultural backgrounds. Most of the children of the Oriental Jews come from feudal Arab countries. Their parents have never learned to believe in the capacity of the individual to change or to determine his own fate, whereas most of the Ashkenazi children come from homes whose parents are interested in social, economic and cultural progress. There is a clash between the two ethnic groups. The problem of the Israeli school is not only to create homogeneity in pedagogical terms but to so "Israelize" all children that they will grow up with the knowledge that they are members of one community. The total number of pupils is 600,000.

Teacher Training

The regular teachers colleges offer a two-year course of study in the theory and practice of education following graduation from a high school. They are the main source of supply for the kindergartens and elementary schools. High school teachers are required to have a University degree. Teachers lacking these qualifications, who were employed under emergency measures, may qualify for teacher diplomas by attending special courses and taking supplementary examinations. Hundreds of teachers are availing themselves of these opportunities. There are eleven state colleges for general teachers and three for state religious teachers.

A great variety of in-service courses and "Pedagogic Centers" are constantly working for the improvement of teaching standards. Eight Pedagogic Centers in all parts of the country provide the teachers with professional libraries and with guidance in the acquisition and application of teaching aids and school equipment.

Higher Education—The Hebrew University

The University was organized in 1925 in Jerusalem. In the 37 years of its existence, it developed into a large academic center embracing all the disciplines of a modern institution for higher learning. The University comprises the following schools: Medicine and Dentistry; School of Humanities (including the Institute of Contemporary Jewry); School of Education; School of Agriculture (at Rehavia); School of Science; School of Law and Economics; School of Social Sciences; School of Pharmacy; Institute of Jewish Studies; Extension and Adult Education Center; Magnes University Press. The number of students is about 7,000. In addition to the Israelis, students are drawn from 45 countries. By the summer of 1960, the University had awarded 5,411 degrees, 1,034 of which were doctoral diplomas.

Technion—Israel Institute of Technology, Haifa

The Technion is Israel's only university for the training and education of engineers, technologists and architects. In the past few years it has deepened and broadened its program of instruction and research. It operates the following departments: Civil Engineering; Architecture; Mechanical Engineering; Electrical Engineering; Sciences; Chemistry and Chemical Engineering; Agricultural Engineering; Aeronautical Engineering; Industrial and Management Engineering. It has an enrollment of approximately 3,500.

The Weitzmann Institute of Science, Rehovoth

The Institute, formally dedicated on November 2, 1949, engages in fundamental and, in some cases, applied research in the exact sciences. There are ten departments and five sections. The departments are: Applied Mathematics, Nuclear Physics, Nuclear Induction, Electronics, X-ray, Crystallography, Isotope Research, Polymer Research, Biophysics, Organic Chemistry, and Experimental Biology. The sections are Photochemistry and Spectroscopy, Infrared Spectroscopy, Biochemistry, Virology and Genetics and Plant Genetics. The Institute endeavours to establish close ties with scientific institutions and individuals overseas. As part of this program of scientific interchange distinguished scientists have visited the Institute to lecture and to attend seminars.

Bar-Ilan University, Tel Aviv

This University was organized in 1950 with the help of the Religious Zionists of America—the Mizrahi. It was patterned after the Yeshiva University in New York, which consists of a synthesis of traditional Judaism and modern science. It is primarily an undergraduate school. It offers a variety of subjects in Judaica, the Humanities and the scientific disciplines.

The University offers a complete curriculum leading to Bachelor of Arts, Bachelor of Science, Master of Arts, and Master of Science Degrees. The enrollment in 1962-63 was approximately 1,100 students, a large percentage of whom were from overseas.

Tel Aviv University

This is a Tel Aviv municipal institution. Since the foundation of the first University Institute in 1953, with 17 students, the number has risen from 17 to 616 in the 1959-60 academic year, and to over 700 in 1961/62. In addition to its departments in Natural Sciences and Humanities, the Tel Aviv University conducts special courses in the study of Israel and maintains a Pedagogic Department and an Academy of Music.

The University confers the degrees of BA, BSc, MA and MSc.

INFORMAL EDUCATION FOR YOUTH AND ADULTS IN DIASPORA

In addition to the thousands of schools for formal instruction in Jewish subject matter, there are numerous facilities for Jewish club activities, most of which are Jewish-content centered. Jewish teenagers and young adults meet in a Jewish community center or in Synagogue-centers for recreational and social purposes and in many instances for discussion of the Jewish past and present. The very fact that young people meet in groups as Jews, no matter how little attention is given to the Jewish content of their recreational and/or social program, is itself a positive educational enterprise. In the United States three distinct types of informal Jewish education are given by the following institutions: The Jewish community center, the synagogue and the independent Jewish youth organization. In the community center, stress is laid on recreational and social activities (swimming, ball games and dances). Teenagers, children and young adults engage in in-door sports, busy themselves in hobby clubs (photography, crafts, etc.) and small groups of youth join debating societies, study and discussion groups, choirs and the like. The National Jewish Welfare Board, the national service agency for all community centers, provides a variety of program materials and convenes regional and national conferences of the center youth groups for discussion of current Jewish problems, an evaluation of the club's programs and formulation of long-range plans for future activities.[28]

The synagogue seeks to train Jewish youth in the values of the synagogue and in their application to daily life. It provides opportunities for recreational and social activities and motivates its youth to engage in Jewish cultural activities and in the religious way of life (worship, holiday celebrations, service to the congregation, and community, etc.). The Conservative synagogue youth groups are affiliated with the United Synagogue Youth—the national organization of teenagers; the Young People's League serves young adults affiliated with Conservative congregations. Both the United Synagogue Youth and the League develop programs for their member groups, publish special bulletins and newsletters, arrange regional and national conferences and in recent years have sponsored pilgrimages to Israel. The same is the case with the Reform group. The Union of American Hebrew Congregations of America sponsors the National Federation of Temple Youth, which services youth groups and stimulates educational activities.

As for the Orthodox group, the Union of Orthodox Jewish Congregations of America, through its National Conference of Synagogue Youth aids Orthodox synagogues in their youth programs and conducts national and regional rallies.

The independent youth groups are not sponsored by either the community center or the synagogue, although in most cases they meet in synagogue or center buildings. They are: (a) the Zionist youth groups affiliated with the various parent organizations, such as Young Judaea and Junior Hadassah, sponsored by Z.O.A. and Hadassah respectively; The Habonim, functioning under the aegis of the Labor Zionists (Farband, Poale Zion and Pioneer Women); B'nai Akiva, serviced by the Mizrahi (Religious Zionists) ; the Trumpeldor Youth, sponsored by the Revisionist organization and the Hashomer Hatzair, a left-wing Labor Zionist youth group, which conducts a boy-scout program and stresses Aliyah (immigration) to Israel; (b) Aleph-Zadik-Aleph (boys) and B'nai B'rith Girls—national organizations sponsored by the B'nai B'rith through its youth division. These youth groups concern themselves with the problems of social welfare, conduct a program of sports and social activities, and sponsor study groups dealing with Jewish life and culture; (c) Young Israel is primarily an adult organization whose purpose is to foster among Jewish youth and adults a loyalty to traditional Judaism. The National Council of Young Israel maintains branches throughout the U.S.A., each branch conducts services in its own synagogue and offers an educational program for teenagers and young adults.

Most of the youth organizations maintain summer camps, an excellent educational means for the enhancement of Jewish awareness.

There is no exact data on the number of young people exposed to the stimuli of the various youth programs. The estimate of 250,000 teenagers and 75,000 young adults is based upon some of the official reports of the sponsoring national bodies. It would be much closer to reality to estimate the total number of active members in the various youth groups in the United States to be approximately 150,000.

In other large Jewish population centers in the Diaspora there are numerous youth groups of various political tendencies within the Zionist Movement. There are also synagogal activities designed especially for the teenagers and community center youth programs. In Western Europe, a number of community centers have been built recently with funds of the Committee of Jewish

Material Claims against Germany and with the assistance of the J.D.C. The Community Center of Brussels, Belgium, established in 1959, where several hundred young people have enrolled as members, is a case in point. There are Jewish community center organizations in 19 countries—all of them affiliated with the World Federation of Y.M.H.A.'s with headquarters in New York.[29] Most of these centers conduct special youth programs endeavoring to meet the socio-cultural needs of their clientele. As for camps, in France alone there were 43 summer camps for children and youth in operation in 1957.[30] Summer camps are being organized in ever-increasing numbers in all large Jewish communities in the Diaspora.

JEWISH YOUTH ON THE CAMPUSES

Special facilities for religious services, formal and informal Jewish education have been organized in a number of countries for the Jewish college students. Initiated by the B'nai B'rith Hillel Foundation, which, in 1924, organized the first cultural, religious and social center on the campus of the University of Illinois, the movement to make Jewish life and culture relevant and meaningful to Jewish college youth gained momentum, and by 1960 there were 75 Hillel centers and 140 counselorships on more than 200 campuses in the United States, Canada, England, The Netherlands, Switzerland, Australia, South Africa and Israel. It is estimated that about 350,000 Jewish students are enrolled in the schools for higher learning in the population centers of the Free World. The Hillel Foundation, sponsored by the B'nai B'rith, is making a concerted effort to provide a Jewish content program, as well as counselling service, to Jewish students in these colleges and universities.

Summary

The cultural life of the Jew has undergone a remarkable change in the last century. The three-fold wall of isolation, consisting of language (Yiddish and Ladino), education (in most cases Heder or Yeshiva) and religion (strict adherence to the Shulhan Arukh) which existed for many centuries, has crumbled. Most of the Jews in the Diaspora mingle freely with non-Jews and participate actively in the cultural life of the general community. The use of the vernacular, and the gradual but continuous adjustment to new surroundings in the newly adopted lands, made cultural assimilation a natural process. A modern Jew had arisen in the Diaspora (after the annihilation of East European communities) who became part and parcel of the larger non-Jewish group, finding ample opportunities for cultural self-expression in fields other than Jewish.

The Jewish home in the large Jewish communities in the Diaspora is, to all intents and purposes, the same as the home of the non-Jew of the same socio-economic stratum. While the decline of old-world Jewish religious culture was offset by the Jewish cultural renaissance of the last fifty to sixty years, and while the new Jewish cultural values enriched Jewish life, revived the people's spirit and enabled further creativeness in the realm of Jewish culture, the process of cultural assimilation was merely slowed, but not altered.

Although it is true that in the last decades neither religious culture nor Jewish secular values could stem the tide of recession from Judaism, there is apparent, almost everywhere in the Jewish world, a genuine desire to cling to some phase of Jewish culture. It is quite evident that the last few years have witnessed the return of many assimilated Jews to Judaism. The new State of Israel has been instrumental in stimulating an interest in Jewish life. Modern anti-Semitism, too, became a factor in the return of many to the fold, and especially the realization that Judaism is not only a heritage from a rich past, but a living force in the modern world.

It goes without saying that with the destruction of the Jewish communities in Europe, age-old institutions of learning have vanished, newspapers, book publishers, and artistic centers were stamped out and the intellectual elite of World Jewry greatly depleted. The intensity of Jewish Life in Europe had considerable influence upon all of World Jewry. There remain now the American and the Israeli communities, which, together, constitute the two creative Jewish centers which are apt to enrich Jewish life the world over through a constant and continuous interchange of ideas and practices.

The Jewish educational enterprise must therefore loom very high on the Jewish horizon. It is the sole guarantee of creative survival in the Diaspora and a strong linkage with Israel. Mr. Abba Eban, Israeli Minister of Education, recently clarified the issue in a statement delivered in Los Angeles on November 29, 1962:

"The Hebrew legacy contains values and ideals, embodied visions of human virtue, equal to the great classical disciplines of the Greek and

Roman civilizations, which inspired and sustained the educative movements in Europe and America through the Middle Ages right up to this century. Nobody can say that those disciplines failed. It was under their impulse that the West made its greatest strides in cultural progress, creativity, and even in material abundance. Whatever could be said then about the virtues of a broad classical discipline can apply to the Hebrew discipline. It is both the credentials of a nation, and also a universal humanism almost unparalleled in its scope, in its range and in its depth, containing models of literary symmetry and esthetic grades of moral depth. Whether you learn these virtues through one medium or another is almost irrelevant. Therefore, I dispute the distinctions which are so often drawn between science and humanism. Science is not inhuman. Scientific proof can be impregnated with cosmic insight and poetic beauty, so as to constitute a humane experience, and the study of great literatures is not really feasible without developing a scientific sense of discrimination and criticism.

The question of the Hebrew legacy in our education constitutes the bridge common to both education in Israel and Jewish education in the Diaspora. It is in our contemplation of our common Jewish heritage that our educational systems meet. I said before that Israel's capacity to be a Jewish state depends upon its sense of attachment to a World Jewish people. But Israel's sense of attachment to a World Jewish people will not have much significance, unless the World Jewish people does us one thing only — and this is all that we ask of it, we ask of it to exist — to survive.

I frankly believe that Jewish survival is in danger. I do not believe that it is in danger through external pressures of hostility. I do not think that American Jews need tremble or crumble very time somebody paints a swastika on a wall, or some vulgar voice evokes Nazi anti-semitic slogans. These things have to be dealt with in a spirit of concern, but they are not symptomatic. The symptomatic trend in American, English and Western society is a trend towards greater liberalism, greater freedom, the dropping of social gaps, the discreditation of incitement. These are the general trends, and I'm speaking of the general rule and not of the exceptions to that rule. The danger to Jewish survival arises not through hostile pressure from outside, but through the absence of hostile pressure — the freedom, the liberalism, the ease with which young Jews can today merge into a broader society, the ease with which they can forget their Jewish identity, and, for the most part, live what they think are normal, happy lives. The allurements, the temptations, the greater accessability of the Gentile society, of Gentile culture, the old fashioned world was a simulation of integration, call it what you will. But there is nothing to compel young Jews in your community to emphasize their specific Jewish identity. In a few generations, the sense of Jewish identity will not exist, unless it is consciously stimulated and organized.

This is the issue of Jewish education in the Diaspora. It is a question of Jewish survival. Israel, I think, will survive despite the factors which I have mentioned. The question is how will she survive? Shall she survive alone, in her East Mediterranean context or shall she survive as part of a world people consciously sharing her memories, her dreams and her hopes? Therefore, I do not believe in the existence of any higher priority in Jewish life in the Diaspora than the problem of Jewish education. If I made a case for its priority in Israel, I think the case could be made even more drastically in connection with Diaspora Jewry. There is a genuine and authentic danger that your children and ours will become foreign to each other—aliens with no common language, sharing no memories, sharing no dreams. You only have to look at current tendencies in the life of Jewry in the free communities to see that this is not an alarmist definition. The question is: to what degree, and in what period of time, can these tendencies be arrested? The previous generation had other sources of Jewish identity and consciousness: the memories of East European Jewry, with its rich, rooted tradition, the Yiddish civilization, the revival of Hebrew, the memory of martyrdom which joined us together, the special solidarity which existed in the process of creating the State of Israel. I'm not sure that we can rely upon any of these things. Eastern Europe becomes an exotic memory; Yiddish is in decline; Hebrew has not sufficiently taken its place; the memories of martyrdom fade, and your children are born in a world in which Israel is one of the other states, like America and Britain. At any rate, its existence is not a special matter of concern or of exhilaration. Israel's establishment can be fully tasted only by those who knew the position when it did not exist. This was our unique generation, *dor-a-haron l'shi-bud v'ri-shon li-g'u-lah* the only generation, in 4,000 years, which has a memory both of statelessness and of statehood, both of exile and of redemption."[31]

TOPICS FOR DISCUSSION

1. Looking at this unit as a whole, do you think that Jewish cultural life in the Diaspora is losing its genuineness?

2. Is continuity of Jewish creative effort in the realms of literature possible in languages other than Hebrew and Yiddish?

3. Could a more intensive Jewish education in the Diaspora prepare (academically) a generation of readers of Hebrew? If so, could the educational institution motivate our youth to want to read Hebrew books?

4. Is it desirable to foster bi-lingualism among certain segments of the Jewish population in the Diaspora? If so, do you think that it is indispensable to Jewish creative survival?

5. Do you think that one may be steeped in Jewish culture without a knowledge of Hebrew and/or Yiddish?

NOTES TO CHAPTER 7

1. Interpretation of Scriptures centering around universal values and eternal virtues.
2. Chomsky, William: "Hebrew: The Eternal Language," Philadelphia, The Jewish Publication Society of America, 1957, p. 227.
3. Spiegel, Shalom: "Hebrew Reborn," Macmillan, New York, 1930, p. 4.
4. It is estimated that almost 80 per cent of all Jews in the United States are native born. Most of them naturally speak English only.
5. The question was formulated as follows: "What language was spoken at your home prior to emigration to the U.S.?" Had this question been asked of all, the number of persons who would have listed Yiddish would have been larger.
6. *Information Bulletin,* Canadian Jewish Congress, February 1, 1963, Montreal, p. 1.
7. Friedland, A. H.: "A Bird's Eye View of Jewish Literature," Cincinnati, 1938, p. 2.
8. Fain, Harry: "Titans of Hebrew Verse," Bruce Humphrie, Inc., Boston, 1936, pp. 62-63.
9. *Ibid.,* p. 92.
10. Friedland, A. H.: "Zalman Shnaiur," Bureau of Jewish Education, Cleveland, 1939, pp. 4-5.
11. Wallenrod, Reuben: "The Literature of Modern Israel," Abelard-Schuman, New York, 1956, p. 79.
12. *Ibid.,* p. 28.
13. Sholom J. Kahn in "Israel Argosy," Jerusalem, 1957, p. 119.
14. Wallenrod, Reuben: "The Literature of Modern Israel," Abelard-Schuman, New York, 1956, p. 202.
15. Massadah was the last Judean fortress defended with matchless heroism against the Roman conquerors (First Century C.E.).
16. Halkin, Abraham G.: "Zion in Modern Literature," Herzl Press, New York, 1961, p. 108.
17. Wallenrod, Reuben: "The Literature of Modern Israel," Abelard-Schuman, New York, 1956, p. 232.
18. Facts About Israel, Ministry for Foreign Affairs, Jerusalem, 1961, pp. 146-148.
19. There were numerous attempts at the publication of Yiddish periodicals at an earlier period. In 1686 there appeared in Amsterdam a newspaper on Tuesdays and Fridays under the name of "Dinshtagishe Kurant"; the first weekly in Warsaw, "Der Beobachter," was published in 1823 in Polish and in Yiddish.
20. Roback, A. A.: "Di Imperie Yiddish," Mexico City, 1958, p. 96.
21. The following are some of the important scholarly works that were published in the last decades in the United States and in England: "Social and Religious History of the Jews," by Salo W. Baron; "The History of Jewish Literature," by M. Waxman; "Judaism as a Civilization," by M. M. Kaplan; a number of studies in Wisdom Literature by Robert Gordis; "Studies in Judaism," by Solomon Schechter; "Legends of the Jews," by Levi Ginsburgh; "Philosophy of Judaism," by Abraham J. Heschel; "The Karaite Halakah," by Bernard Revel, "The Megillat Taanit," and "The History of the Second Jewish Commonwealth," by Solomon Zeitlin; The Soncino books in Judaaica consist of unabridged translations of the Talmud, the Zohar, tractates of the Talmud which consist of the Hebrew text with Rashi and Tosaphoth commentaries with the corresponding English translation of the text facing each page, Midrash Rabbah, Soncino Books of the Bible, (14 volumes).
22. Roth, Cecil: "Jewish Contribution to Civilization," Cincinnati, 1941, pp. 367-68.
23. Levitan, Tina: "The Laureates," Twayne Publishers, New York, 1960, p. 20.
24. Bentwich, Norman: "The Jew of Our Time," Penguin Books, Ltd., Harmondsworth, Middlesex, 1960, p. 121.
25. The language of instruction in most cases is Yiddish.

26. & 26a. Engelman, Uriah Z.: "Jewish Education in the Diaspora," Jerusalem, World Conference of Jewish Organizations, August, 1962, pp. 111-139.
27. Much of this chapter is based on the article "Education in Israel," in *The Pedagogic Reporter,* January, 1957, American Association for Jewish Education, New York, N. Y.
28. For a detailed analysis of the center program, see: *Jewish Community Centers* by Herbert Millman, American Jewish Year Book, 1958, pp. 186-200.
29. American Jewish Year Book, 1962, p. 271.
30. American Jewish Year Book, 1957, p. 251.
31. Bulletin of the Bureau of Jewish Education, Los Angeles, December, 1962.

BIBLIOGRAPHY

General

Baron, Salo W.: "A Social and Religious History of the Jews," Jewish Publication Society, Philadelphia, 1952.

Bentwich, Norman: "The Jews in Our Time," Baltimore, Maryland, Penguin Books, 1960.

Cohen, Israel: "Contemporary Jewry: A Survey," Methaen, London, 1950.

Cohen, Israel: "Jewish Life in Modern Times," London, 1929.

Elbogen, Israel: "A Century of Jewish Life," Jewish Publication Society, Philadelphia, 1944.

Engelman, U. Z.: "The Rise of the Jew in the Western World," Behrman's Jewish Book House, New York, 1944.

Federbush, Simon (ed.): "World Jewry Today," Thomas Yoseloff, New York-London, 1959.

Finkelstein, Louis (ed.): "The Jews, Their History, Culture and Religion," Harper Brothers, Vols. I and II, New York, 1949.

Grazel, Solomon: "A History of the Contemporary Jews," Philadelphia, Jewish Publication Society of America, 1960.

Greenberg, Louis: "The Jews in Russia," New Haven, 1944.

Hermann, Lewis: "A History of the Jews in South Africa," Johannesburg, 1935.

Janowsky, Oscar I.: "The Jews and Minority Rights," New York, Columbia University Press, 1933.

Janowsky, Oscar I. (ed.): "The American Jew: A Composite Portrait," New York, 1942.

Learsi, Rufus: "A History of the Jewish People," Cleveland, 1949.

Robinson, Nehemiah: "European Jewry Ten Years After the War," World Jewish Congress, New York, 1956.

Ruppin, Arthur: "The Fate and Future of the Jews," Macmillan, London, 1939.

Sachar, Howard M.: "The Course of Modern Jewish History," World Publishing Company, Cleveland and New York, 1958.

Sack, Benjamin G.: "History of the Jews in Canada," Montreal, 1945.

Schwartz, Leo W.: "The Root and the Bough, the Epic of an Enduring People," New York, 1949.

Tenenbaum, Joseph: "In Search of a Lost People: The Old and New Poland," New York, 1948.

Tenenbaum, Joseph: "Races, Nations and Jews," New York, 1934.
Waxman, Meyer: "A History of Jewish Literature From the Close of the Bible to Our Own Days," 4 volumes, New York, 1930-41.
Zeitlin, Solomon: "The Jews: Race, Nation or Religion," Philadelphia, 1938.
Zeitlin, Solomon: "Who Crucified Jesus?" New York, 1942.
Saron, Gustave and Hotz, Louis (eds.): "The Jews in South Africa," Oxford University Press, 1955, London.

Chapter 1

Kulischer, E. M.: "Jewish Migrations," New York, 1943.
Lestschinsky, Jacob: "Jewish Migrations, 1840-1946," in *The Jews*, edited by Louis Finkelstein, Harper Brothers, New York, 1949, Vol. II, pp. 1198-1238.
Robinson, Nehemiah: "The Jewish Communities of the World," Institute of Jewish Affairs, World Jewish Congress, New York, 1959.
Ruppin, Arthur: "The Fate and Future of the Jews," Macmillan, London, 1939.
Wishnitzer, Mark: "To Dwell in Safety," Philadelphia, The Jewish Publication Society of America, 1949.
American Jewish Year Books, 1957–1962, The American Jewish Committee, New York and The Jewish Publication Society of America, Philadelphia.
Facts About Israel, Ministry for Foreign Affairs, Jerusalem, 1961.
Papers in Jewish Demography, Part I, Association for Jewish Demography and Statistics, 1961.
The Institute Anniversary Volume, Institute of Jewish Affairs, World Jewish Congress, New York, 1962.

Chapters 2 & 3

Cohen, Israel: "Jewish Life in Modern Times," Dodd, Mead & Co., New York, 1929.
Goldberg, Israel (ed.): "The Massacres and Other Atrocities Committed Against the Jews in Southern Russia," American Jewish Congress, New York, 1920.
Golding, Lewis: "The Jewish Problem," Penguin Books Ltd., Great Britain, 1938.
Hay, Malcolm: "The Foot of Pride," Beacon Press, Boston, 1950.
Hilberg Raul: "The Destruction of European Jewry," Quadrangle Books, Chicago, 1961.
Isaac, Jules: "Has Anti-Semitism Roots in Christianity," New York, National Conference of Christians and Jews, 1961.
Lowenthal, Marvin: "The Jews of Germany," Philadelphia, 1936.
Pinson, Koppel S.: "Anti-Semitism After World War I," in Encyclopedia Britannica, 1952 Edition, Vol. II, pp. 78-78j.
Pinson, Koppel S. (ed.): "Essays on Anti-Semitism," New York, 1942.
Poliakov, Leon: "Harvest of Hate," Philadelphia, The Jewish Publication Society of America, 1954.
Radin, Paul: "The Racial Myth," New York, 1934.
Robinson, Nehemiah: "The Jewish Communities of the World," Institute of Jewish Affairs, World Jewish Congress, New York, 1959.
Roth, Cecil: "The History of the Jews in England," Oxford, 1941.
Roth, Cecil: "The Spanish Inquisition," London, 1937.

Roth, Cecil (ed.): "Ritual Murder Libel and the Jew," The Report by Cardinal Lorenzo Garganelli (Pope Clement XIV), London, 1934.

Sachar, Abraham L.: "Sufferance Is the Badge," New York, 1939.

Samuel, Maurice: "The Great Hatred," Knopf, New York, 1940.

Sassoon, David Solomon: "A Short History of the Jews of Baghdad," Letchworth, England, 1949.

Schwartz, M. Solomon: "The Jews in the Soviet Union," Syracuse University Press, 1951.

Segel, B. W.: "The Protocols of the Elders of Zion—The Greatest Lie in History," New York, 1934.

Simmel, Ernst: "Anti-Semitism: A Social Disease," New York, 1946.

Yarmolinsky, Avram: "The Jews and Other National Minorities Under the Soviets," New York, 1928.

European Jewry Ten Years After the War, New York Institute of Jewish Affairs, World Jewish Congress, 1956.

Chapter 4

Engelman, U. Z.: "The Rise of the Jew in the Western World," Behrman's Jewish Book House, New York, 1944, pp. 71-98.

Fortune: "Jews in America," New York, 1936.

Lestschinsky, Jacob: "Dos Nationale Ponim fun Golus Yidentum," (Yiddish), Buenos Aires, 1955, pp. 87–105.

Marcus, A.: "Jews as Entrepreneurs in Weimar Germany," *YIVO Annual of Jewish Social Studies,* New York, 1952, pp. 175-203.

Reich, Nathan: "The Economic Structure of Modern Jewry," in *The Jews: Their History, Culture and Religion,* Edited by Louis Finkelstein, Harper Brothers, New York, 1949, Vol. II, pp. 1238-1260.

Robinson, Nehemiah: "European Jewry Ten Years After the War," World Jewish Congress, New York, 1956.

Rosenberg, Louis: "Canada's Jews," Montreal, 1939.

Ruppin, Arthur: "The Jews in the Modern World," London, 1934, pp. 109-226.

Tartakower, A.: "Ha-Hevrah Ha-Yehudit," (Hebrew), Massadah, Tel Aviv, 1959, pp. 100-143.

Zweig, Ferdynand: "The Israeli Worker," Herzl Press and Sharon Books, New York, 1950.

Facts About Israel, Israel Ministry for Foreign Affairs, Jerusalem, 1956.

Israel Government Year Book, (5722) 1961–62, Central Office of Information, Jerusalem, pp. 45-85.

Chapter 5

Agus, Jacob B.: "Modern Philosophies of Judaism," Behrman's Jewish Book House, New York, 1941.

Badi, Joseph: "Religion in Israel Today," New York, Bookman Associates, 1959.

Baeck, Leo: "Judaism and Christianity," Philadelphia, The Jewish Publication Society of America, 1958.

Bamberger, Bernard J.: "The Story of Judaism," Union of American Hebrew Congregations, New York, 1957.

Cohen, A.: "Everyman's Talmud," London, 1934.

Freehof, Solomon B.: "Reform Jewish Practice and Its Rabbinic Background," Cincinnati, 1944.

Ginsberg, Louis: "Students, Scholars and Saints," Philadelphia, 1928.

Heshel, Abraham J.: "The Philosophy of Judaism," Philadelphia, 1956.

Kaplan, Mordecai M.: "Judaism as a Civilization," Macmillan, New York, 1934.

Landis, Y. Benson: "1962 Yearbook of American Churches," New York, Office of Publication and Distribution, National Council of the Churches of Christ in the United States, 1961.

Lowenthal, Marvin: "The Jews of Germany, A Story of Sixteen Centuries," Philadelphia, 1936.

Miller, Milton G. and Schwartzman, Sylvan D.: "Our Religion and Our Neighbors," Union of American Hebrew Congregations, New York, 1959.

Montefiore, Claude G. and Loewe, H.: "A Rabbinic Anthology," London, 1938.

Newman, Louis and Spitz, Samuel: "The Talmudic Anthology," New York, 1945.

Sassoon, David Solomon: "A Short History of the Jews of Baghdad," Letchworth, England, 1949.

Schechter, Solomon: "Studies in Judaism," Three Series, Philadelphia, 1908-24.

Silver, Abba Hillel: "Where Judaism Differed," New York, The Macmillan Company, 1957.

Steinberg, Milton: "Basic Judaism," Harcourt, Brace & Company, New York, 1947.

Strock, Hermann: "Introduction to Talmud and Midrash," Philadelphia, 1945.

Chapter 6

Bavli, Hillel: "The Modern Renaissance of Hebrew Literature," in *The Jews: Their History, Culture and Religion*, Edited by Louis Finkelstein, Harper Brothers, Vol. I, New York, 1949, pp. 567-602.

Chomsky, William: "Hebrew: The Eternal Language," Philadelphia, The Jewish Publication Society of America, 1957.

Chomsky, William: "Teaching and Learning," Gratz College Book Shop, Broad and York Streets, Philadelphia 32, Penna.

Dushkin, Alexander M.—Engelman, Uriah Z.: "Jewish Education in the United States," Vol. I, New York, American Association for Jewish Education, 1959.

Engelman, Uriah Z.: "Jewish Education in the Diaspora," Jerusalem, World Conference of Jewish Organizations, August, 1962, pp. 111-139.

Frank, M. Z. (ed.): "Sound the Great Trumpet," Whittier, New York, 1955.

Gannes, Abraham P.: "Central Community Agencies for Jewish Education," Philadelphia, Dropsie College, 1954.

Goodman, Henry (ed.): "The New Country," (Stories from Yiddish), YKUF Publishers, New York, 1961.

Halkin, Simon: "Modern Hebrew Literature," New York, 1950.

Halkin, S. Abraham: "Zion in Jewish Literature," New York, Herzl Press, 1961.

Howe, Irving—Greenberg, Eliezer: "A Treasury of Yiddish Stories," Viking, New York, 1954.

Kahn, Shalom J. (ed.): "A Whole Loaf: Stories from Israel," The Vanguard Press, Inc., New York, 1962.

Kallen, Horace M.: "Of Them Which Say They Are Jews," New York, Bloch Publishing Company, 1954.

Kaplan, Mordecai M.: "The Future of the American Jew," New York, Macmillan, 1948.

Katzoff, Louis: "Issues in Jewish Education," New York, Bloch Publishing Company, 1948.

Klauzner, Joseph: "A History of Modern Hebrew Literature," London, 1932.

Levitan, Tina: "The Laureates," Twayne Publishers, New York, 1960.

Pilch, Judah: "Changing Patterns in Jewish Education," *Jewish Social Studies*, Volume XXI, No. 2, April, 1959, pp. 91-117.

Pilch, Judah: "Jewish Religious Education," *Religious Education: A Comprehensive Survey*, Edited by Marvin J. Taylor, Abingdon Press, New York-Nashville, 1960.

Pilch, Judah (ed.): "Jewish Education Register and Directory," New York, American Association for Jewish Education, Volume I, 1951, Volume II, 1959.

Raisin, J. S.: "The Haskalah Movement in Russia," Philadelphia, 1913.

Rappaport, Israel R.: "Education for Living as American Jews," New York, American Jewish Committee, 1946.

Ribalow, Harold U. (ed.): "A Treasury of American Jewish Stories," New York, Thomas Yoseloff, 1958.

Roback, A. A.: "History of Yiddish Literature," New York, 1940.

Roth, Cecil: "The Jewish Contribution to Civilization," Cincinnati, 1940.

Samuel, Maurice: "The World of Sholom Aleichem," New York, 1943.

Schwartz, Karle: "Jewish Artists of the 19th and 20th Centuries," Philosophical Library, New York, 1949.

Swartz, Leo (ed.): "A Golden Treasury of Jewish Literature," Rinehart, New York, 1937.

Simon, Leon: "Studies in Jewish Nationalism," London, Longmans, Green and Company, 1920.

Spiegel, Shalom: "Hebrew Reborn," Macmillan, New York, 1930.

Wallenrod, Reuben: "The Literature of Modern Israel," New York, Abelard Schuman Publishers, 1956.

Israel Government Year Book (5722), 1961–62, Central Office of Information, Jerusalem, pp. 111-139.

Survey of Jewish and Supplementary Schools in Western Continental Europe, Education Department, American Jewish Distribution Committee, Geneva, October, 1962.

The Jewish People: Past and Present, Vol. II, Jewish Encyclopedic Handbooks, New York, Central Yiddish Culture Organization (CYCO), 1948.

Index